The Great Match Race

BOOKS BY JOHN EISENBERG

THE LONGEST SHOT: LIL E. TEE AND
THE KENTUCKY DERBY

COTTON BOWL DAYS: GROWING UP WITH
DALLAS AND THE COWBOYS IN THE 1960S

FROM 33RD STREET TO CAMDEN YARDS: AN
ORAL HISTORY OF THE BALTIMORE ORIOLES

NATIVE DANCER: HERO OF A GOLDEN AGE

THE GREAT MATCH RACE: WHEN NORTH
MET SOUTH IN AMERICA'S FIRST
SPORTS SPECTACLE

THE GREAT MATCH RACE

WHEN NORTH MET SOUTH IN AMERICA'S FIRST SPORTS SPECTACLE

JOHN EISENBERG

HOUGHTON MIFFLIN COMPANY

BOSTON · NEW YORK

2006

For information about permission to reproduce selections
from this book, write to Permissions, Houghton Mifflin Company,
215 Park Avenue South, New York, New York 10003.

Visit our Web site: www.houghtonmifflinbooks.com.

Library of Congress Cataloging-in-Publication Data

Eisenberg, John, date.
The great match race : when North met South in America's
first sports spectacle / John Eisenberg.
p.   cm.
Includes index.
ISBN-13: 978-0-618-87211-4

1. American Eclipse (Race horse) 2. Sir Henry (Race horse)
3. Race horses — United States — Biography. 4. Horse
racing — United States — History. I. Title.
SF355.A45E37 2006
798.40092'9 — dc22 2005031540

Book design by Robert Overholtzer

QUM 10 9 8 7 6 5 4 3 2 1

With love to my home team:
Mary Wynne, Anna, and Wick

Contents

American Eclipse, the majestic champion representing the North, had never come close to losing a race. Painting by Alvan Fisher.

Courtesy of the National Racing Museum and Hall of Fame

Sir Henry was the South's astonishing young star. No horse had ever raced faster. Painting by Edward Troye.

Courtesy of the National Racing Museum and Hall of Fame

Prologue

It was a new sound for American ears: the lusty, clattering, sports-stadium roar — sixty thousand people shouting, whistling, stomping, and rattling cowbells, raising a din so forceful it shook the wooden beams supporting the grandstands. The noise was audible for miles, rolling across the countryside like booming thunderclaps in a boot-soaking rainstorm. It would become a familiar sound in the distant future, an archetype of autumn football weekends and summer baseball nights. But in 1823 it was a new phenomenon, a startling sensory assault never heard before.

A horse race, of all things, was the occasion, luring a tumultuous horde of sports fanatics that was almost larger than the combined populations of Illinois and Delaware. Before this time, political rallies, prayer revivals, and holiday parades had brought together the largest crowds of Americans, but a ballyhooed duel between the fastest thoroughbred in the North and the fastest in the South had improbably attracted a mob that dwarfed all earlier crowds. Suddenly, on a sunny spring afternoon, a racetrack on Long Island was the nation's fourth-largest city.

The country came to a standstill, sweating the outcome of the race between Eclipse, the North's dark, snorting, undefeated champion, and Henry, the South's precocious, brilliantly fast darling. Congress shut down because so many politicians had tickets to see them run. The New York Stock Exchange was closed. Andrew Jackson interrupted his presidential campaign to attend.

Public support was evenly divided, and as the animals circled the all-dirt track at the Union Course in Jamaica that day, little business was conducted anywhere else in the twenty-four states. People from

Maine to Alabama found their minds drifting to a race that had been anticipated for months and exhaustively analyzed and debated. Many fans had invested more than just their emotions. They had bet hundreds, even thousands, of dollars or, in a few cases, everything they owned.

In hindsight this outbreak of raw, irrational passion, a premature burst of American sports mania, was almost an apparition, appearing out of nowhere and vanishing just as quickly. Hoarse, purple-veined sports fanaticism was a concept whose time had not come. Baseball, football, and basketball would not even be discovered for decades, much less organized into popular cultural institutions. Stadiums packed with tens of thousands of noisy fans would not become commonplace until the 1900s. In 1823 the idea of sixty thousand people coming together to watch a sports event was only slightly more fathomable than the idea of a man flying to the moon and walking across a crater.

But a boiling brew of intense, hardheaded loyalties had turned the race into more than just a sporting event, setting the stage for this circus to unfurl. The race had become a national referendum on what was right and just, a symbol of the developing dispute between northerners and southerners that would eventually tear the country apart.

It would be many years before North and South shed blood, but the joy of their celebrated union was already flickering, as evidenced by their increasingly shrill and incessant arguments about slavery, politics, business, morals — any issue that could be dredged up, really. Southerners were smugly accustomed to the upper hand; they had controlled the presidency for almost a quarter-century, easily protected their right to own slaves, and farmed the crops that were helping the fledgling nation rise to its feet. But northerners were rising up against slavery now, fighting back politically, and shrewdly betting their future on industry, not agriculture.

America's political, social, and economic winds were slowly shifting. The race between Eclipse and Henry was like a leaf picked up and carried in those breezes, a palpable metaphor of coming change. Southerners, steeped in horse-racing expertise, nuance, and history, saw themselves as the rightful bearers of America's equine legacy, superior in every way to the northerners, whom they saw as clueless dabblers. Yet several of the South's finest horsemen had recently taken on the North's indomitable Eclipse and failed to win, delighting northerners and making southerners increasingly unhappy.

After the last southern defeat, William Ransom Johnson decided he had to step in. A charismatic forty-one-year-old Virginia plantation owner, politician, and gambler, Johnson was most of all a cunning and dominant racehorse trainer. He arranged a new challenge to Eclipse and spent months preparing for it, drawing the entire South into his thrall. Because of his uncanny instincts and unmatched record — in one two-year span, horses wearing his sky blue colors had won sixty-one of sixty-three races — southerners thought Johnson's horse surely would crush Eclipse and deliver a triumph reasserting their superiority.

Northerners, meanwhile, never thought Eclipse could lose. Yes, the nine-year-old horse was near the end of his racing days, but he was still strong and fearsome. His fans had faith in him and in his human support team; his chief financial backer, John Cox Stevens, was a millionaire sportsman. Cornelius Van Ranst, the self-doubting old horseman who owned and trained Eclipse, was the only one worried that the horse might in fact be too old and that this match against Henry would push him beyond his limits.

With both sides viewing the race as a chance to have their region's superiority affirmed, a spectacle ensued. For days ahead of time, steamships and stagecoaches brought thousands of southern race fans to the streets of New York. Hotels, bars, and taverns filled. Northerners and southerners, jammed shoulder to shoulder, exchanged taunts and punches, certain their side would win the race.

Hanging in the air, almost tangible enough to grasp, was the combination of energies that would later serve as the foundation of the modern sports experience: the power of regional pride, the thrill of shared passions, the ability to see a contest as an allegory. And the intense desire to win.

On race day, as tens of thousands of people crossed the East River on dangerously overloaded ferries from New York City and journeyed to Jamaica along dusty dirt roads, it was as if all the armies in the world had gone on maneuvers together. In the end, everyone somehow fit inside the Union Course's rickety fences, a sweltering rabble with eyes fixed on the oval dirt track in front of them.

Then the nation stopped to pray, the horses started to run, and the roars of the great crowd began to thunder. Goodness, who had ever heard such noise?

The Great Match Race

1

Eclipse Against the World!

S IR CHARLES came to a halt a half-mile from the finish. The southern horse stood forlornly on the grassy track, his sinewy right foreleg dangling awkwardly as his grooms raced to help him. His thousands of supporters abruptly fell silent, shocked by his abject failure.

The northern horse, Eclipse, hurtled ahead, a streaking dark brown blur bathed in sunshine as he bore down on the finish at the National Course in Washington, D.C. There was no doubt now that he would win again, and his outnumbered fans, mostly visitors from New York, began to hurl taunts at the southern hordes around them. Look at that, you sons of Dixie!

William Ransom Johnson jerked his head away, almost physically ill as he sat in the grandstand calculating the extent of the South's humiliation. Its horses had now lost four straight races to Eclipse in the past thirteen months, and Sir Charles, the pride of Virginia, was not even going to finish — a new low by any reckoning. Soon northern pockets would bulge with thousands of dollars dolefully handed over by southern tobacco planters who had expected to celebrate that night but would instead just turn and slink home, leaving New Yorkers to rule the nation's capital. Johnson could barely tolerate the thought.

A pair of northerners sitting behind him began flinging insults, unable to contain their joy.

"What dare say ye today, sirs? That only southern men know of horses?" one shouted.

"Let no man say so now, friend," the other replied.

Their shrill voices cut through the stark silence of southerners coming to terms with another defeat.

Hearing them, Johnson cursed so hard he shook the thick mane of prematurely white hair that fell down his back. He wanted to turn and spit a reply at the obviously ignorant Yankees. It was a fact that horse racing in the South was infinitely more popular and sophisticated than that in the North, and superior in every respect. Southerners had better horses and could talk rings around New Yorkers on the subject. Everyone knew it.

But rather than rebuke the Yankees (because what could he say, really, after such a pathetic race?), Johnson began to formulate a plan for revenge. Then and there he decided he had stood aside long enough while other southern horses and horsemen fell to Eclipse. It was time for the South to take this challenge more seriously, time for Johnson — a horseman so renowned he was known as the Napoleon of the Turf — to get involved.

Johnson started concocting a new challenge to Eclipse even before the indomitable northern horse reached the finish of this one. His many years of arranging (and usually winning) races enabled him to instinctively shuffle through the important questions that had to be answered. Where should the race be held? Which horse should represent the South? How much money should be staked on the outcome?

His close friend William "Racing Billy" Wynne, another Virginia plantation owner who owned and raced horses, sat beside him. Equally disgusted, Wynne blurted that one of their slaves (they owned some five dozen between them) probably could have trained a southern horse to give Eclipse a tougher fight. Johnson nodded distractedly and did not reply; he was busy studying Eclipse's running action as the horse passed in front of him on the way to the finish.

Eclipse was formidable, for sure. An eight-year-old with a well-muscled dark coat broken only by splashes of white between his eyes and on his rear left ankle, he stood more than fifteen hands tall and possessed a palpable competitive thirst — the more his jockey, Samuel Purdy, whipped and spurred him, the harder he ran. He had never come close to losing a race, often intimidating opponents with his mere appearance, hoofs pounding and nostrils flaring.

He had now soundly beaten three top southern horses: the once great filly Lady Lightfoot and colts Sir Walter and Sir Charles — all sired by Sir Archie, a legendary southern stallion beloved by Johnson. Lady Lightfoot and Sir Walter had lost at the Union Course in New York. This latest defeat at the National Course was so much worse, Johnson felt, that it demanded a response.

For starters, President James Monroe himself was on hand, sitting in a private grandstand with his secretary of war and fellow Virginian, John Calhoun. Like most Virginians, they had doubted that Eclipse could prevail on southern soil against a fine runner such as Sir Charles. The sight of a southern president galled by defeat was sufficient motivation in itself, Johnson thought.

The race also had attracted quite a crowd, surely one of the largest ever to see horses run in America. There had to be six thousand people, or maybe more! Johnson looked around and saw northern and southern men and women of all colors — black, white, brown, and red — many of the men wearing top hats, jackets, and high collars, the women in bonnets and full-length dresses. That morning the spectators had clogged the streets around the course with their horse-drawn coaches, chariots, carts, buggies, and wagons, causing such a backup that some people had just abandoned their vehicles and walked to the course. For the South to have experienced total humiliation in front of such a gathering was, Johnson felt, just not acceptable.

The crowd's mood had been relatively sporting until now, but when Sir Charles stopped running, the insults suddenly began to fly. These northerners supporting Eclipse were so smug it was disgusting, Johnson felt. But should the South just give up and admit the northern horse was too good? Absolutely not, Napoleon thought. The South had better sires, better-bred horses, and shrewder trainers than the North. It also had a long history of commitment to racing excellence. Surely, Johnson thought, he could marshal those many advantages in another race, beat Eclipse, win back the South's money, and shut up these infernal Yankees. It was not even a fair fight, really.

Save for this one horse, northern racing was inferior and inconsequential. Johnson could easily handle it.

As soon as the race was over, Cornelius Van Ranst and John Cox Stevens, the northerners in charge of Eclipse, leapt down from their grandstand seats and jogged across the grass, anxious to pat their horse and congratulate Purdy. They made an odd-looking pair as they ran, the sixty-year-old Van Ranst hobbling, Stevens young and athletic. But they were a fine team.

A lifelong thoroughbred breeder and trainer, Van Ranst was a rare northerner devoted to racing. More than a century after his great-grandfather had emigrated from Holland to the New World, he was a distinctive and original figure, an old wizard of the turf, his bony frame often swathed in a long, thick coat and a fur hat; his pale skin, pointed white goatee, and thin layer of wispy white hair gave him a magician's air.

Stevens was a robust millionaire industrialist whose financial backing enabled Eclipse to run. The son of one of the pioneers of steamboat travel, he liked horse racing, sailing — just about any sporting endeavor. Mostly he liked to turn a profit. Whenever owners agreed to run their horses, they put up money — and now the stakes were higher than ever, it seemed. The original stakes for the race between Eclipse and Sir Charles had been $10,000 a side, quite a sum. Although Van Ranst, who was wealthy in his own right, and other northerners had contributed, Stevens was the main money man.

Purdy had dismounted by the time Van Ranst and Stevens reached them. Eclipse, barely breathing hard, was held by his grooms, who would soon take him away for a bath and a meal, his reward for having run so hard. Van Ranst nuzzled him and spoke softly to him. So did Purdy, who had ridden him in almost all of his races. The trainer and jockey felt a keen attachment to the horse. Where others saw a fearsome beast, they saw a smart old animal with eyes so bright and alert they almost seemed to suggest that human thoughts and feelings lurked inside.

Eclipse had never set foot outside of New York before this race. A week beforehand, he had traveled from Van Ranst's private stable at

Harlem Lane, a small racecourse in northern Manhattan, to a se-cluded barn near the National Course. A decade earlier, he would have had to walk the entire two hundred miles, a prospect that likely would have kept the race from taking place. But now, tended by a team of Van Ranst's stable hands, Eclipse had traveled most of the way by steamship. This mode of transportation had become popular in the past decade on many of America's waterways. The broad, flat-bedded vessels were ideal for moving racehorses, as the ride was smooth and the animals could lie down in open-air stalls. They arrived rested and ready to race rather than exhausted and doomed to defeat.

Eclipse's trip was chronicled in northern newspapers, which "pay as much attention to his movements as court gazettes in different parts of the world bestow upon the perambulations of crowned heads," as one Washington newspaper stated. New Yorkers might not understand racing, but they loved their horse. They sighed with relief when he reached Washington "as quiet as he would have been in his own stable, and in as fine a condition as when he left," according to Van Ranst.

After such an authoritative victory, the trip home promised to be an even more kingly procession. Standing on the National Course grass — southern soil! — and listening to the cheers of the northern fans, Van Ranst and Stevens shook hands as Eclipse was led away. Van Ranst commented that the trip had been a glorious one. Stevens nodded and congratulated him for having prepared the horse so bril-liantly for the race. The old wizard smiled. In all his years of racing horses, he could not remember a finer day.

Like most southerners, Johnson blamed the debacle on Sir Charles's owner, James Junkin Harrison, a showy, cocky Virginia plantation owner who bet so much at the races that he would eventually lose one million dollars. An avid horseman, Harrison would later show a seri-ous side by funding some of the first research into American thor-oughbred pedigrees. But his behavior throughout this challenge to Eclipse had been appalling, Johnson felt.

Harrison had itched to take on Eclipse for more than a year, since the northern horse's defeat of Lady Lightfoot in October 1821. Harrison was sure Sir Charles could succeed where the ten-year-old mare had failed. Sir Charles was a durable, mature bay that had run for three years at southern tracks from Maryland to Georgia, almost always winning. Eclipse, though older, had raced only a few times in New York. Sir Charles was more seasoned, and his running times compared favorably with Eclipse's.

Harrison had almost taken Sir Charles up to the Union Course for a race against Eclipse in October 1822, but the owner of Sir William, another leading southern horse, suggested that their horses race in Lawrenceville, Georgia, in September to find out which was faster. Harrison felt compelled to accept the challenge; Sir William had won two of three previous races between the horses, and his owner had crowed a little too loudly about it, claiming Sir William was a "golden horse" so fleet he "commanded the wind to stand still."

In Georgia, Sir Charles took off from the start and raced so far ahead that Sir William became discouraged and all but quit. The day ended with spectators laughing as Sir William's jockey fell off, sending the horse on a wild dash around the grounds.

Returning to Virginia after that triumph, Harrison decided Sir Charles was ready for Eclipse. He wrote a letter to Van Ranst and sent it to the *Petersburg* (Virginia) *Intelligencer,* with orders to publish it and forward it to the *New York Evening Post,* where Van Ranst would see it.

Brunswick, Virginia
30th September 1822

To the Owner of the American Eclipse:

Sir — I did have a great desire to attend the Long Island races this fall, and in all probability, should have done so, if the owner of the golden Sir William had not given notice. I met him with Sir Charles, and sir, I have to inform you, that the golden horse, which commanded the "wind to stand still" and all creation to bend before him last winter in South Carolina, has now taken a western direction to seek his level with the depreciated currency of that part of the country.

As I have been told that Eclipse is a fine race horse and would be benefited by southern fame, I have thought it proper to offer you the only opportunity in my power. Now you have it in your power to try his superiority, for if he can beat Sir Charles, he may stop his running career as he stands victor in the southern states.

I will run Sir Charles against him on the Washington Course, agreeable to the rules of the course, on the 15th or 16th of November, for five or ten thousand dollars.

Now, sir, you have it amply in your power to test Eclipse as a race horse, and I think the world will not say the proposition is illiberal, as Sir Charles has already run two races this season and in all probability will run two more. Admit you accede to the proposition and I propose to meet you halfway.

I am, respectfully,
James J. Harrison

Johnson knew Harrison well — they had competed for years (with Johnson's horses usually winning), dined together, and sold each other horses — but he believed Harrison's letter was haughty and mean-spirited. It was enough to make any respectable southern horseman cringe. Why disparage another man's horse as Harrison had disparaged Sir William?

Although Sir Charles had won their most recent race, Sir Charles and Sir William were close competitors, having split four races in all. As for the inference that Sir Charles's latest victory had persuaded Sir William's owner to seek easier competition in the "western states," it simply was not true. Sir William's owner had told Johnson the horse was ready to run again.

Johnson suggested to Sir William's owner that he send Harrison a caustic letter through the newspapers; Harrison deserved such a public rebuke, Johnson believed. The letter ran in the *Petersburg Intelligencer* and other southern papers.

Sir — It would have been candid and liberal of you to have acknowledged that Sir William and Sir Charles have twice beaten each other. Delicacy should have dictated silence on your part on the subject of the Lawrenceville race, inasmuch as Sir William was deprived of his rider. As for your fulsome challenge to the owner of Eclipse, it is misinformation to state that Sir William has retired to the West. Sir William is on his way to South Carolina, which you knew before publication of your challenge. But sir, since victory over Sir William is so necessary to establish the fame of Sir Charles, and that in his retirement from the turf (which will shortly be) he may carry with him the reputation of the Virginia champion, which you so much covet, I am disposed again to give you an opportunity to evince Sir Charles' superiority, after which you may blaze forth his fame unmolested.

Harrison paid no attention to this challenge for a fifth and deciding race between Sir William and Sir Charles; he was too busy with Eclipse. His letter to Van Ranst had run in the *Evening Post,* accompanied by a sarcastic editorial. "If Sir Charles comes in contact with Eclipse, he will be compelled to follow Sir William to the western country to seek his level with the depreciated currency of that region," the *Post* wrote. Northerners were proud of their horse.

Van Ranst smiled as he read the letter and the tart commentary. He liked the idea of another challenge and was instantly ready to accept. Eclipse surely could beat another southerner, just as he had beaten all the others.

The old wizard jotted a quick reply to Harrison and sent it to the *Evening Post* with instructions to forward it to the *Petersburg Intelligencer.*

New York, October 15, 1822

To James J. Harrison, Esq.

Sir — The confident terms of the challenge seemed to require deliberation on my part before I determined that my horse should come in contact with the "victor of the southern states." I have duly deliberated and now agree to meet you on the terms you have proposed, and as in naming two sums, you leave the choice with me for which to run, I choose the greatest, that the object of the contest may correspond with the fame of the horses.

Respectfully, yours,
C. W. Van Ranst

In further correspondence, Harrison and Van Ranst finalized the terms and conditions of the race. Each would deposit $5,000 in the Bank of the United States, payable to the other side in the unlikely event of a forfeit. The overall stakes would be $10,000 a side. The race was scheduled for November 20, a day before the start of the fall meeting at the National Course. The event would consist of four-mile heats with half-hour breaks between them. The first horse to win two heats would take the stakes.

Later generations would consider it sadistic to make horses run a dozen miles to win a purse. By the end of the century most American races would be run over no more than two miles; a twelve-mile event would be considered a death sentence. But such conditions were standard in the 1820s, which racing historians later called the "heroic age" because of the grueling distances. To decide a sweepstakes event involving a large field, occasionally five heats were needed. Those horses had to run twenty miles in an afternoon.

To prepare for the National Course race, Harrison raced Sir Charles twice more in the weeks beforehand. That, Johnson believed, was a mistake even more grievous than Harrison's first letter to Van Ranst. Even though Napoleon believed in pushing horses to their limits, he felt that Sir Charles had been raced too hard for too long. The horse had been training and racing since early spring, winning seven straight events, an impressive total. Sir Charles had to be tired, and a tired horse not only ran slower but often changed its running motion and overused some muscles, resulting in pulls and tears.

Sure enough, Sir Charles ran into trouble. Harrison, confident of victory, brought the horse to Washington a week before the race and put him through daily training sessions at the National Course. But during a morning gallop two days before the event, Sir Charles took an awkward step. Although he did not fall, he could not continue.

Harrison, watching the workout on horseback, raced across the grass, dismounted, and assessed the horse's right foreleg. When he knelt to feel the tendons, Sir Charles flinched. Harrison's face was ashen as he rose. The horse was seriously injured.

The timing was horrendous. Washington's hotels, inns, and rooming houses were filling with racing fans. A Georgetown newspaper had predicted "the greatest concourse of people ever witnessed in this district." But Sir Charles was in no shape to run.

Johnson arrived in Washington on the eve of the race. He was in a sour mood, for he believed Sir Charles was destined to lose. That day a Washington newspaper had printed a rumor about the southern horse suffering an injury, and while the paper discounted the rumor, Johnson wondered if it were true.

The next morning Napoleon and Racing Billy walked in silence to the course, unable to relate to the festive atmosphere around them. The course was located on a hill overlooking downtown, on property belonging to the Holmead family, Washington's largest landowners. An oval track, a mile long and thirty feet wide, was marked in grass that was half gone to autumn brown. Twin rows of connected wooden rods formed inner and outer railings. Three small wooden stands, including one for President Monroe, stood near the finish.

A line of fans formed at the entrance. They paid fifty cents to get in and ran to find standing room with a good view of the course. Men on horseback were also allowed in, shunted to the ground inside the oval. Hawkers in temporary wooden booths selling food, liquor, and carriage rides tried to attract the fans' attention as sheriffs wandered through the crowd, looking for pickpockets.

As Johnson and Billy took their seats, they listened to dozens of northerners and southerners arranging bets around them.

"Sir Charles to win! The North to fall in flames!" southerners shouted, holding up fistfuls of money to lure northerners into making wagers.

"Eclipse to prevail! The South to leave the course in shame!" northerners replied, showing their money.

Thousands of dollars were staked by one o'clock, when the race was supposed to start. But no horses appeared on the course. Harrison finally arrived after twenty minutes, but his dour expression as he approached the judges quickly quelled any southern cheers.

Only a few fans standing near the finish could hear the conversation between the subdued Virginian and the trio of judges, but it was clear from Harrison's body language that something had gone terribly wrong.

Harrison told the judges Sir Charles had met with misfortune; an injured leg would keep him from running. The lead judge, Charles Ridgely, a sixty-three-year-old former governor of Maryland, asked about the stakes. Harrison paused, crushed that it had come to this, and confessed that the forfeit would have to be paid.

The judges spoke briefly among themselves. Ridgely climbed down from his seat and stood in front of the stand. He cleared his voice and announced that Harrison was forfeiting and would pay the northern side $5,000, as per the terms of the challenge.

The southern fans' mouths fell open. How was this possible? Northerners in the crowd, a decided minority, began to shout. News of the forfeit quickly circled the course. Northerners demanded payment from the southerners with whom they had just bet. Some paid, but others refused, pointing out that this result was a cancellation, not a defeat. Sheriffs tensed, sensing trouble.

"A two-hundred-mile journey to see nothing but grass grow!" one fan cried as Harrison walked away.

Humiliated, Harrison turned and went back to the judges. He had an idea. What about a substitute contest, a single four-mile heat? He pointed out that while Sir Charles was too injured to attempt a series of heats, he probably could run one, for he was a champion who would rise to the occasion. Ridgely asked about the stakes. Harrison suggested $1,500 per side. Van Ranst and Stevens were called over and quickly agreed to the conditions. The race was announced to the spectators.

Johnson and Racing Billy exchanged glances. It seemed obvious to them that Harrison had proposed the new race strictly to satisfy the fans who wanted to see a race; Sir Charles had been forfeited and was in no shape to test Eclipse. Nonetheless, the fans were soon treated to the high drama of a start.

Eclipse was presented first to the judges. His grooms were dressed in work clothes matching his colors. Purdy shone in a shirt of Van Ranst's maroon. The northern fans applauded, whistled, and exhorted their horse. Eclipse snorted and stomped as beads of sweat rolled down his flanks. He was all heated up and ready to run.

Sir Charles arrived moments later, tended by a pair of unkempt slaves belonging to Harrison, who suddenly was nowhere to be found. The horse was limping and had a thin, tattered blanket thrown over him, his appearance itself an embarrassment. His jockey was a white boy from Virginia whom Johnson did not know.

The shocked southern fans made little noise. Johnson was speechless.

The race was to consist of four trips around the oval, a total of four miles. The horses were aligned at a starting point, and a brief silence swept across the course as all eyes focused on a drummer standing with the judges, clutching a stick above his instrument. When his hand came down and a loud tap sounded, the jockeys whipped and spurred their horses, which took off running. The spectators on both sides screeched their support.

Eclipse immediately took the lead, with Purdy working him hard. His legs blurred as he dug deep into the turf and sent clumps of grass flying behind him. Sir Charles never had a chance. Game but failing, the southern horse managed to be within five lengths of Eclipse after two miles, but it was clear that his right front leg was injured. His breathing became labored, and he dropped farther and farther behind. Finally, his jockey eased him and then halted him altogether on the final lap, refusing to go on pushing the injured horse or participate in such a sham.

After Eclipse crossed the finish line alone, Johnson glumly watched Van Ranst and Stevens celebrate their latest success. Only a fool would suggest that it meant the North was now superior to the South as a thoroughbred region; this result was meaningless in that sense. But it was equally foolish, Johnson conceded, to deny the North's rising threat. What else could one infer from the fact that the North had a horse the South seemingly could not beat?

Johnson usually was at his wiliest after a defeat. Although he was no scholar — like his friend Andrew Jackson, he proudly stated he "had never read a book through" — he had a knack for negotiating winning challenges. His mind raced as he watched southerners digging into their pockets to pay their debts. His eyes lingered on the celebrating northerners. The outline of a strategy began to form. He knew the Yankees would be supremely confident after winning again, even though this race had not been a real test. Meanwhile, Eclipse would be nine years old by next spring, surely more vulnerable than the Yankees realized. Maybe in their overconfidence, Johnson thought, they would consent to lopsided racing conditions that favored the South.

It was worth a try.

When he outlined his thinking to Billy, his friend's eyes came alive for the first time all day. Billy suggested that Johnson seek an agreement immediately, while the northerners were still basking in this triumph.

There was no time to waste. Johnson set out to find the southern horsemen who backed him in his racing ventures. They had business to discuss.

A private carriage transported Van Ranst and Stevens back to the elegant Mansion Hotel in downtown Washington. As their driver navigated streets overrun with racing fans, some exuberant, others despondent, Van Ranst and Stevens smiled and waved at supporters.

That evening they ate in a private dining room with other northerners, including Michael Burnham, the publisher of the *New York Evening Post*, and Stephen Price, the manager of the Park Theater. All were members of the New York Association for the Improvement of the Breed of Horses (NYAIBH), the horseman's group that owned and operated New York's Union Course. Their dinner was understandably festive, as they had collected twice that afternoon, earning $5,000 when Harrison forfeited the original race and then another $1,500 when Eclipse won the substitute contest.

A succession of hard raps on the door silenced the conversation. A waiter walked to the door and opened it.

Johnson entered briskly, hat in hand, white hair flowing down his back. The northerners instinctively stood out of respect for the well-known southern horseman.

Without offering greetings, Johnson began to speak. "Is it not true that Eclipse is the swiftest horse in all of the North?" he asked.

"Aye," replied Van Ranst, dabbing his mouth with a napkin. "Has he not just proved it this afternoon against the proudest boast of Virginia?"

"Very well," Johnson said. "Here is something for Eclipse and his friends to consider."

Before leaving the National Course that afternoon, Johnson and Billy had met with a group that felt as strongly as they did about reaffirming their region's supremacy, men such as John Randolph, the fiery Virginia congressman, and John Tayloe III, whose family had bred and raced champions since the 1750s. Johnson knew they would back another challenge and contribute to the stakes, but since his idea for a new race was so bold, he had wanted to confirm their support.

Johnson's plan centered on the fact that the Union Course was barely a year old, and the northerners, especially Stevens, really wanted to make it profitable. By offering to hold a major, expensive race there, Johnson figured he could lure the northerners into agreeing to disadvantageous racing conditions. He wanted to be able to pick the southern horse from a large pool of candidates, and he wanted time to train the horse to win. By offering to run a $20,000-a-side event at the Union Course, Napoleon figured he could get everything he wanted. The northerners, he guessed, would be so confident in Eclipse — foolishly so, in his opinion — and so excited about running such a race on home ground that they would not even realize they were selling out the old horse.

Randolph and Tayloe had enthusiastically agreed to back the race, seeing the genius of Johnson's thinking. They then helped Johnson finalize the conditions he now proposed to the northerners at the Mansion.

"For $20,000 a side," Napoleon stated, "I pledge to bring a horse to the Union Course next March and challenge your fine Eclipse. My horse will be the best I can find from anywhere in the land beyond the confines of the North. I shall name the horse on the day of the race."

None of the northerners spoke. Had Napoleon lost his mind? Not only were stakes that large unheard of, but Johnson was giving himself the right to consider every horse in America's expanding and prosperous South and West. And he would not have to name a challenger until the day of the race! In return, he was offering to race in New York, an admittedly attractive proposition. But was that enough to offset the advantages he was giving himself?

Van Ranst asked if he could deliberate privately with his northern partners. Johnson left the room. Stevens immediately shouted that the race must take place — it was too attractive to turn down. Van Ranst did not reply at first. Though as a horseman he was not as eminent as Johnson, he was the North's closest equivalent. And he was skeptical about this challenge. He had confidence in Eclipse, but he was concerned. It was asking a lot of a horse who would be nine in the spring to endure the trip back from Washington to New York and then to take on the horse selected by Johnson — out of a pool of hundreds, no less — in an afternoon of four-mile heats before winter's chill had vanished.

A younger horse could handle such a strain, Van Ranst warned the group, but a horse as old as Eclipse might struggle. Johnson was being given a great deal of latitude. Did everyone understand the extent of this southerner's horsemanship?

Stevens did not want to hear such talk. A challenge this attractive could not be rejected, he felt. He had invested heavily in the Union Course and was sure the proposed race would help the track. Interregional contests were becoming popular, as evidenced by the crowd that had gathered at the National Course that day. A Union Course race might attract an even larger crowd.

Stevens suggested they compromise. He and Van Ranst discussed the conditions and settled on an offer clearly weighted in Stevens's favor — but mainly slanted to Johnson's desires. Van Ranst shrugged, realizing he could not win this argument.

The northerners brought Napoleon back into the room and gave him their counterproposal. The $20,000-a-side race could take place at the Union Course on the last Tuesday in May, giving Eclipse two extra months to rest. In exchange, Johnson was free to scour the entire world for a horse, not just the South and West.

Johnson remained outwardly impassive as he listened. Gambler that he was, he did not want to reveal his emotions. But his insides tingled with excitement. He wanted to shout his joy. He had gambled and won on all counts, he believed. The northerners had been willing to agree to almost anything to have a major race staged at their track. They were too confident in Eclipse.

With six months to find and prepare a horse from just about anywhere, Napoleon had no doubt he could present a challenger capable of beating a nine-year-old.

Remaining calm — barely — he nodded to the northerners that an agreement had been reached, and said that racing itself surely would benefit from the excitement of such a challenge.

After handshakes and a round of toasts, Johnson went off to tell his friends about the new race. They would be flabbergasted. The New Yorkers finished eating and went out into the balmy November evening to announce the news. Their unbeaten horse would face still another challenge, the most daunting ever.

Eclipse against the world!

2

If Civil War Must Come

A T NOON ON THE DAY after the race between Eclipse and Sir Charles, a crowd gathered at the base of the one-hundred-foot Liberty Pole in Brooklyn. William Niblo, owner of Manhattan's Bank Coffee House, had gone to some lengths to have the race results from Washington delivered as quickly as possible. A rider was supposed to have left the National Course on horseback immediately after the race. After riding all night, he would signal a watchman as he neared Brooklyn. The watchman would send one of two flags up the pole: white if Eclipse had won, red for Sir Charles.

Niblo, a tireless Irish-born entrepreneur who was prominent in the New York Association for the Improvement of the Breed of Horses, was still in Washington, but he had enthusiastically touted his Liberty Pole arrangement for weeks, telling his coffee-house customers — and anyone else who would listen — that they could be the first people in New York to know the winner of the race if they came to the pole at noon.

Now several hundred people — Eclipse fans and transplanted southerners rooting for Sir Charles — waited together for Niblo's rider, nervously exchanging taunts, boasts, and bets. "The news of Eclipse's demise will soon make our pockets fatter than a hibernating bear!" one southerner shouted, causing the other southerners to laugh and applaud. Factory jobs had brought them (and thousands of others from Virginia, Georgia, and the Carolinas) to New York, and even though they lived far from home, they were still loyal to the South and relished the idea of walking around Manhattan after a momentous southern victory.

The northerners hooted back, daring them to support their swaggering boasts by putting more money on the table. "Do any of you dare double your wager? My guess is you don't have the stomach," one exclaimed.

A northern cheer arose at noon when a white flag went up, but it immediately came back down — the watchman had mistaken a windmill's wing on the New Jersey shore for a sign from the courier. The correct winning flag was still expected to rise at any moment, but agonizing hours passed without any sign of the courier. The afternoon slipped away, tempers shortened, fights broke out. "Anxiety is great among the sportsmen of the city," one afternoon newspaper reported.

The northerners grew quiet and finally scattered, having convinced themselves that Niblo's courier bore sad news and had chosen not to deliver it rather than face those who had bet heavily on Eclipse and now had to pay. Southerners, on the other hand, stayed by the pole, eyes sparkling as their long wait slowly turned into a celebration. One afternoon paper gloomily opined that Sir Charles had won.

The courier never arrived, seemingly having defrauded Niblo. Southerners went to bed believing they had won bragging rights and stacks of northern money. But their dreams turned upside down when mail carriers, returning race fans, and the next morning's papers delivered the stunning news from Washington. Sir Charles had forfeited the original race and then failed to finish a single-heat event? Who could believe it?

Finally, a white flag went up on the Liberty Pole, flapping in the wind for all of New York to see. Niblo returned from Washington and raised a second white flag over his coffee house. The transplanted southerners skulked back to work, having read a depressing account of the race in a morning paper: "The very appearance of Eclipse, his bright eyes and distended nostrils breathing defiance, produced lameness in Sir Charles and induced his owner to leave the field and his $5,000 stakes in the bargain. And now the faces of southerners in New York are quite as long today as those of the Gothamites were yesterday."

It was time for New Yorkers to celebrate. They praised Eclipse when they met on the street that afternoon, and they drank to him that night in their homes and at turf-friendly establishments such as Niblo's. "To Eclipse, the pride of New York, who has exhibited the estimable character we all possess," said Niblo as he bought a round at the Bank. Similar toasts echoed across the city. Eclipse's victory was a triumph for all of the North. He had traveled into the heart of America's slaveholding territory and defeated the southerners at their own game. What could be better?

News of the victory spread through the rest of the country in the coming days. Mail carriers navigating their routes in stagecoaches and on steamships brought newspapers and personal correspondence containing details to smaller towns and remote outposts. In town after town, fathers and sons waited for the carriers and accosted them: "Sir, do you bear the information of Eclipse and Sir Charles?" The news produced wildly different reactions, depending on the region. Northern tavern owners rang bells and put out maroon flags honoring Van Ranst. Southerners were stunned. Many had recently seen Sir Charles in action and believed he was invincible.

Some southerners did not want to pay off their gambling debts; the substitute race was not what they had bet on, they said, and the best two-of-three event never took place. The judges at the National Course had sided with them, declaring all bets void. But northerners scoffed at such a judgment coming from Washington, a southern jurisdiction. They pointed out that English gamblers typically paid half the stakes on a forfeit. "Harrison has done so and so should you," the exasperated northerners said. Some did, but many continued to balk. The disputes would endure for months.

In Charleston, South Carolina, Alvan Fisher, a young Massachusetts artist, received a letter about the race from one of his patrons. Fisher, known for his paintings of animals and landscapes, had been commissioned to produce portraits of several horses, including Eclipse, and had gone to Charleston to spend the winter studying the thoroughbred form. He teased his hosts about the race.

"The éclat Old Eclipse has gained over the 'ancient dominion' has given me great joy,'" he wrote to a northern patron. "I can assure you, I laugh without mercy at these boasting southerners in consequence of our northern victory. I crack them for their arrogant assumptions. I sincerely hope the North will retain the character it has gained for superior speed, and which it always had for superior bottom. This last remark, by the way, applies to the sciences and literature as well as the turf."

A bitter dialogue erupted between northern and southern newspapers, underlining the increasing hostility between the regions. Some three hundred American papers were being published in 1822, many overseen by strong-willed editors doggedly advancing a point of view. The *Richmond Enquirer*, for instance, was fiercely loyal to slavery and the South, while the *New York Evening Post* was run by Federalists from New England. Although such papers disagreed politically, they printed opposing views found in other papers, knowing such controversial columns would attract readers.

The *Albany Daily Advertiser* wrote:

When we consider, on one hand, the time and manner of Mr. Harrison's challenge, the language in which it was expressed, and the large amount offered on his horse; and on the other hand, the modest and unassuming reply of Mr. Van Ranst, the heavy expenses he incurred in taking Eclipse southward, the disadvantages, danger, and risk of such a journey, and the cool steadiness with which he was backed by his friends, we can assure Mr. Harrison that his challenge was extremely ridiculous, and Mr. Van Ranst that his victory was nobly deserved.

We trust modesty and a sense of decency will prevent the southern gentlemen from raising their usual outcry against the North. The challenge came from the South, and the friends of Eclipse had to act under many disadvantages. Though all are gentlemen of fortune, none had cotton plantations to risk or bands of negroes whose liberties could be staked on a horse. We are sorry Sir Charles fell down in his training. If he should ever recover from his lameness, we propose Lady Lightfoot as a competitor. We think he will find this beautiful creature quite equal to his happiest efforts.

Southerners could only shake their heads at the references to their "usual outcry" and their "bands of negroes." Northerners were nothing if not smug in victory. How dare they suggest ancient Lady Light-foot as an appropriate opponent for Sir Charles?

The *Petersburg Intelligencer* responded, summing up the prevailing southern attitude: "Owing to an accident, the Virginia horse has lost the forfeit, but not his reputation. The New Yorkers, to be sure, have won some thousands of dollars; but if they rejoice with exceedingly great joy, the sporting world will remember that their triumph was one of four legs over three. Let them raise their flags and ring their bells; they are welcome to such a victory."

Years later, when northerners and southerners were firing guns at each other rather than insults, it would all make better sense: they were never meant to be countrymen, at least not originally, when they were colonists, or during the long prelude to the Civil War, when their differences were so obvious.

In hindsight, the idea that they could coexist was almost absurd, an ill-fated ideal encouraged by naive nationalists. Northerners and southerners were different fundamentally, organically, not just on the surface. Southerners were descended from fun-loving Colonial-era British loyalists who had supported the crown and the Church of England. Northerners belonged to socially conservative groups such as the Puritans and Quakers, who had opposed the crown and even briefly overthrown it in the 1600s.

They were polar opposites who had little in common and wanted nothing to do with each other. Southern plantation owners were the heirs of English aristocrats who had obtained their land from royal governors; northerners had fled the crown's rule. Southerners farmed (thanks to better weather and richer soil) and emulated their wealthier forefathers, racing horses, chasing foxes, and staging cock fights with a wink from the Church of England, which tolerated drinking and gambling. Northerners, forced inside by harsher weather, left their farms, formed communities, and worked together, forging the barest outline of the urban industrial life that would later characterize them. Informed by stricter churches, they generally disapproved of southern-style fun. Puritans outlawed sex and idle conversation on Sundays. William Penn, founder of Pennsylvania, declared, "The best recreation is to do good."

A desire for independence eventually engulfed the South, of course, and the shared goal enabled southerners and northerners to fight alongside each other during the Revolutionary War. But they were at odds again as soon as independence was won. The 1787 constitutional convention was divided over how to value slaves when determining taxes and congressional representation. Northerners believed slaves were property that should be taxed but not represented. Southerners claimed that their large slave population should be represented but not taxed. In a compromise, each slave was valued at three-fifths of a person.

They also argued over the right to navigate the Mississippi River and the effects of several international treaties. In the late 1790s, southerners were convinced that President John Adams, from Massachusetts, favored northern commerce over southern agriculture. "We are completely under the saddle of Massachusetts and Connecticut. They ride us very hard, cruelly insulting our feelings as well as exhausting our strength and subsistence," Virginia's Thomas Jefferson said.

The 1796 presidential election, in which Adams narrowly defeated Jefferson, vividly illustrated the enduring sectional divide. Adams won all fifty-one electoral votes available north of Pennsylvania. Jefferson won fifty of fifty-two electoral votes south of Maryland. The thirty-six votes in the middle states (New Jersey, Maryland, Pennsylvania, and Delaware) were split equally. Though northerners and southerners shared a loathing of the British and an effective business partnership — tobacco and cotton produced on southern plantations were exported through northern ports — the country was still split.

There was no doubt which region had the upper hand. Jefferson's victory in the 1800 presidential election began what historians later called "the Virginia dynasty," a twenty-four-year run encompassing six presidential terms, two apiece by Jefferson, James Madison, and James Monroe, all Virginians. Their southern Democratic-Republican party was so popular it almost put the northern Federalists out of business. In 1822 the U.S. Senate consisted of forty-four Democrat-Republicans and four Federalists. Commentators claimed the nation was in an "era of good feelings" because of the apparent political harmony and the absence of a war to fight.

But in reality that tranquillity was ebbing. The public was, in fact, sharply divided over who would succeed Monroe as president in 1824. Candidates included Kentucky's Henry Clay, former speaker of the U.S. House; Georgia's William Crawford, a U.S. senator backed by the Virginia dynasty; Massachusetts's John Quincy Adams, Monroe's secretary of state; and Tennessee's Andrew Jackson, a war hero. The Virginia dynasty was facing its most serious threat of the century.

Also, northern opposition to slavery was finally beginning to swell, launching the core conflict that would eventually bring on the Civil War. Slavery was a constitutionally protected southern institution, legal in a dozen states, Washington, D.C., and all of the two million square miles acquired in 1803 in the Louisiana Purchase. In 1822 there were one and a half million slaves on American soil, almost all in the South. Slaves outnumbered whites in South Carolina and made up 15 percent of the overall national population. Jefferson, Madison, and Monroe owned them, as did other wealthy southerners, including William Ransom Johnson.

Enlightened southerners recognized the immorality of buying and selling fellow humans — Jefferson termed it "deplorable" — but maintained it was an unfortunate necessity. Plantation owners could not pay field workers and still turn a profit, they said. Freeing slaves might ease their consciences, but it would destroy the region's economy.

Northern protests occasionally arose. "How long will the desire for wealth render us blind to the sin of holding the bodies and souls of our fellow men in chains?" asked Samuel Livermore, a Federalist senator from New Hampshire, in the late 1700s. But with slaveholders running the country, dissent was almost nonexistent. A proposal to outlaw slavery in all new states was easily quashed in Congress in 1818. The next year Missouri, a territory in the Louisiana Purchase, applied to join the union as a slaveholding state, expecting no opposition. Missourians already legally owned two thousand slaves.

But northern politicians abruptly drew the line at tolerating a practice many of their constituents quietly abhorred. It was as if the lawmakers finally decided they had stayed silent long enough. After a bill authorizing Missouri to write a state constitution was presented to the House, James Tallmadge, a New York Republican, introduced an amendment prohibiting new slaves in the state and also granting freedom at age twenty-five for children born in Missouri to slave parents.

Southerners were shocked. "If you persist, the union will be dissolved," a Georgia congressman railed. But northerners suddenly were not afraid to fight. Tallmadge responded, "If disunion must take place, let it be so. If civil war must come, I can only say, let it come."

The controversial amendment passed in the House, which was controlled by the more populous North, but failed in the Senate, equally divided between states for and against slavery. Virginia's John Randolph illustrated the South's determination to maintain the status quo when he roared during the House debate, "There can be no compromise on this question! God has given us Missouri and the devil shall not take it from us!"

A solution presented itself when Maine applied to join the union in 1819 as a nonslave, or "free," state. The Senate passed an amendment allowing both into the union with slavery prohibited in Maine and permitted in Missouri. That would maintain equality, with a dozen slave and a dozen free states. But a new debate erupted when an Illinois senator added an amendment banning slavery in the rest of the Louisiana Purchase, destined to be divided into many states. Southerners feared that limiting slavery's western growth would turn the nation toward eventual eradication. The *Richmond Enquirer* asked, "Shall we surrender so much of this region that was nobly won by the councils of a Jefferson and paid for out of a common treasury? If we yield now, beware; they will ride us forever."

In another compromise, Missouri was allowed to join the union as a slave state, but slavery was banned in much of the rest of the Louisiana Purchase. The *Enquirer* wrote, "We scarcely ever recollect to have tasted of a bitterer cup. The door is henceforth slammed in our faces." Many southern politicians offered similar laments. One stated that northerners had "kindled a fire which all the waters in the ocean" could not put out.

Missouri and Maine were in the union by August 1821, but the political struggle, which one historian later called "the first clear demarcation between the sections," had left raw scars. Northerners and southerners now understood that their disagreement on this fundamental issue ran dangerously deep. Different to begin with, the two sides sensed that loyalty to their region and their way of life might outweigh loyalty to the nation as a whole. A sectional dispute had boiled their blood; nationalism barely trickled through their veins. "This momentous question, like a fire bell in the night, awakened and filled me with terror," Jefferson said.

America, unmistakably, was starting to come apart.

As the only tangible contests between the regions, horse races were the only places other than Congress where northerners and southerners could see, hear, and feel their differences. Although the races were basically lighthearted diversions, lacking any real social or political significance, both sides envisioned in their horses the qualities that had made their regions distinct — the brilliance of untamed southern speed, the resolve of northern "bottom," or stamina — and saw the races as a chance to emphasize their superiority, win money, and, if necessary, punch a rival's jaw.

Coming in the immediate aftermath of the Missouri crisis, the race between Eclipse and Sir Charles stirred enough emotions on both sides to cause sensible men to lose their heads. "Many who have bad-betted large sums are unable to pay their honest debts to their mechanics, grocers, and even their washer-women," wrote Hezekiah Niles, editor of *Niles' Weekly Register,* a popular news gazette.

William Ransom Johnson instinctively grasped that it was imperative that his horse beat the other side. But he avoided the caustic public aftermath of the National Course fiasco. Although he was known to write letters to newspaper editors when an issue moved him (any horseman who dared disparage Sir Archie was assured of receiving a fiery rebuke from Johnson), he let the angry southern editors and other letter writers vent the South's frustrations.

He did read every word, however, carefully monitoring reactions to the race just finished and the one now on the distant horizon. One editorial in a Maryland newspaper almost moved him to applause. "As southlanders we regret that the reputation Virginia has so long and deservedly maintained, of raising the best horses, should have been risked on the foolish boastings of any individual," the paper stated. Harrison deserved that, Johnson felt.

As for the swaggering northern editorials, he found them end-lessly amusing; the New Yorkers certainly seemed to believe they had learned everything about racing in the few months since their state government had reopened the sport in 1821. When a Baltimore paper dared suggest that Eclipse had never really been tested because Lady Lightfoot was old, Sir Walter a mediocrity, and Sir Charles injured, the *New York Evening Post* fired back as if it were an all-knowing rac-ing authority: "What do the southern papers mean he has never been tested for speed and bottom? Did he not give a specimen of both when he defeated the great Lady Lightfoot, who had not lost a single race in the South in three years?"

You could put their knowledge of racing in a thimble, Johnson thought. But the assumptions of many of his fellow southerners also troubled him; those who doubted Eclipse's chances were as foolish as the northerners. Although he was sure he could beat the aging northern star, he knew he would have to present a top-notch op-ponent. He had seen enough at the National Course to know that Eclipse was a commendable runner. Even if Sir Charles had not been injured, Eclipse would have trounced him.

The most insightful column Johnson saw — one he could have written himself — was an anonymous letter to Washington's *Na-tional Intelligencer*, in which a southerner warned that overcon-fidence could lead to another disaster:

> Many gentlemen in my part of the country are still under the impres-sion Eclipse is not a first rate horse. This delusion, if persisted in, may be fatal to the southern horse in the next Great Race in May. I consider it ungenerous as well as injudicious to lessen the merit of the New York horse, as he is not only first-rate but extraordinary. At the same time, I indulge a confident expectation that in the upcoming contest the gen-tlemen of the South will make every exertion to procure a race horse capable of sustaining our heretofore unrivaled reputation.

When Johnson read that editorial in his study at Oakland, his sprawling plantation near Petersburg, Virginia, he stood up, energized for the fight ahead. There was just one "gentleman of the South" empowered to find the right horse — Johnson himself. He would find that horse, he vowed.

The next day he took a tandem carriage to nearby Dinwiddie County to visit Racing Billy Wynne, whose estate, Raceland, sat on the site of a famous Colonial-era tavern. His driver knew the route, so Johnson could sit quietly in the carriage and contemplate what lay ahead. He stared out at bare tree limbs and the dull, gray-green December landscape, knowing he would have to have a challenger in mind by spring, when the limbs would be full of leaves again and the landscape alive with color.

Wynne, who kept a race track and immaculate barns at Raceland, had trained some brilliantly fast horses over the years. His colt Timoleon had once run a mile in 1 minute 40 seconds, believed to be the fastest mile ever run in America. Now Billy had a couple of horses he felt might be able to represent the South at the Union Course, a four-year-old colt named John Richards and a six-year-old named Flying Childers.

Johnson and Billy spoke briefly in the parlor and then headed for the track to see the horses. The tobacco harvest was months away, but slaves still toiled in the fields, wearing thin shawls against the cold. The two men situated themselves near the finish line of the track. Billy ordered slave stable boys to bring the two horses out for Napoleon to observe. He walked around them slowly, inspecting the shine in their eyes and the conformation of their bones. He knelt and rubbed his hands up and down their legs, searching for deformities.

As he rose, he congratulated Billy. Both horses were fine specimens.

Billy ordered slave jockeys aboard the horses and barked instructions. They were to jog their animals around the oval and then accelerate into a hard sprint. Stable boys led them to the start and sent them running.

The horses raced around the oval, their rhythmic breathing audible in the quiet country air, muscles straining against their dark hides. John Richards ran ahead of the older horse, eyes ablaze with excitement as his jockey urged him with each stride, "Git, bo', git, git."

Napoleon watched wordlessly. Both horses obviously had potential. But he knew he could not take just any horse to New York.

Standing in the heart of Virginia horse country, Johnson began hatching his plan to find the right horse to silence the cocky northerners.

3

The Only Legitimate, Respectable Sport

I N 1822 MOST AMERICANS worked a minimum of ten hours a day, six days a week, grinding away monotonously at sweaty, exhausting jobs in fields, mills, or factories. Most made just enough money to get by and had little free time. During their rare chances to relax, they went out to taverns and theaters, read books by James Fenimore Cooper, Washington Irving, and Sir Walter Scott, played cards, attended fairs, and argued about politics. The newest rage was singing at home, made possible with music sheets sold in mass-market songbooks.

Spectator sports, which would become a cultural cornerstone, were not yet leisure-time options. It was impossible to envision the thunderous, addicting, billion-dollar sports world that would develop in the twentieth century. There were no leagues, teams, or touchstone events, no seasons, statistics, or superstars. Baseball, football, and basketball did not exist. National tennis and boxing champions would not be crowned for another half-century. Even simple exercise faced occasional resistance from conservatives who believed it was a waste of time and even perverted, dangerously arousing men's sexual desires. Princeton's faculty had banned ball playing in the 1780s, claiming it was "beneath a gentleman."

Bowling games such as ninepins and skittles were popular, as was a horseshoes-like game called quoits, in which people threw metal rings at targets. Swimming and running races were common, as were forerunners of baseball known as town ball in Philadelphia and Boston and as two old cat and four old cat (depending on how many bases were used) in the South. But while Americans enjoyed playing these games, they seldom gathered in groups to watch others play. Who had the money or time for spectator sports?

"Blood sports," such as cockfighting and bullbaiting, did attract large crowds. Hundreds of rowdy, liquored-up men would sit around rings fenced with barbed wire on Saturday nights and bet on which farmer had the toughest cock or how long it would take a bull to kill a pack of stray dogs. Sometimes they strung up a live goose on a wire and bet on how many passes a horseback rider would need to pull off the head. Such evenings were no argument for the societal value of "sports."

The only legitimate, respectable sport that consistently drew large crowds of fans — the only game with any semblance of tradition or organization in 1822, the only sport that could persuade a man to leave home and shell out his hard-earned cash on a ticket to a contest — was horse racing.

Americans treasured their horses, regarding them as both indispensable and magical. As much as they were needed for dragging farm plows, powering tobacco presses and cotton gins, and pulling carriages, they also were revered as "angels without wings," having deep souls and profound character. A litany of almost mythical American horses already existed; heroes such as the Narragansett pacer ridden by Paul Revere as he warned of advancing British troops in 1775, the Revolutionary War cavalry horses that bedeviled the British, and now fast racehorses were elevated to the same acclaimed status later generations would reserve for football and baseball stars.

Although opposition to the sport persisted, mainly in the North, because of the gambling involvement, many Americans believed there were few better sources of excitement and drama than a close race between fast horses. In the racing-mad South, it was said that a man left home for only three reasons: to worship at church, appear in court, or attend a race.

Many major cities had privately owned courses that held racing sessions or "meetings" every spring and fall, attracting as many as several thousand people for four or five straight days. Crowds filled the stands at Newmarket, an elegant course near Petersburg, Virginia; the Central Course in Baltimore; the Fairfield and Tree Hill courses in Richmond; the Washington Course in Charleston, South Carolina; the National Course in Washington; and the new Union Course on Long Island, the first with an all-dirt racing surface. There also were smaller country tracks in such places as Nottoway, Virginia; Lawrenceville, Georgia; and Lexington, Kentucky.

The major tracks were modern establishments with clubhouses, grandstands, kitchens, dining halls, sleeping quarters, barns, and immaculate grassy racing surfaces. Each was run by a local group of men, mostly wealthy tobacco planters, who bred and raced the horses that competed. Their groups were known as jockey clubs, even though the men deemed riding in the races so far beneath them they ordered slaves to do it.

Although no national jockey club existed to oversee the local clubs, compile records and statistics, and settle disputes, the clubs worked together to organize and promote the sport. (Some planters belonged to three or four clubs.) Their meetings unfolded on a set schedule every year, never conflicting. The racing calendar began every February with the Charleston meeting, followed by the Fairfield and Tree Hill meetings in early spring, and then the Newmarket races, the most prestigious, in May. Baltimore and Washington held meetings as spring gave way to summer. Autumn brought another round of meetings.

The races themselves were far more demanding than the contests that later generations of horsemen and fans would consider typical. A single race consisted of heats lasting two, three, or four miles apiece, with just a short rest between heats. Some races attracted as many as eight entries, while others were match races between two horses. But no matter how many animals were entered or how long the race was, the first horse to win two heats won the purse money put up by the jockey club. A purse could be as low as $50 or as high as $1,000 — princely sums in an age when a man could live on $500 a year.

Most horses began competing in two-mile events at three years old. The three-mile and four-mile events were for older, stronger horses. Four-mile racing was seen as the real test of a horse's mettle. England had long ago done away with such marathon events, shortening the Epsom Derby and other major races to single heats of a mile and a half or two miles; anything longer was deemed cruel. But Americans continued to use what they called the "heroic" distances, intent on proving they could breed better horses than the English. Certainly, the winners of four-mile races were formidable animals.

Leading horsemen, such as Johnson, Wynne, Harrison, and the New Yorkers Van Ranst and Stevens, traveled the entire circuit, running animals of different ages and abilities in various events. Most meetings lasted four or five days. The two-mile, three-mile, and four-mile events each had their own day, with other days allotted for handicap sweepstakes and one-mile sprints for two-year-olds. Racing usually began at noon and lasted several hours with all the heats and breaks.

Wherever and whenever a race was held, it was as if a holiday had been declared. Local fans took time off from work. Hundreds of visitors came from out of town. Hotels and taverns filled. People attended the races during the day and socialized at night. Jockey clubs put on elegant dinners and balls. The races dominated all talk.

The sport was unmistakably a rich man's game; only the wealthy could afford the extravagance of owning horses just to race them. Little had changed since 1674, when a Virginia tailor wanting to race his horse against a doctor's was fined and warned that the sport was "for gentlemen only."

But people in the middle and lower classes, who needed their horses for work and transportation, were just as crazy about fast races. They bought tickets (usually with a poorer view than the planters had), cheered just as hard, and bet as heavily as they could afford. Even slaves were occasionally allowed off from the fields to watch. Everyone had favorite owners, trainers, and horses.

The scale of the sport was still relatively small; millions of Americans paid little attention, either offended by the noise and gambling, uninterested, or more concerned about earning a living. But many people saw racing as a good time, a rare chance to spice up the monotony of daily life with an event that was unscripted, interactive, and dramatic. Horse racing connoted fun, purely, simply, and almost unfailingly.

Decades later, Americans would obsess over sports such as football and baseball because they enjoyed the games and the sense of belonging to a greater group of fans. In 1822, long after the first horses competed in the colonies but long before the beginning of America's sporting age, those fans had only one sport to follow and enjoy: horse racing.

Horses raced for the first time in the New World in 1665, less than a year after the British took New Amsterdam from the Dutch. The royal governor of New York ordered a track laid out on a grassy Long Island plain. But the disapproving attitudes of the Puritans and Quakers soon chased the sport out of the northern colonies. Boston banned it in 1677 because of the gambling, drinking, and general rowdiness associated with horse racing. Philadelphia sought a ban in 1695. New York and Rhode Island were the only northern colonies that tolerated it, and they ran hot and cold.

The sport then drifted south to Maryland, Virginia, and Carolina, finding a more broad-minded public and better weather. Southerners loved to line up their horses and see which was fastest. Their churches smiled on it, and the farming culture held horses in high esteem. A southerner with the perfect life had fertile soil for growing tobacco or cotton and a fast horse for winning grudge matches with neighbors on Saturday afternoons.

Swells of northern-style resistance occasionally arose in the South. In 1696 Virginia's governing House of Burgesses heard complaints from Northumberland County residents about rowdy Saturday races that resulted in all-night partying and Sunday rematches. But the sport's popularity easily overpowered such opposition. No southern county fair was complete without a set of races. Many towns had a Race Street for conducting quarter-mile sprints in which horses pounded down a narrow, straight path, surrounded by gamblers hurling bets and insults back and forth.

A more sophisticated version of the sport developed in England after Queen Anne, a horse enthusiast, opened a mile-long oval track at Ascot in 1711. Quarter-mile racing disappeared in England in favor of

longer contests in which horses circled oval courses vying for tro-
phies and money while carrying weight allotments determined by
their ages. The older the horse, the more weight it would carry.

The concept was soon exported to America, where racing ovals
materialized on burned-out tobacco fields across the South. A four-
mile race between horses representing Maryland and Virginia lured
hundreds of spectators to a hilly race ground in the Virginia Tidewater in 1752. A Maryland-based mare named Selima won, infuriat-
ing Virginians and sparking a racing rivalry between the states that
lasted until the eve of the Revolutionary War.

As racing's popularity increased, the first American jockey
clubs organized in Charleston and in Annapolis, Maryland. Others
sprouted elsewhere. In sophisticated Annapolis, where it was joked
that people were more British than the British, the social season
peaked with parties and theater performances organized around the
races. George Washington attended the Annapolis meeting and
listed his gambling record in his diary.

With more money and prestige at stake, planters inevitably sought
to breed faster horses. Until the 1750s, American runners came from
a blend of smallish breeds, including the Scottish Galloway, a popular
horse in England. Breeding specifically to produce a racehorse was
seen as wasteful, an affront to the men striving to make America
better. Horses were for work, not sport.

The demise of quarter-mile races in favor of longer, oval-course
events merged the owners' desire for more formidable horses with
the general public's enthusiasm. Planters could breed horses specifically to race without being criticized. A new, vastly superior breed,
the thoroughbred, eventually became the dominant American racehorse.

Like most aspects of American racing, thoroughbreds origi-
nated in England, where soldiers returning from desert battles in the
late 1600s kept talking about astounding Arabian horses sprinting
through the sand. Three of these horses imported to England — the
Byerley Turk, the Darley Arabian, and the Godolphin Arabian —
sired fleet youngsters when bred to Galloway mares, providing the
genetic foundation of the new breed.

The Byerley Turk was captured in 1686 during the British siege of Buda, Hungary; a guardsman named Robert Byerley took him as booty, rode him in battle, and brought him home. A few years later Thomas Darley, a businessman serving as the British consul in Aleppo, Syria, eyed a yearling in the desert, convinced a reluctant sheikh to part with it, and sent it to his brother in England; that was the Darley Arabian. The last to arrive, the Godolphin Arabian, was a dark beauty foaled in Yemen and shipped through Syria and Tunis before landing in France's royal stable. The king disliked him and supposedly consigned him to pulling a water cart, but an Englishman, Edward Coke, spotted him, bought him, and sent him to England, where he ended up in the Earl of Godolphin's stable.

The descendants of these sires were taller, thinner, and faster than any Galloway. A son of the Godolphin Arabian offered the first example of the developing genetic magic. He was a bright bay with a white blaze across his forehead and four white ankles. No one had ever seen a horse run so fast. His name was Childers but, seeing him run, his fans called him "Flying" Childers. He beat all comers in England from 1721 to 1723, winning races by as much as a quarter-mile.

Americans visiting England saw these spectacular horses and wanted them for their stables. Samuel Gist, a tobacco merchant from Hanover County, Virginia, imported a horse named Bulle Rock in 1730 — the first thoroughbred to reach America. Other early importers included Samuel Ogle, the royal governor of Maryland; Ogle's bachelor brother-in-law, Benjamin Tasker, Jr.; and John Tayloe II, owner of the Mount Airy estate in Richmond County, Virginia.

Imports soon dominated American breeding and racing. Of 175 horses imported before the Revolutionary War, more than half went to Virginia, and many won races. Although colonists still believed horses were for business rather than sport, racing boomed in Virginia. In 1774 Philip Fithian, a noted tutor to aristocrats, wrote in his diary about attending a race in Richmond with a crowd that was "remarkably numerous." The planters whose horses populated the races believed they were on the verge of gaining their own version of independence, breeding high-caliber horses without help from England.

But the Revolution devastated American racing and breeding. The Continental Congress halted racing in 1774, and once the war began, most swift American horses were either killed in battle or stolen by

British troops, wiping out decades of genetic development and any semblance of a sport. The only horses spared were impotent stallions and mares unfit for motherhood.

Many of the proud stables of the Tidewater suffered such horrific losses that they never recovered. America's racing center shifted to lower Virginia and upper North Carolina, an area known as the Piedmont, where the plantations and horses experienced less devastation. (Soldiers under the British general Charles Cornwallis supposedly were too depressed to pillage and plunder when they passed through the Piedmont on the way to surrendering in Yorktown, Virginia, in 1781.)

When racing resumed after the war, the social climate had changed. The racing-friendly Church of England was no longer as dominant in the South, replaced among the lower classes by conservative Protestant sects. The leaders of these sects opposed racing, deeming it a pointless pastime of spoiled elites. The sport virtually disappeared in the North and struggled as never before in the South. North Carolina's General Assembly passed a bill designed to repress racing in 1790. Even in turf-happy Virginia, the General Assembly passed a law in 1792 prohibiting bets of more then seven dollars. That pushed some horsemen to go farther west, to Kentucky and Tennessee. The first course west of the Allegheny Mountains opened near Louisville in 1788, and Kentucky eventually replaced Virginia as America's racing hotbed.

Though it was foundering, American racing survived because of the persistence of planters who imported new thoroughbreds. Conducting business with their former motherland was tricky after the war, but horsemen maintained cordial relations with English breeders. The war had diminished neither their passion for the turf nor their desire to prove they could produce runners equal to those in England.

In 1796 the famed English architect Benjamin Henry Latrobe, who had come to America to direct the building of a canal, attended a racing meeting in Petersburg, Virginia. The level of interest in the races astounded him. Petersburg's taverns were so crowded with sportsmen that he had to sleep in a garret with seven other men (becoming an expert on snoring, he noted in his diary). Everyone was so focused on the races, he wrote, that he was as lost for conversation as if he had been among the Hottentots.

New sires imported from England included Medley, a gray so popular with Virginians that he was sold for 29,000 pounds of tobacco, valued at $7,000. Another gray named Messenger satisfied the few active northern breeders.

But the most important import was Diomed, an aging chestnut who arrived in Virginia in 1799 with little expected of him, only to prove wrong the many horsemen who had doubted him. John Hervey, a twentieth-century American racing historian, called him "the greatest progenitor that ever crossed the Atlantic." William Woodward, owner of Belair Stud, a twentieth-century racing dynasty, said, "Diomed is the horse above all others that we Americans should respect — one might say, worship."

Foaled in England in 1777, Diomed had been handsome and fast in his youth, a horse marked for greatness. With an upright bearing, a white star between his eyes, and the kind of natural speed horsemen dream about, he won seven straight races as a three-year-old, including the first running of what became the Epsom Derby, England's premier race. Fans grew accustomed to seeing his chestnut coat streaking far ahead of the competition.

But then his owner, Sir Charles Burnbury, the president of England's Jockey Club, took him out of action for a much-needed rest, and when he returned to racing, his speed was mysteriously gone. Horses he had easily beaten began finishing ahead of him. He still managed to win a few events, but then he lost eight in a row, with increasingly dismal efforts. Whatever magic he had possessed was gone.

Burnbury retired him and stood him at stud, but the trajectory of Diomed's stud career followed a familiar arc — early promise followed by a decline. His descendants proved high-strung, obstinate, and mediocre at the races, and his allure faded. By the spring of 1798 Burnbury was ready to unload him, believing the horse had little remaining use. His stud fee was down to two guineas, or $10, little more than tip money. It was also rumored that infertility was impending. When a pair of horse traders offered Burnbury $250, he accepted. The horse traders then put Diomed back on the market.

That spring, two Virginia horsemen, John Hoomes and John Tayloe III, needed a stallion. Hoomes, the operator of a profitable stagecoach line between Alexandria and Richmond, imported thoroughbreds and resold them. Tayloe, the scion of America's greatest prewar racing family, ran a successful racing stable that won 113 of 141 races between 1791 and 1806. The two men co-owned a breeding business, offering stallions to the public, and one of their sires had died unexpectedly, leaving customers waiting.

Hoomes and Tayloe wrote to their London equine agents about Diomed, having seen the traders' advertisements for him in the London papers. The agents replied that the old horse was indeed available but was hardly a wise investment. Tayloe's agent warned that Diomed was "a tried and proved bad foal-getter" — a producer of useless horses — and added that James Weatherby, the influential publisher of England's General Stud Book, which traced thoroughbred lineages, believed it was pointless to breed any mare to Diomed.

The Virginians ignored the warnings. Like many American horsemen, they respected the British but believed they knew as much, if not more. They paid $5,000 for Diomed and booked him on a boat for America.

The English horse community laughed. Burnbury, who had sold the horse for a fraction as much just weeks earlier, was incredulous. Weatherby and the equine agents shook their heads; Hoomes and Tayloe were good customers and seemingly astute horsemen, but this was ridiculous. It wasn't even certain that Diomed, at age twenty-one, would survive the difficult three-month trip across the Atlantic. Diomed left England in ignominy, his early brilliance long forgotten. Fans who knew him only in his recent incarnation as a cheap stallion, not even worth his meager stud price, were amazed that anyone wanted him.

But something inexplicable happened as he crossed the Atlantic, one of those magical mysteries of the horse world. Diomed had been creaky and sleepy when he left England, but when he arrived in Virginia, his coat shone and his eyes sparkled as he bounded off the ship in Norfolk, resembling a colt more than a disconsolate old codger.

When Hoomes went to the dock to greet the horse, he sent an excited letter to Tayloe. "I wish you could see Diomed. I really think him the finest horse that I ever saw," Hoomes wrote. The men began accepting mares for their new stallion. Diomed proved popular. The bane of England became the talk of Virginia. Horsemen lined up to breed their mares to him. His sons and daughters inherited his upright bearing and went out and won on the turf. Hoomes and Tayloe made back six times their investment when they sold him.

What made Diomed great again? It is impossible to know for sure. The sea air seemed to revive him, as did the changes in geography and feed once he was in Virginia. Being bred to the best mares in America's top racing state certainly helped his chance of producing better runners; he had not seen top mares in England for years, the breeders there preferring more respected sires.

Whatever the explanation, Diomed became a star again. His last years in America resembled his early life, when fans were excited just at the mention of his name.

In 1805 a large crowd gathered at a course near Richmond for a match race between two of Diomed's sons, colts named Florizel and Peacemaker. Florizel, owned by William Ball, was undefeated, but Hoomes intended to beat him with Peacemaker. Peacemaker had been forced to forfeit a sweepstakes to Florizel the year before because of an injury, and Hoomes, in frustration, had issued a high-stakes challenge to Ball. Each man put up $3,000 for a race hailed as the Virginia championship.

To help prepare Peacemaker, Hoomes brought in Tayloe and the young William Ransom Johnson. The trio's combined expertise easily outweighed Ball's, but Ball had the faster horse. Florizel won with a smooth, effortless running action. The line of horsemen bringing mares to breed to Diomed lengthened.

That same year a Diomed-sired colt named Truxton, owned by Andrew Jackson, the future war hero and president, competed in a match race in Tennessee that attracted what Jackson described as "the largest concourse of people I ever saw assembled, unless an army." Truxton won a competition so bitter it escalated into a pistol duel between Jackson and the owner of the opposing horse. Jackson took a bullet in the chest but delivered a fatal shot to his foe.

Truxton went on to win more races and glory for Diomed, as did the Piedmont's fastest colts, Sir Archie and Wrangler, and a brilliant mare, Haynie's Maria. Diomed's offspring brought excitement back to the sport when it was desperately needed. He produced so many winners in slightly less than a decade of American stud service that it became rare for a top horse not to trace back to him.

Englishmen who had dismissed Diomed years earlier waved a white flag of defeat, admitting he had made fools of them. His death in 1808 was regarded as a tragedy among the planters who had relied on him to improve the quality of the horses in their barns.

But he left behind a dynasty.

His presence was still so powerful in 1822 that it was as if he were still alive. Eclipse, the great northern star, was descended from him, as were all the southern horses Eclipse had beaten in match races and all the horses William Ransom Johnson would consider for the Union Course race.

Northerners and southerners were at each other's throats, but they shared an eternal debt to Diomed, the horse that, more than any other, saved American racing when it was at its lowest ebb, laying the groundwork for what was to come.

4

A Fine Ole Gen'leman

HE WHITE-GRAY REMAINS of a recent heavy snowfall blanketed the ground when Racing Billy's two horses, John Richards and Flying Childers, were moved from Raceland to Johnson's estate in early January 1823. They arrived on a cloudy afternoon, their riders jogging them beneath the sign over Oakland's front gate, which read THERE IS NOTHING SO GOOD FOR THE INSIDE OF A MAN AS THE OUTSIDE OF A HORSE.

The estate, which ran for three miles along the Appomattox River, was more a tree-shaded horse haven than a tobacco plantation, featuring immaculate stables, a two-mile straightaway training track, pristine fields, and an eighteen-room mansion with two great halls. Johnson kept his stallions and mares on the property. Horses in training for the races were stabled at his private barn adjoining the nearby Newmarket track.

Napoleon had asked Billy to bring the horses over so he could take a more serious look at them as possible challengers to Eclipse. He had liked what he saw when he inspected them in December at Raceland, but he wanted to know if these two really had potential to represent the South in New York.

Arthur Taylor, a diminutive ex-jockey who was Johnson's long-time second-in-command, joined Napoleon and Billy to watch the horses work out the next morning. The three men stood on a raised stand by the finish, bundled in long-tailed, high-collared sheepskin coats. Johnson and Wynne chewed braided twists of cured tobacco leaves from the most recent harvest.

Johnson ordered slave jockeys onto John Richards and Flying Childers and had the horses run separately and then together. The solo dashes on the straightaway track were strictly for Johnson to inspect their running action. Some horses run gracefully, with seemingly minimal effort, legs and torso almost a single unit. Other horses, even some fast ones, run awkwardly, hamstrung by odd bone structure or natural hitches in their gait that either slow them or limit their potential to run long distances without tiring.

Johnson observed that Flying Childers was slightly pigeon-toed in front, but he seemed to overcome it and cover ground rapidly. John Richards, the four-year-old, was a muscular, heavy-shouldered bay with a wild-eyed look and impeccable action, his legs a blur as he ran, his thick torso muscles straining against his hide. Johnson watched him in silence, concentrating, impressed.

When it was time for the horses to compete against each other, the jockeys jogged them down to the far end of the two-mile track, then turned and came back running. At first they were just specks in the distance — Johnson, Billy, and Taylor strained to see them — but they came into focus as they neared the finish, their hurried breath forming clouds in the chill air, their rhythmic exhalations the only sounds in the wintry scene.

They ran together most of the way, but John Richards, legs pumping, surged ahead near the finish and came in ahead. He was an equine teenager if ever there was one, loose and long-limbed and slightly out of control. He had paid little attention to his jockey until near the end of the trial, when he finally obeyed a call to run. The horse was obviously in need of exacting instruction, but he brimmed with potential.

After the trial the men watched the horses cool down from the workout, which had totaled some four miles of running. Johnson always watched to see how horses reacted to exercise, gleaning from their responses whether they had the capacity to handle an afternoon of four-mile heats. John Richards clearly did; his chest barely heaved, as if all that running had barely bothered him.

After the grooms bathed the horses and led them away to their sta-

42

bles, thick pillars of steam rising off their hides, Johnson asked Taylor for an opinion. Quiet and knowing, Taylor could not match Johnson's dramatic persona, but he was every bit Napoleon's equal as a horseman.

Taylor had emigrated from England as a boy and been taken in by Johnson after showing an aptitude for race riding. Known for wearing ratty rabbit and coonskin caps cocked at an angle, he rode winner after winner in the early 1800s and then took up training when he outgrew the saddle. For years he had run Johnson's barns at Oakland and Newmarket and traveled with him to the races, leaving an assistant in charge. He lived with his family on a small neighboring property that Napoleon had given him as a reward for his years of service. Johnson teased him about his British roots, calling him "guvna," but he valued Taylor's opinion.

Taylor said John Richards's raw talent was impressive, but the horse clearly needed schooling. Billy nodded, pleased to hear the generally positive reaction. Johnson said he believed both were good horses.

After dinner that night, Johnson and Billy relaxed in the library, with a great fire crackling in the massive hearth. The men sat in ornate, high-backed chairs and looked through tall windows at the snowy ground outside, lit by a full moon on a cold, clear night. Warmed by the cozy surroundings, Johnson was in an expansive mood. As Billy listened, the trainer explained that he was just beginning his search for the right horse. He planned to view the fastest horses of many men, including John Tayloe III and John Randolph. Why not scour the whole countryside? The race was still months away. He had plenty of time.

Billy agreed, pointing out that the North had given him "the world" from which to pick a challenger.

Johnson eyed his friend before responding; this was a subject that moved him. He did not need the world, he sniffed. The fastest horses in America were right here in the Piedmont. The finest descendants of Sir Archie roamed the fields of Virginia and the Carolinas, and in those fields he would find a horse that could defeat Eclipse. He was sure of it.

Billy agreed that Virginia and Carolina had many fine horses but wondered if it was wise to ignore the larger territory the northern group had ceded to him. Johnson smiled. The South still had an ample advantage, he said. An assortment of America's finest equine blood was available within a day's carriage ride of where they sat.

In the next few weeks Johnson entertained more horsemen at Oakland, studying their animals, seeking their opinions, and raising the money to cover the $20,000 stakes. (Billy returned several times, offering another set of eyes at the workouts.) John Randolph agreed to put up thousands of dollars during a brief stopover on his way from Roanoke to Washington for the congressional session. Johnson's father, Marmaduke, a voracious gambler, also agreed to contribute.

Johnson knew that bringing horsemen to Oakland would increase their excitement for the upcoming race. He had inherited the plantation from his father-in-law, a doctor, and made it into a showcase for entertaining visitors as well as training horses. He lived splendidly there with his wife and four children. The precision of the slaves and staff, the easy atmosphere, and the cordiality of the hosts were widely recognized. Randolph, Andrew Jackson, and Henry Clay — all horsemen as well as politicians — were among Johnson's closest friends, and they often visited. Johnson was himself a politician, having held state-level offices in Virginia and his native North Carolina.

In the end, even as he culled the opinions of others, Johnson alone would pick the horse to challenge Eclipse. The southern side of the race was his fiefdom. He would select the horse and jockey, oversee their training, and manage them on race day at the Union Course. The decision to grant him such power had been made by acclaim, without debate; the other horsemen just bowed to his superiority. Of the one and only Napoleon, it was said, "If not born in a manger, he was raised in a stable." And no one deemed it sacrilegious to invoke the Lord when explaining his prowess.

Animals racing in Johnson's sky blue colors had so dominated the American turf for two decades that it was just assumed they would win whatever events they entered. Between 1807 and 1809 they lost just twice in sixty-three starts, evoking the comparison to France's emperor Napoleon Bonaparte, then lording it over Europe. Johnson, not yet thirty, was lording it over American racing with the same fe-rocity, showing up at meetings with a half-dozen hungry runners that squashed everything in their path.

Now, when southerners heard that Johnson finally was chal-lenging Eclipse, they were ecstatic. Their disappointment over Sir Charles's embarrassing defeat was replaced by a sense of confidence that rolled through the region like an ocean tide. The horsemen Eclipse had defeated so far were no match for Napoleon. Johnson had dominated them for years in conditions that were, if anything, fair. With six months to sort through candidates and find the right one to beat a nine-year-old, he was almost certain to win.

At any time his stable included between thirty and fifty horses. Many were his own, either bred or bought by him, sometimes right on the track after beating his horse. Others belonged to rival horse-men who gave him their best runners to train, believing he could do more with them. He turned down a fair share of such offers, his sta-tus enabling him to pick and choose.

His mythic horsemanship was a popular topic of conversation among his rivals, who studied him and sought unsuccessfully to imi-tate him. He alone could look at a field of indistinguishable yearlings and pick out the ones that would eventually race with the most heart and bottom. His secret? It was not always the most muscular horses, those a layman might pick, but rather those that breathed most easily and still displayed determined expressions after long training runs — the signs of endurance and competitiveness.

Johnson also had an uncanny knack for entering his runners in the events to which they were best suited. Some excelled at two-mile heats, others at longer distances. Some preferred particular tracks. Some hated to train but raced brilliantly. Every horse generated questions. When was it mature enough for the races? When was it ready for the heroic distance? Where could it win if it was of just av-erage ability? Knowing the answers to those questions often sepa-rated winners from losers, and Johnson always knew the answers.

He never raced a horse unless he was sure it was ready to perform at its best, a determination other horsemen seldom considered. His training schedules were notoriously rigorous, consisting of long morning runs with staccato bursts of sprints mixed in, emphasizing stamina where other trainers focused on speed. American horsemen were obsessed with measuring their horses against the clock (unlike their British counterparts, who did not use watches), but Johnson went by his instinct. Only after a horse could effectively run double the distance of an upcoming event (for instance, eight miles in training for a four-mile event) would he consider running it for money.

For years he had run horses at major courses from Georgia to Maryland and had regularly sent runners to Tennessee and Kentucky. It took a sizable staff to maintain the far-flung operation. Johnson employed a team of trustworthy white assistants who had grown up with horses on surrounding farms, but he plucked his grooms and jockeys from his multitudes of dark-skinned slaves.

Some slaves excelled at feeding and cleaning the animals and were canny horsemen themselves, able to offer Johnson advice. A few were natural jockeys, small but strong and shrewd amid the noise and fury of a race. Most lived right in the barns or in nearby outbuildings, sleeping on pallets and rising before dawn to guide the horses through their daily training sessions. It was hardly an easy life, but it beat the depressing servitude of the fields and it offered the exciting chance to travel and deal personally with the master (and maybe gain his favor). Slaves competed for Johnson's attention and the chance to work in his stable; in return, he was constantly on the lookout for slaves who exhibited a knack with horses. In an 1884 magazine article Charles Stewart, a slave jockey who proved so successful that he eventually gained his freedom, recalled joining the stable. (Stewart, more than seventy years old, spoke to an interviewer, who printed his recollections in dialect.)

> De Colonel he jes' dashed his eyes ober me — I was monst'ous lean fur twelve year ole — an' says "Here's a light weight [rider] for my stables. Do you know a horse when you see one, boy?" I says, "Yas, sir. I knows a horse rum a mule jes' as far as I kin see 'em bofe walk." Dey all larfs at dat, an' de nex' thing dey gives me some new clo's all fixed up, an' I was sent down to de great big training stables my new marster owned at New Market, an' I was set to wuk. Dar was a big force of boys an' men at wuk on dem horses, two boys to each an' another white man second in charge. Jehu! How we did wuk on dem horses.

The depth of Johnson's stable was astounding. He always had different horses ready to dominate at every distance from one to four miles. The jockey clubs at some tracks finally stopped giving him the winning purse after each race; instead they waited until the end of the meeting to hand him the stacks of bills and coins he had earned. A few clubs quietly asked him to stay away so that other horsemen would have a chance to win, but most eagerly sought his presence, which confirmed their track's importance.

With his fierce dark eyes, strong jaw, and flowing white hair, Johnson possessed the looks and reputation that drew all eyes to him as he strode across a track. His female admirers called him "Irish Beauty." His manners were impeccable, his dress stylish but not pretentious, his innate humanity plainly evident in his treatment of his slaves, which Charles Stewart recalled:

> My marster was de picter of a fine ole gen'leman; he was a fa'r-lookin' man, with thick white hyar, an' eyes datjes' snapped fire at you; he was what you calla plain gen'leman, an' didn't b'lieve his coat an' pants was de makin' of him; he treated his servants like dey was de prime cut, an' dey all loved him. He was a yearthly gen'leman, an' ef dere is any good place anywhere, it 'pears to me like he ought to be in it.

In a way, Johnson's lifelong love affair with horses and racing was attributable to fate. He happened to grow up in north-central North Carolina in the late 1700s, just as that region emerged as America's racing capital, replacing the war-ravaged Tidewater.

Born in 1782, he was raised on a tobacco plantation close to the Virginia state line. His father, Marmaduke, was the Warren County clerk, an educated man who had married into a wealthy family that owned a dozen slaves. Like many men in the region, Marmaduke became an avid horseman in the 1780s, breeding and training animals and then gambling on them.

Marmaduke's interest dated to his purchase of a mare to lead his carriage, a seemingly insignificant acquisition at the time. Waiting for the carriage by his front door one morning, he was told by a slave that the mare had been difficult to catch in the field, outrunning everyone who chased her. Having watched his neighbors run their fastest horses on straightaway quarter-mile tracks on Saturday after-noons, Marmaduke decided to give his mare a shot. He took his carriage to a tavern and found a friend who owned a speedy horse named Bessy.

"How about a race?" Marmaduke asked.

"Ah, yes. What will you start?" the friend replied with a smirk.

"My nag against your Bessy," Marmaduke said.

"Done, sir," the friend said. "Your nag against the best riding horse in town."

Marmaduke had a quarter-mile track cut on a burned-out tobacco field at the back of his property. (Oval tracks were not yet popular in North Carolina, as they were in Virginia.) The friends of both men heard about the race and came to watch.

The horses, restrained by slaves holding ropes, were aligned at a start and then set loose to cheers. Marmaduke's mare broke quickly, hurtled down the track, and finished well ahead of Bessy. Marma-duke smiled broadly as he collected his winnings from his friend. The experience thrilled him, and he soon had a stable of horses running at the oval courses that sprouted around the Piedmont. The Cottage Course in Warrenton was his favorite.

It was hard to say what excited Marmaduke more, training a fast horse or winning money with it. His appetite for betting was seem-ingly limitless. He enjoyed the challenge of arranging favorable odds and proving he knew best. On his deathbed years later, having over-heard his doctor predict that he would not live past noon, Marma-duke bet the doctor fifty dollars that he would make it — and he hung on just long enough to collect.

His son William attended Warrenton Academy, where Marma-duke was a trustee. Marmaduke tried to encourage William to take up various careers. Learn how to run a business, he said. Study law, read books. William heeded his father's suggestion that he have varied interests. He would later hold political offices, run a planta-tion, and oversee a vast land deal in Texas. He could do anything, it seemed. But he was always a horseman first.

His upbringing coincided with Marmaduke's increased interest in racing and gambling in the late 1700s. He listened to his father go on and on about how to train horses, when and where to race them, and how to win money. As soon as he was old enough, William disappeared into the stables and, in essence, never came out.

He related instinctively to horses, demonstrating a precocious knack for understanding them. Accompanying Marmaduke to training sessions, he was soon telling his father which horses had the most potential and how to coax their best effort from them. Marmaduke was pleased about his son's knowledge but worried that the youngster was a little too enthusiastic.

Marmaduke demurred at first when William, then fourteen, began pestering to let him train a horse without help from adults. But he eventually relented and gave his son a colt. Within months William challenged his father to a race. Marmaduke smiled, sure that he knew more than his son. Their horses were lined up opposite each other at the Cottage Course one Saturday afternoon.

William's horse won easily. Seeing that, Marmaduke decided to focus on breeding, leaving the training to his son.

As he grew into a tall and handsome young man with long dark hair and twinkling eyes, William started out running horses at local tracks but was soon drawn to the higher caliber of racing in Virginia. He moved easily between the two states and strengthened his ties to Virginia when he married a girl from there in 1803. He became, in effect, a resident of both states, stabling horses at Oakland as well as at Marmaduke's plantation.

In Virginia he was soon known as one of the shrewdest trainers available. Some of the state's most avid breeders, including John Hoomes, sought his services. His stable swelling, he sent winner after winner to tracks ranging from elegant city circuits in Richmond and Petersburg to remote wooded outposts. Meanwhile, he was so popular in North Carolina that he was elected in 1807 to represent Warren County in the state legislature. He was twenty-five years old, and his hair was already turning white.

In 1809 Johnson took over the training of a young horse that would become his equine counterpart. Sir Archie was a strapping son of Diomed that had bounced around before coming to Johnson. Bred by Archibald Randolph, a Virginia war hero and tobacco planter, the young horse had been foaled in 1805 out of a losing race mare named Castianira that had gone blind. Randolph originally named the foal

Robert Burns after a friend, but when he encountered money trouble he sold it to John Tayloe III, who renamed it Sir Archie to boost the spirits of the troubled Randolph. Tayloe then sold the horse to his nephew, Ralph Wormeley, for $400 and a mare that proved worthless. Wormeley soon lost interest in racing and put his horses up for sale. Sir Archie attracted no buyers even though ads extolled him as "vigorous, clean-limbed, and swift, of ideal proportions."

Still under Wormeley's care, Sir Archie was ready for the races by the fall of 1808. A bout of distemper slowed preparations for his debut at the National Course, but Wormeley ran him anyway, not wanting to pay the forfeit. Not surprisingly, Sir Archie lost. He was then entered in a four-mile sweepstakes at Fairfield that attracted seven entrants, including True Blue, a Johnson-trained colt, and another speedy colt named Wrangler.

The sweepstakes drew more than a thousand spectators to Fairfield on a sunny fall afternoon in 1808. Wrangler won the first heat by three lengths, showing no evidence of tiring near the end, but he fell during the second heat and was withdrawn from the event. Johnson's True Blue decisively won the second and third heats to take the purse. Sir Archie, obviously still affected by his recent illness, was never in contention.

Of all the horses in Johnson's stable, True Blue was the best, a natural speedster with an upright carriage and running action so graceful it almost seemed he was floating above the grass rather than racing across it. Although he had lost the first heat, he was clearly superior to the other horses in the sweepstakes. Ordinarily, Johnson would have been watching him proudly as he ran away from the field, but the great horseman found himself focusing on Sir Archie, running well behind.

What a specimen, Johnson thought.

Sir Archie was indeed quite a sight, even at less than 100 percent. His bones were long, his musculature thick, his eyes clear and alive, taking in everything around him. And his running action was perfectly synchronized, the equine equivalent of a classical orchestra.

That's royalty, Johnson thought. It didn't matter that the horse was outclassed in the race; he was obviously not fully recovered from his illness. But given time to heal and months of training, he could be a formidable four-mile runner with that frame and action. A horse like that could win a man a lot of money. Like Marmaduke, Johnson was an eager gambler, always operating with wagers and profits in mind. Four-mile racing always attracted the biggest bettors and highest stakes.

After pocketing the sweepstakes purse, Napoleon sought out Wormeley and offered $1,500 for Sir Archie. It was not a very high offer, but Wormeley was anxious to sell and quickly agreed to the price. Johnson left the course with Sir Archie.

The young horse spent the winter at Marmaduke's estate in North Carolina. Johnson gave him time to recover from his illness and then began training him to run strictly in four-mile races. As he healed and filled out, Sir Archie was even more impressive than Johnson had expected. The horse seemed almost human at times. His eyes sparkled when he recognized someone. He quickly learned his feeding routine and let grooms know when they were late putting a meal on the table. He paused when his jockey took him for an extra lap of training, as if to note that he understood this was a departure from the norm. But then he lowered his head and gave his best throughout the extra mile, carrying himself low to the ground and vaulting forward on strong shoulders while pushing off with his hind legs.

Johnson had never been around a horse with so many physical and mental assets. Sir Archie had everything a champion should possess. His appetite for hard work was staggering; the harder he was pushed, the more he seemed to enjoy it.

Napoleon usually avoided getting emotionally involved with his horses — they would break your heart if you were not careful, breaking down or running so poorly you had to unload them — but he could not help himself now. If you appreciated talent in a horse, as Johnson did, you could not help falling for Sir Archie.

By spring the horse was ready to race. His comeback took place at Fairfield, where he had lost the previous fall. This time, he won, defeating Wrangler in successive heats in a four-mile event. He raced just as well as Johnson had thought he could, all but eating up the ground without tiring. The hundreds of fans at the course murmured in surprise. What had happened to this horse that had lost so dully before?

Wrangler had an excuse for losing, having raced and won just the day before, and his owner, Miles Selden, asked for a rematch. The horses met again a week later at Newmarket, again at the four-mile distance. Wrangler, a smallish gray, was up to the challenge this time. He held a narrow lead throughout the first heat and fought off a rally from Sir Archie to win it. The two then traded the lead back and forth through the second heat and appeared to reach the finish in a tie. But instead of declaring a dead heat, the judges said Wrangler had won.

Johnson, annoyed, immediately asked for a rematch consisting of a single four-mile heat, with a large private bet on the line. Selden turned him down, knowing his chances of beating Sir Archie again were slim.

The horses ran into each other again that fall in a four-mile event at Fairfield that drew five entries and more than a thousand fans. Johnson approached Selden before the start and negotiated a $1,000 side bet. He was so certain of winning he gave two-to-one odds.

Wrangler took off from the start at a full sprint, his jockey seemingly asking him to go as fast as possible, saving nothing for the end. The horse covered the first two miles in 3 minutes 46 seconds. Two minutes per mile was the standard for superior racing at any distance, so 3:46 was exceptional.

Johnson was alarmed to see Sir Archie fall farther and farther back and trail by fifteen lengths midway through the heat. But then the big horse started coming. As Wrangler slowly ran out of steam, having started too hard, Sir Archie cut the lead to ten lengths, then five, pulling even as the final lap started. The race was effectively over. Sir Archie took the lead and moved so far ahead that Wrangler became discouraged, stopped running, and was disqualified. (Horses finishing far behind the winner in a heat were said to have been "distanced" and not allowed to continue.) It was Sir Archie's day. He easily won the second heat to take the purse.

Johnson stroked and nuzzled the horse as fans applauded after the race. Sir Archie's eyes softened when he saw his mentor. Their kinship was palpable. Sir Archie enjoyed running for Johnson, and Johnson had never trained a horse with such a towering blend of speed, stamina, character, competitiveness, and intelligence.

Sir Archie won another race at Newmarket the next week to improve his career record to three wins in six starts. Word began circulating among rival horsemen and fans: Napoleon preferred this big horse with an inauspicious record to any other he had trained.

That was enough to frighten almost all comers. Horsemen figured that if Johnson was so sure about Sir Archie, there was no use taking him on. Sir Archie's final race of 1809 — and the last of his career, it turned out — was scheduled for Scotland Neck, a track in Halifax, North Carolina, not far from Warrenton. Only one opponent was offered, a fine colt named Blank. Sir Archie prevailed in successive four-mile heats, finishing the first in 7 minutes 52 seconds — the fastest four-mile heat ever run south of the James River.

Hundreds of fans watched the race, including William Davie, a wealthy planter and politician who sought out Johnson after the race and offered to buy Sir Archie for $5,000. The offer staggered Napoleon. He loved the horse but could not turn down that kind of money. Sadly, he reminded himself why he tried never to get too attached to his horses: they always broke your heart.

Davie, a Revolutionary War hero later credited with founding the University of North Carolina, immediately retired Sir Archie and stood him at stud at his son's Halifax County plantation beginning in the spring of 1810. Johnson sent Davie a signed letter of recommendation to show to prospective clients:

> I have only to say that in my opinion Sir Archie is the best horse I ever saw, and I well know that I never had anything to do with any that was at all his equal. This I will back, for if any horse in the world will run against him at any halfway ground, four mile heats, according to the rules of racing, you may consider me $5,000 with you on him. He was in good condition this fall and he has not run with any horse that could put him at half speed toward the end of the race.

Johnson's wistfulness was evident in the letter. Sir Archie was retired from racing and owned by someone else, but Napoleon was still trying to issue challenges on his behalf, obviously wishing he could still race the horse. The trainer could not help himself; he loved Sir Archie that much.

To remedy his sadness, Johnson arranged to lease the horse in 1811. Sir Archie was brought back to Oakland and bred to Johnson's best mares as well as those from surrounding plantations. Just being around the horse again made Johnson happy. He put on his riding breeches and boots and took Sir Archie on long country rides, relishing the chance to commune with a horse so wise.

But the lease agreement lasted just one year, and then Davie accepted another horseman's offer to stand the horse in 1812. After Sir Archie left, Johnson realized he had to let go of his attachment to the horse. Now Sir Archie should produce as many fast sons and daughters as possible, proving his greatness in a new way. The horse stood in numerous locations in Virginia and North Carolina in the coming years, but never again at Oakland. Davie sold him to the Amis family of North Carolina in 1818, and he remained in their possession until his death at age twenty-eight in 1833. Johnson visited him whenever he was in North Carolina. They would spend time in a paddock, with Johnson nuzzling and patting the great horse.

Starting with his first foals, which began racing in 1814, Sir Archie dominated the American turf as a sire more than he ever did as a runner. His sons and daughters won race after race, then were retired and produced winners themselves. Sir Archie so infused his descendants with speed and stamina that he was later recognized in England's General Stud Book as "the Godolphin Arabian of America," essentially the starting point for the breed on his side of the Atlantic. It was primarily his success that transmitted Diomed's influence. "He filled the hemisphere with his blood," one historian wrote.

Johnson remained closely associated with Sir Archie. The talents of the horse and the man became intertwined, with Sir Archie known for siring horses that excelled at four-mile races, and Johnson known for developing four-mile stalwarts.

In 1815 Johnson gave up his seat in the North Carolina House of Representatives, sold his holdings in Warrenton, and moved his family to Oakland. Although Virginians and North Carolinians had their differences, Johnson's move from one state to the other was seamless. He quickly reentered political life and was elected to Virginia's House of Delegates, representing Petersburg and then Chesterfield County starting in 1818. He later took a seat in the state's prestigious upper house, the Senate.

During these years Oakland's pastures filled with runners sired by

Sir Archie. Vanity and Reality, full sisters bred by Marmaduke, were brilliant race mares and quite capable of beating the boys. Timoleon was the speedy colt later owned and trained by Racing Billy. A hardy colt named Walk-in-the-Water went to Tennessee and raced for years; it was said that "he won more races, ran more miles and traveled farther than any other horse that ever lived." Lady Lightfoot, the filly that took on Eclipse in 1821, started out at Oakland, as did Sir Charles.

By the early 1820s the competition in most races was between Sir Archie's sons and daughters, with Johnson somewhere in the fray and usually the winner. Southerners came to view Sir Archie's blood as hallowed, and no southerner believed that more than Johnson himself. Sir Archie was his greatest creation, the embodiment of his legacy. He was devastated by Eclipse's recent success against the great sire's descendants, viewing it as a direct challenge to Sir Archie, for while Eclipse was a grandson of Diomed, his sire was a lesser horse named Duroc.

Until now no sane man would have dared suggest that Duroc belonged in the same realm as Sir Archie. But in the wake of Eclipse's success, some northerners now believed Duroc was a worthy competitor, or perhaps even Sir Archie's superior. Johnson took this as a personal affront. How dare anyone castigate Sir Archie!

That emotion, which had simmered inside him for a year, came to a boil in Washington and led him to issue his challenge to Eclipse. He had to set the record straight and reaffirm Sir Archie's superiority.

The public saw the challenge in plainer terms, as a tangible representation of the North–South feud; Johnson, as a loyal, slaveholding southerner who had known only one way of life, understood that. He surely wanted to win for the South. But he had competed against northern horsemen such as Van Ranst for years, and frankly, he liked and respected many of them. He did not loathe the North, as some of his southern friends did. But he was as passionate about Sir Archie as he was about any aspect of his life. That was why he had no interest in scouring "the world" for a challenger. He wanted to run a horse that would make the South proud but, more important, do justice to Sir Archie.

When the Union Course race was over, he told himself, northerners would never again mention Duroc in the same breath with Sir Archie.

"When we are finished in May, the South will stand above the North, and the South's eminent bloodline will be hailed by all as the royal influence it surely is," he said to Taylor one morning while watching a workout at Oakland.

Taylor, hearing the passion in his boss's voice, blandly replied that he was confident the South would win.

"I dream of it!" Johnson shouted, his voice echoing through the trees. "I dream of scoring a triumph that sets straight the blind and foolish judgments of all those who dispute us!"

5

His Excellency

ONE MORNING IN EARLY JANUARY, as a steady snowfall covered New York, Van Ranst slept late. He ate a leisurely breakfast at his Manhattan home, then ordered his carriage driver to take him up to the Harlem Lane track. His stable boys waited for him, having prepared Eclipse for a training run despite the harsh weather. Van Ranst, as always, barely acknowledged the people around him before stepping into the horse's stall. Stable boys came and went, but there was only one Eclipse.

The old wizard patted the horse and made an affectionate clucking noise. Eclipse nodded forcefully, approving of the attention. What a pair we are, Van Ranst mused. An old man and an old horse. Two wrinkled, worn-out codgers who would prefer not to have to rise before the sun to get their day's business done. It was amazing, really, how alike they were.

They had been together since 1819, when Van Ranst purchased Eclipse as a five-year-old from Nathaniel Coles, the Long Island mill owner who had bred the horse. At the beginning of his time with Van Ranst, Eclipse had been a little-known success in an illegal sport. Now he was a hero throughout the North. His return trip from the National Course in November had amounted to a royal procession. Baltimore's *Morning Chronicle* depicted his brief stopover in that city:

On Saturday there passed through, on his way to his country seat in New York, in high health and spirits, the celebrated champion of the North, the denominated Eclipse. His Excellency appeared to wear his honors proudly, was superbly caparisoned, and was attended to the steamboat in which his passage was bespoken by a large, respectable cavalcade of our fellow citizens. Surely, we thought, pride was not made for man when it sits so gracefully upon horses.

The procession had continued in that spirit until Eclipse was safely back at Harlem Lane. He had almost six months to rest and get ready for his May race at the Union Course, which his northern fans assumed would result in another triumph, a rousing valedictory.

But then winter set in, and the newspapermen, noise, and excitement drifted away from Harlem Lane, and the doubts that had crossed Van Ranst's mind as the race was being arranged began to seem more justifiable — and ominous. The old horseman wondered if he had been foolish in allowing Stevens and the other zealous northern managers to sell out his grand champion, entering Eclipse in a race that was more than he could handle — all so they could put on a big event at the Union Course.

Eclipse was still a majestic athlete, no doubt about it. He had been in a robust state since returning from Washington, his appetite enormous as he exercised lightly in the mornings and otherwise lazed through his days. Even at nine years old, he made the task of running a four-mile heat seem like a leisurely Sunday gallop; other horses were glassy-eyed and panting at the end, but Eclipse just casually stopped, barely out of breath, and all but tapped his toes while waiting for the horses he had beaten to catch up.

Van Ranst had been around horses long enough to know better than to imagine human qualities in them, but he swore Eclipse took pleasure in outdistancing rivals to the point that they become discouraged. He was obviously intelligent, with clear eyes and a feisty personality — he nipped at anyone he did not know who tried to feed him — but he was especially jaunty at the end of a heat, as if he were laughing about how easily he had won.

But was there a limit to what he could take on? This dark, snorting beast, widely viewed as fearsome — a horse that would not only beat you but also maybe bite your head off if you salted it just right — was surprisingly vulnerable. For instance, though his muscular body was still rippled and imposing, his flesh subtly sagged, especially around his jaw, where a geriatric roll announced that his best running days were almost over, if not already behind him.

He was also rather inexperienced for such a well-known runner, having raced just seven times. True, he had never lost a heat and sometimes finished hundreds of yards ahead of his opponents. Of such performances were legends made, and Eclipse's now circulated widely. But what would happen if he was really tested? How would he react if some fast young horse raced in front of him and kicked dirt in his face, daring him to respond?

At the age of sixty, after a long life in racing, Van Ranst could contemplate such questions with more insight and sophistication than anyone else in the North. He had been breeding and racing horses since the 1780s, thanks to a generous inheritance that enabled him and his wife to live with their now-grown children in several residences, including a Long Island estate and a grand home in Manhattan. For years he had dominated the limited northern racing circuit and had taken his best horses to southern tracks, seeking the most challenging competition available.

Around the barn he was prone to barking at his jockeys and stable boys; they did his bidding silently, afraid to speak around a boss who always believed he knew best. But he paid them well and kept them on even after they made mistakes; he was softer than they knew and plagued by self-doubts that lingered below the surface. He knew that the real turf aficionados (that is, southerners) did not care who the North's best horseman was; he had compiled far more losses than wins on his southern trips, his horses often finishing well behind their southern opponents.

Still, he knew his stuff, and if it had been left up to him to decide whether Eclipse should race again in May, he would have said no. The horse had accomplished enough, he believed. Seven wins was not that many, but each had been better than the one before, and in the last four he had obliterated top southern horses. His legend was assured; asking him to try to take it further was a threat to it, a gamble in which the risks conceivably outweighed the rewards. Giving William Ransom Johnson six months to find and train a top opponent was a scary proposition. Van Ranst knew that better than any other northerner, having lost many times to Johnson on southern tracks. Napoleon was certain to come armed.

Van Ranst had wanted to retire Eclipse after the National Course race and make him a stallion in 1823. The horse had stood at stud before, servicing more than 150 mares, and had proved to be a popular and efficient sire. The whole point of legalizing racing again in New York supposedly had been to improve the quality of the horses in the region, and spreading Eclipse's seed around surely would help.

Standing in Eclipse's stall on a snowy January morning, Van Ranst took a brush and idly began to sweep it through the horse's dark tail. He wondered why he had not stood firmer and turned down the race, adding up the litany of factors working against Eclipse in the upcoming race — his age and relative inexperience, Johnson's presence on the other side, the South's freedom to scour "the world," and the fact that he had been a stallion not so long ago. When you added it all up, Eclipse had far more going against him than anyone in the North realized.

But Stevens had persisted that evening in Washington, stressing the many positives of such a race, which Van Ranst understood. He knew the event would give the Union Course a boost and promote Eclipse's name, likely increasing his stud value. And Van Ranst had to admit that the thought of taking part in a $20,000 wager intrigued him. He was as competitive as anyone, and while Johnson was far more gracious than cocky James Junkin Harrison, this new challenge was audacious, and Van Ranst was stirred by it.

Deep down he believed that Eclipse deserved the chance to prove his greatness once and for all, in daunting circumstances, against the greatest challenge the South could offer. As forbidding as he was, Eclipse was also a long shot, a bright star that had somehow risen in the otherwise dim sky of northern racing. He had emerged from a region that barely tolerated racing and had soared beyond what his fans had any right to expect, taunting and continually disappointing the hopes of those in the South. His long-shot story would be complete, Van Ranst figured, once he defeated "the world" in conditions weighted so heavily against him.

When the small coterie of active northern horsemen heard about the match race planned for the Union Course, they almost danced with delight. Southern horsemen had long disdained their racing, believing that not only was the caliber of events inferior but the caliber of the horses was as well. Van Ranst and his colleagues had gone south for years to compete, but southerners had never returned the favor, sniffing that such trips were pointless.

Nathaniel Coles, the mill owner and retired military hero who had bred Eclipse, sought out Van Ranst to congratulate him just for arranging the Union Course race. Like Van Ranst, Coles had taken his share of disappointing trips to southern tracks. When Coles suggested that it was a victory in itself that the South finally was coming north to race, Van Ranst smiled and said, "I must admit, I hope their journey is as long and dusty as those we have taken."

Southern notions about the inferiority of northern racing were hardly unfounded. Unlike the South, with its numerous tracks and vibrant racing culture, the northern racing world was sparse indeed, with only one minor racecourse in Pennsylvania, two in New Jersey, none in New England, and just one in New York, the Union Course, operating legally. Most northern meetings were illegal, hardscrabble affairs so insignificant that lawmakers just looked the other way rather than interfere, choosing to let the country gentry have their little fun.

The entirety of the North's racing history was not quite so bare. In earlier times the sport had achieved popularity in some pockets of the region. Colonial New Yorkers had generally supported racing, their population being more diverse and open-minded than those in other colonies. A few Rhode Islanders had raced avidly. A succession of tracks had come and gone on the Long Island plain where the first American track was built in 1665.

Before the Revolutionary War, one of America's top horsemen was James DeLancey, Jr., a New Yorker of immense wealth. Educated in England and loyal to the crown, he ran a stable that was equal to any in the South. His horses dominated the competition around New York and even won in Maryland and Virginia. But DeLancey sold his property, including his stable, and sailed to England as the Revolutionary War neared. His loyalties were clear.

Ironically, New York probably had the best American racing during the war. The British occupied Long Island, erected a depot for horses and munitions, and staged races at Jamaica, their headquarters. They also raced north of New York at Beaver Pond and Ascot Heath.

But after the war, with the British gone and conservative churches gaining influence, the sport dwindled badly in New York and the rest of the North. New York State banned it in 1802 because of what one newspaper later termed "intoxication, riot, and lewdness" at local tracks. The ban would remain in place for nineteen years. Also in 1802, some two thousand mechanics and manufacturers in Philadelphia signed an antiracing petition complaining that the sport would "tend to our ruin if not removed." Pennsylvania later outlawed the sport.

The superiority of southern racing was reaffirmed whenever northern horsemen went south. Even the best northern horses usually failed. After a speedy Pennsylvania bay named First Consul scored twenty-one straight victories in the North, his owner proposed to race Florizel, Virginia's unbeaten champion, for $10,000 a side in 1806. Florizel's owner ignored the challenge, so First Consul ended up in Baltimore, taking on the fastest horse in Maryland — and losing in successive four-mile heats.

Northern racing was so insignificant that few breeders even attempted to produce winning runners, preferring the sturdiness and strength of workhorses to the lightness and agility desired in racing. Speed was just not valued, as evidenced by the peculiar contests that northern horsemen occasionally staged instead of traditional races. Some were laughably pathetic. A group of men would each enter a horse and then ride one they did not own — the horse that came in last was the winner. Or they rode old, infirm, and useless horses around and around a track until the animals dropped dead one by one; the last one standing won.

Southerners were not wrong to believe their racing was vastly superior, but their disdain for northern horses was an increasingly un-informed generalization. Although the number of racehorses being produced in the North was small, the quality was improving, thanks to the influence of one sire in particular — Messenger. He had injected valuable traits such as quickness, size, and stamina into the region's pedigrees. A few northern horses were more capable than anyone south of New York knew, and Eclipse, a product of the Messenger bloodline, was seemingly unbeatable.

Like Diomed, Messenger had been imported from England. But unlike Diomed and almost every other import that came to America after the Revolutionary War, Messenger went north instead of south. He first came to public attention as an eight-year-old stallion advertised in 1788 in Philadelphia newspapers:

> Just Imported! The Capital, Strong, Full-Blooded English Stallion, Messenger! To cover mares this season at Alexander Clay's, at the sign of the Black Horse, in Market Street, at the very low price of three guineas each mare, and one dollar to the groom. The performance of Messenger has been so very great that there only need be a reference to the [British] racing calendar for the years 1783, 1784 and 1785.

Messenger's English racing career had indeed been successful, although not quite as wildly as the ad suggested. He won ten of sixteen races in three seasons, excelling at shorter distances, and was "entitled to the rank of thorough respectability without attaining the rank of great distinction," the historian John Hervey wrote. How he reached America is a mystery. His whereabouts was unrecorded for two and a half years, from the time of his last race in England to the first mention of him in Philadelphia. His importer was later identified as Thomas Benger, an estate owner and slaveholder in Bucks County, Pennsylvania, who stood Messenger around Philadelphia and southern New Jersey from 1788 to 1793.

When Benger fled during a yellow fever panic, the horse was taken to New York and sold to Henry Astor, a prosperous butcher and the brother of John Jacob Astor, a fur trader who later purchased large tracts of Manhattan real estate and left $20 million to his heirs. Henry Astor stood Messenger for two years, then in 1796 sold a share to Van Ranst, who controlled the rest of Messenger's stud career. The horse stood at Van Ranst's Long Island estate, Pine Plains, and was leased to other northern breeders, such as John Cox Stevens and Townsend Cock.

David Jones, a son of one of the era's leading horsemen, recalled Messenger in a letter to a friend a half-century later:

> He had a large bony head, rather short straight neck, with windpipe and nostrils nearly twice as large as ordinary, with his low withers and shoulders somewhat upright, but deep, close, and strong. Behind these lay the perfection and power of the machine. His barrel, loin, hips, and quarters were incomparably superior to all others. His hocks and knees were unusually large; below them his limbs were of medium size but flat strong and remarkably clean, and either in standing or action, their position was perfect. Taking him all in all, he is unquestionably the best race horse ever brought to America.

At the peak of his popularity in 1796, Messenger carried a thirty-dollar stud fee. Covering thoroughbred mares as well as mixed breeds, he sired horses that eventually produced a new breed suited to harness racing — the standardbred. Messenger was that breed's foundation sire. He also sired thoroughbred winners, including a mare named Miller's Damsel that was foaled in 1802 and became known as the "Queen of the Northern Turf." Notoriously high-strung, she was by far the fastest mare around, winning many races, especially at four miles. Although she worked herself into a sweaty lather before a race, she usually settled down and won.

When Miller's Damsel retired, her owner, Nathaniel Coles, bred her to Diomed's son Duroc, who had been purchased in Virginia and brought to Long Island. Duroc had also been a high-strung runner with talent (evidenced by several four-mile victories), but his temperament was unfortunate. He had a nasty habit of bolting off the racecourse before an event, seemingly fleeing the scene.

Before dawn on May 25, 1814, Miller's Damsel delivered her foal by Duroc at Coles's Long Island estate. Coles was curious to see how a horse with such high-strung parents developed. The youngster was extraordinary from his first steps, seemingly having inherited his parents' natural athletic gifts but not their temperament.

At five months old, he showed such promise running through

fields that Coles named him Eclipse, after England's greatest thoroughbred. The British Eclipse, so named because he was foaled during a total eclipse of the sun in 1764, had won eighteen straight races without his jockey ever using a whip; he was often so far ahead of the field that his owner famously said his races consisted of "Eclipse first, the rest nowhere." Believing his young Eclipse had the potential to reach similar heights, Coles meticulously recorded the horse's early life:

> The colt was weaned on November 10, 1814. At the commencement of winter he was fed with four quarts of shorts which was increased during the winter to eight quarts per day; hay, clover, dampened.
>
> Second year (1815) in the spring, he was turned to grass with no grain. November 10, put up, fed with eight quarts of shorts per day, during winter shorts was increased to ten quarts.
>
> Third year, turned to grass with four quarts of shorts per day. Sept 1, commenced breaking; fed eight quarts oats; through the winter hay as formerly, grain, ground corn, and oats, equal to 11 quarts.
>
> On March 1, 1817, commenced training and was trained for nine weeks. Then gave a trial of two miles and was found to be very superior.
>
> Fourth year, in the summer turned to grass; fed with ground oats and corn equal to nine quarts oats; in the winter hay as formerly, with nine quarts oats per day til late March 1818, when commenced training; feed, oats and cracked corn equal to 12 quarts oats.

Four years old, Eclipse began racing in May 1818 at an illegal meeting on a Long Island course known as Newmarket. Coles entered him in a three-mile event against a pair of experienced runners, a colt named Sea Gull and a mare named Black-Eyed Susan. Eclipse was calm before the race (unlike his parents) and easily outran his rivals in successive heats to win $300. He did not race again that year, Coles deeming him still too young to be pushed.

Coles abruptly sold Eclipse to Van Ranst for $3,000 early the next year; he was in his fifties and was scaling back, getting out of the racing game. Van Ranst, who was about the same age as Coles, also occasionally thought about getting out but had not entirely lost the urge to run fast horses.

Van Ranst thought about taking Eclipse south to compete in 1819, but decided against it; he was weary of making the long trip to Virginia just to get beaten. Instead, he entered the horse in a four-mile race held in June at the Bath Course, another small Long Island track. Eclipse, with jockey Samuel Purdy guiding him, easily won the $500 purse, destroying a field that, oddly, included another horse named Eclipse. Van Ranst's Eclipse shot ahead of the others at the start and never looked back, winning by several hundred yards. Purdy, an old hand long associated with Van Ranst, started off using a whip and boot spurs as encouragement but quickly realized they were unnecessary. Eclipse never stopped running hard and never seemed to tire. A sprinkling of fans salted around the little track watched with wide eyes, aware that they had seen few better runners, if any.

Four months later Eclipse beat the same field in another race at the Bath Course, winning another $500. As 1820 dawned, Van Ranst pondered whether he should take Eclipse south. There was no competition whatsoever for him in the North, but Van Ranst did not have the energy to make the journey, and he was tiring of the racing scene. It would be easier, more profitable, and potentially more interesting, he thought, to pull the horse out of training and stand him at stud. Van Ranst had actually experienced more success over the years as a breeder than as a racing trainer. Southerners may have beaten him on the turf, but going back to the days when he stood Messenger, he had bred many stout horses. Eclipse — with Messenger as his maternal grandfather and Diomed as his paternal grandfather — surely would enhance his record.

Van Ranst's other option was to continue racing Eclipse at the same little Long Island meetings he had already dominated. That prospect paled beside the vision of owners waiting in line with cash in hand to have their top mares bred to Eclipse. Van Ranst decided to go in that direction. He took Eclipse out of training and groomed him for the life of a stallion.

Some northern horsemen were surprised to see newspaper ads for Eclipse. Why take a horse so gifted out of the running after just three races? The sad state of northern racing had left him with no choice, Van Ranst explained. And Eclipse could serve the whole of northern society better in this new role.

Northerners were indeed starting to care more about the quality of their horses, after lagging for so long behind the agricultural South. But the value of good horses was becoming clearer — horses powered mills, for starters — and owners were looking to improve their breeding overall. Eclipse obviously could help. That spring fifty northern men brought their best mares to Van Ranst's estate and paid $12.50 for a breeding session with Eclipse. They were not attempting to produce horse-racing stars; they wanted workhorses.

Eclipse's racing days were over, it seemed.

That same spring John Cox Stevens convened a meeting of New York's most avid racing men, which included Van Ranst. They decided to start a group called the New York Association for the Improvement of the Breed of Horses. Other horse-friendly northern associations had also recently started up, but NYAIBH, while proclaiming that improving the breed was its chief concern, was slyly focused on the turf.

With friends in high places and their own clout, the wealthy horsemen succeeded in having the legalization of racing brought up in the state legislature in March 1821. They lobbied hard to have the nineteen-year-old ban overturned, and in a vote taken near the end of the session, the ban was narrowly defeated.

That state legislators were deeply conflicted about the turf was apparent. They voted to permit just two racing meetings a year at the all-dirt course in Jamaica that NYAIBH intended to erect, and the vote for that limited amount of racing was just fifty-three in favor to fifty opposed. (Just enough nay voters were swung the right way when clauses were added to the proposal mandating that sheriffs be present at the Union Course to "protect the public" from racing's corrupting influences.) In the same session a similar proposal to allow racing in a neighboring county was denied.

It was not exactly a warm welcome. But NYAIBH had what it wanted, a license to hold races. The group had already purchased land in Jamaica, eight miles from the East River, and drawn up plans for the course. It would be the first attempt since the Revolutionary War to reestablish New York as a serious racing state. NYAIBH intended to offer large purses, attract southern horsemen, put on first-class racing, and draw crowds.

Publicly, NYAIBH's position was that racing had been revived primarily to improve the breeding of horses. Drawing up its racing rules, it heeded an idea offered by John Jay, the famous statesman, former governor of New York, and first chief justice of the U.S. Supreme Court. Now seventy-seven, Jay suggested that horses at the Union Course should carry more weight than horses at southern tracks because the additional weight would make them tougher. His idea was adopted.

Stevens and his cohorts spent six months getting the course ready for racing, concentrating on laying and leveling the dirt track, which was expected to lead to faster running times. The inaugural meeting was scheduled for October 1821, and NYAIBH wanted to make a splash. Stevens asked Van Ranst if he would consider bringing Eclipse out of retirement to race. Few northern horses had achieved any popularity while competing illegally before small crowds, but Eclipse was at least known.

Van Ranst initially said no. Eclipse, now seven, had spent two springs at stud, covering 150 mares. Coles had tried bringing Duroc back to the races from stud a few years earlier, and the experiment had failed miserably. Duroc would bolt off the course before he could run, seemingly hearing voices. Van Ranst was hesitant to follow that dubious lead. "The friends of Eclipse questioned the policy of running him again," Van Ranst wrote later, "believing from the long, cherished opinions of sportsmen on the subject, and those who had written on the economy of the horse, that covering [mares] rendered him unfit to contend in a race. The practice has been never to run a horse that has covered."

But Van Ranst experienced a change of heart as he watched Eclipse running in a field one day. The big horse still ran with that rare blend of elegance and power he had shown before, sprinting across the grass as if the goal were to see how far he could fly with each step. He was flabby around the middle after two years out of training, but Van Ranst could see his muscles pushing and pulling just as hard behind the extra weight, which surely would come off with more exercise. Why not try bringing him back?

Van Ranst mulled the question for a week, seeking no one's counsel — this was a decision he alone had to make. Finally, he jotted a note to Stevens. Yes, Eclipse would come back to run in the four-mile event at the Union Course in October. Van Ranst immediately felt good about changing his mind. He enjoyed standing Eclipse at stud, but part of him had always regretted retiring such a fine athlete so soon.

Van Ranst went in knowing that the experiment might end miserably, but long before October, he knew it would succeed. He sent Eclipse on long training runs through the Long Island countryside during the summer and early fall, and the horse rose to the challenge. Purdy, who knew the horse almost as well as Van Ranst, came out to help. Some of their conditioning jaunts lasted an hour, a tall order under the summer sun. But Purdy's presence seemed to excite Eclipse. His weight dropped, his stamina increased, his ears pricked. He craved food and exercise, heeded orders and instruction, and exhibited his familiar feistiness. It was as if he had never stopped running.

He was, at seven, totally in tune with what Van Ranst wanted — the perfect racing specimen.

The Union Course opened for business on October 15, drawing a crowd of several thousand fans. The sun was shining, and a four-mile sweepstakes with a distinct North–South flavor was scheduled. The $500 purse had attracted the Virginia horseman J. D. Sleeper, who owned Lady Lightfoot. Eclipse was entered along with two lesser northern runners, Flag of Truce and Heart of Oak.

Lady Lightfoot had enjoyed a long, brilliant career, winning races from South Carolina to Pennsylvania and attracting a loyal following. Even though she was now nine, she was generally favored by two-to-one odds before the first heat as bettors heatedly arranged terms. Eclipse, though seven, seemed a neophyte by comparison, coming off a two-year layoff with just three career races. (The two-to-one odds meant that those backing Eclipse would receive twice as much if their horse won the heat — quite a show of confidence by Lady Lightfoot's supporters, who would win $50 on a $50 bet if their horse won but lose $100 if Eclipse won. Most bettors would then settle up and make different bets on the second and third heats, with different odds.)

After the starter sent the horses running, Lady Lightfoot broke quickly and led by four or five lengths throughout the first three laps around the oval as her cocky fans cheered. Northern fans commented that she was indeed a sleek, beautiful horse with a fluid running action. But she tired on the fourth lap, and Eclipse made a charge. As Purdy flailed his whip and spurs, Van Ranst's horse bore down on the mare and pulled even on the final turn. Seemingly surprised to have company, Lady Lightfoot flinched, losing her stride. That was all Eclipse needed. He shot past the mare and reached the finish three lengths ahead, with Purdy driving hard the whole way.

As the jockeys eased the horses, northern fans clapped and whistled, somewhat startled that their horse had won. Their southern opponents had been so confident when making bets beforehand and seemed to know so much more about horses and racing. But look whose horse had won.

During the thirty-minute break between heats, northerners asked their southern rivals if those two-to-one odds would remain in effect for the second heat. The southerners grimly shook their heads. Were the Yankees dreaming? Their horse had just won the heat! If anything, the northerners should be giving them favorable odds now.

In the end, most bets on the second heat were made at even-money odds. The southern fans, having seen Eclipse's winning charge to the finish in the first heat, seemed to know what was about to happen, and it was not good news for their side.

Lady Lightfoot started out strongly again in the second heat, taking a small lead on the first lap. But Purdy kept Eclipse closer this time and, sensing weakness in the mare, charged after her on the second lap. Eclipse pulled even and sprinted ahead. Lady Lightfoot relaxed, seemingly admitting defeat. The outcome was never in doubt after that, as Eclipse's lead increased to five, ten, and finally fifteen lengths at the finish. His time for the heat was about eight minutes, fast for a horse returning to the turf after such a long layoff.

Having watched from the grandstand, Van Ranst bounded across the dirt to congratulate the horse and Purdy. The jockey beamed down at him as he patted Eclipse. They shook hands across the saddle. What a feat! Lady Lightfoot was the pride of the South; Virginians and Carolinians uttered her name with reverence. But Eclipse had demolished her.

The old wizard could not remember experiencing a grander racing moment. How smart did he look for bringing Eclipse back to the races? The horse had surpassed all reasonable expectations, returning from stud duty and a long layoff to beat a superb horse. Van Ranst thought back to all those tough afternoons at southern tracks when his horses had finished far behind their southern rivals. What sweet revenge this was! His enthusiasm for the turf was restored. How could he have thought about scaling back? A triumph like this made him hunger for more.

For the first time, Eclipse's name reverberated beyond the narrow boundaries of the northern turf. Southerners wondered about this horse that had unexpectedly trounced Lady Lightfoot. Van Ranst was known to southerners from his many sojourns to their region, but this horse had never come and, in fact, had not even raced recently. Who was he?

Van Ranst did not breed Eclipse to mares in 1822, preferring to keep him in training. Spring and fall meetings were scheduled for the Union Course that year, and it was hoped that Eclipse could run in both.

In the spring Bela Badger brought his fastest horse, Sir Walter, up from Pennsylvania for a test. Though technically a northerner, Badger was closely aligned with William Ransom Johnson and was considered a southern horseman. His horse Sir Walter was a speedy five-year-old son of Sir Archie. His challenge to Eclipse was highly anticipated. Northerners and southerners bet sizably and bantered loudly beforehand, and Badger and Van Ranst agreed on a $750 side bet. But the race was a mismatch. Eclipse was easily the better horse. With Purdy driving him hard, he lowered his head, took the lead early, and won the first heat in 7 minutes 54 seconds. Sir Walter was never close. Eclipse then won the second heat the same way to take the $700 purse. Southerners left the course quietly.

A rematch was arranged for October 1822 at the Union Course. A $1,000 purse attracted several horses besides the two rivals. Eclipse was far superior to them all. He won the first heat in 7 minutes 58 seconds, with Sir Walter well behind. The second heat disintegrated as Eclipse raced so far ahead that the others, including Sir Walter, became discouraged and quit.

That victory inspired James Junkin Harrison to issue the challenge that led to the match with Sir Charles at the National Course. Van Ranst trained Eclipse for the race, and Stevens jumped in to handle the money, raising the $10,000 stakes, with much of it coming out of his own pocket. The victory gave Eclipse a career record of seven wins in seven starts, including four in a row over southern horses.

Privately, Van Ranst held his breath every time Eclipse raced; he feared the horse was too old to be running this well and this often, and he was playing an increasingly risky game of chance with the odds. When would those years of stud service catch up with him? Van Ranst had nightmares about that. Horsemen had long avoided bringing a sire back to racing because stud service supposedly ruined a horse's concentration and conditioning. Eclipse had not experienced any such problems so far, but what if they arose abruptly in the middle of a race?

The old wizard tried to put such thoughts out of his mind. His decision to bring Eclipse back to the races was widely acclaimed. He had gambled and won. The horse had still been largely unknown coming out of stud in 1821, but now, with the rise of the Union Course and his succession of triumphs there and in Washington, he had supporters throughout the North. The idea of a horse captivating that region, historically lukewarm about racing, might have seemed preposterous until now, but Eclipse's victories had generated countless smiles and filled countless pockets. Northerners everywhere relished beating the South at its own game — again and again. They had grown accustomed to seeing Eclipse win, and they now expected it every time he ran.

His success was laced with symbolism. The South had dominated American horse racing since the turn of the century, much as it had lorded over the national political scene and dictated economic policy. The endurance of slavery, despite northern objections, underscored the fact that the South ruled the country. But sweeping changes were afoot. A northern presidential candidate, John Quincy Adams, was faring well in the polls. The pending opening of the Erie Canal would increase the flow of goods to New York and bolster the city's position as America's economic hub. The South seemed stuck in the past; it expected to win the presidency because it always had; continued to rely on slavery to make its economy profitable; and believed it would continue to rule the turf because, well, the North had never mounted a challenge.

But just as Adams and the Erie Canal represented threats to southern visions of superiority, so, clearly, did Eclipse. Southerners were almost apoplectic about his four straight wins over their horses. Their refusal to concede that the North had produced America's fastest thoroughbred was telling; they knew deep down it was true, but their pride would not allow them to admit it.

In reality, Van Ranst's horse was vulnerable. He was like an aging gunfighter beating off youngsters while trying to stave off the day when a faster one came along. But that day had not yet come, and maybe it never would. Eclipse was every bit the equal of the best the South could produce, and then some.

6

This Plan Will Work

B Y EARLY FEBRUARY Johnson had decided on a plan for challenging Eclipse. Befitting a man nicknamed Napoleon, it was masterful — precise, comprehensive, and designed to make the most of the available variables. Anyone else might simply pick a horse to represent the South and train it. But Johnson was dead set on masterminding a victory.

Selecting the horse now, almost four months before the race, made no sense, he thought. According to the conditions both sides had agreed to, the South did not have to name a horse until he presented it to the judges at the Union Course, moments before the start. That, Johnson believed, was his greatest advantage. Others thought it was the chance to search "the world" for a horse, but that was just a northern stunt intended to increase public interest in the event — it was obvious he would use a southern horse. Waiting until race day to name the challenger had much more valuable benefits. He could keep the other side guessing and off balance until the end. And, most important, he could select the horse from a pool of candidates.

That thought — a brilliant one, he had to admit — had occurred to him one morning at Oakland as he studied several horses being auditioned: he should take more than one to the Union Course. In fact, he should take three, four, maybe even five, all trained and ready to run. That would eliminate any chance of a forfeit; if his favorite contender pulled up lame at the wrong time, as Sir Charles had in Washington, another could step in — and yet another if a second problem arose.

Explaining his idea to Arthur Taylor, Johnson compared it to being allowed to cheat at poker. If men sitting around a card table represented horses, the North was limited to having just one hand — Eclipse — playing for the pot, but the South could have four or five hands and choose the best one. Any man who proposed such conditions at poker would be shot dead and buried in an unmarked grave — the unfairness was obvious. But the North had foolishly agreed to it, and now Johnson wanted to make the most of it.

He decided to select five finalists and train each as if it were going to run at the Union Course. He would station them at Oakland and Newmarket and put them through a months-long course of workouts and private trials while also racing them publicly at the February meeting in Charleston and the Virginia meetings in April and May. The finalists would compete against each other and other top horses, and then, in mid-May, Johnson would take them to the Pennsylvania estate of his friend Bela Badger for a week of final training. From there all five would travel to Long Island, where Johnson would make his final choice on May 27, race day itself.

Taylor's eyebrows rose when Johnson outlined the plan. Five horses for one race! Who had ever heard of taking such precautions?

Johnson smiled. He had counted on the northerners' overconfidence tipping the scales in his favor. Here was a prime example of how the conditions favored him. Why not make the most of it?

Of course, he had to select the right five horses. He had been working on that since December, entertaining horsemen, soliciting opinions, and observing the training sessions of several dozen animals, male and female, young and old, big and little, fast and slow. Visitors to Oakland had included John Randolph, John Tayloe III, James Junkin Harrison, Racing Billy, and others. A wealthy rice planter from South Carolina had sent a fine mare named Betsey Richards for a tryout. A Kentucky horseman had brought an interesting gray colt. Johnson had traveled to North Carolina to scrutinize candidates; he saw his father's horses and visited John Amis, who owned Sir Archie.

The southern turf community included hundreds of thorough-breds owned by dozens of planters, and while Johnson could not consider them all, he sought to personally judge as many as possible. With Taylor by his side, he spent morning after morning studying horses at Oakland and Newmarket. As he had with Billy's two horses in early January, he watched them run alone on the track, studying their running action, and then had them race against others in brief trials.

Bundled up in a thick coat and a hat to ward off the cold, he dictated his observations to Taylor, who wrote them down on sheaves of paper, using a quill pen. "This one labors. Look, he's big but awkward," Napoleon barked one morning as a horse jogged past. Taylor watched, agreed, and wrote it down. The next day, a fast young colt with a startling lump on a rear ankle ran past. "Pity. Whatever distresses that ankle forbids him," Johnson commented.

Day after day, as horses worked out and cooled down from the exercise, Johnson assessed their action, their size, their bone structure, their stamina, their eyes — anything that could help him make a decision, positive or negative. Taylor jotted down every word and also occasionally added his own comments.

Napoleon could not help wondering what some of the planters who brought horses had been thinking; he eliminated their horses after seeing them take three plodding steps. Others were viable candidates, gracefully gliding across the grass. A few were so gifted they raised Johnson's eyebrows.

On most days, Johnson returned home after the morning session, warmed up by a fire, ate lunch, and retreated to his study to read the notes he had dictated. Taylor often joined him, as did the horsemen who had brought their animals for him to observe. In the late afternoon he went back to the stables to check on the horses as they ate and slept, curious to see how they reacted to the training session. A horse that lost its appetite concerned him; if exercise dulled its system, it probably would not hold up through hard training. Horses that seemed tired also went down in his estimation; he needed animals with stamina to survive the next four months.

Then it was back to Oakland for an elegant dinner with other horsemen around Johnson's long table, raising toasts to the South, their host, and the upcoming event.

"To Virginia, mother of the American thoroughbred!"

"To the South, may her honor be regained!"

"To the Napoleon of the Turf, who shall restate our dominance for 'the world' to see!"

By early February Johnson needed to pick the finalists. His barns were overcrowded, not only with his own animals — a smaller complement than usual, as it happened, without a star capable of being a finalist — but also with more than twenty others that had auditioned. Their owners had left them in case they were selected. The size of the herd was testing the limits of Johnson's operation; a small army of stable boys and jockeys tended to the horses around the clock.

Knowing it was time to cut the field to five, Johnson retreated to his library one afternoon. He wanted silence and a clear head to remember all he had observed during the past month. A stack of papers containing Taylor's scrawled notes lay on a table beside him.

He knew he could not select Sir Charles, Lady Lightfoot, or Sir Walter; southerners would think he had lost his mind if he proposed running any of them against Eclipse again. He also quickly eliminated about half of the horses he had observed recently, the ones that clearly did not have what it took.

Contemplating the remaining choices, he sat alone in his library for hours as the light faded to dusk and then disappeared. When a servant knocked on the door and announced dinner, Johnson declined, saying his work was unfinished. No one knocked again, and the library door remained closed as the house quieted later, when his wife and children retired to bed. Not until after midnight did Johnson end his deliberations, climb the stairs, and fall asleep himself.

He was up at dawn, ready to announce his decision to Taylor during training hours. As the sun rose and horses raced up and down the Oakland track, tended by slave grooms and jockeys, Johnson beckoned for Taylor to join him on the stand by the finish.

"I have narrowed the pool of candidates to the five we shall train for the Union Course," he said.

"I am anxious to hear the names," replied Taylor.

Johnson started reeling them off. "Both of Billy's are in — John Richards and Flying Childers," he said. "The younger one has enormous potential. And the older one is small but runs hard every time."

Taylor nodded in agreement.

"The fine race mare from South Carolina is also in. The one called Betsey Richards," Napoleon continued.

Taylor smiled. They had discussed her at length. The mare was an elegant specimen, the obvious heir to Lady Lightfoot as the South's leading female runner.

"She's a wise choice, sir," he said.

"The final two have not run for us here. I saw them when I was in North Carolina last month," Johnson said. "Both are young colts — very young, in fact. One belongs to my father. His name is Washington and he has already won several races. The other belongs to a friend of my father's. The horse goes by the name of Sir Henry."

Taylor nodded. "I saw them when they raced at Newmarket last fall," he said. "They are indeed precocious. But their talents speak loudly."

Johnson continued. "All five are blessed with Sir Archie's blood, as you might expect," he said, a smile forming. "My beloved Archie is the sire of four, with Washington the lone exception. And Washington was sired by Timoleon, so Sir Archie is his paternal grandsire. This pedigree is essential, as you know, for surviving a day of four-mile heats with Eclipse."

Taylor did not reply, although he agreed. For several moments the two men silently watched the horses jogging in front of them as they contemplated Johnson's choices. The morning was bright blue but cold. The rhythmic breathing of the animals and the shouts of slaves filled the air.

"What do you think of the five?" Johnson finally asked.

Taylor, as always, spoke frankly. "The choices are commendable. But, sir, I must ask: what of Sir William? And what of Muckle John?"

Other southern horsemen were certain to ask the same questions. Sir William was the hard-running eight-year-old that had beaten Sir Charles twice in four tries and "commanded the wind to stand still," according to his owner. He had raced and won at all the distances, including four miles. So had Muckle John, a six-year-old that had beaten Sir William.

"With all due respect, sir, John Richards, Washington, and Sir Henry have barely raced," Taylor continued. "Is it wise to go with them instead of horses more proven on the turf?"

Johnson smiled. "This issue kept me up past midnight last night," he said. "I have, in fact, thought hard about Sir William. How could I not consider a horse with more than twenty race victories? No southern horse has a better record. Muckle John is also a worthy candidate. But I have turned them down because I have made what I believe is the fundamental assessment of this challenge, the key to beating Eclipse."

He paused and looked hard at Taylor. "This race is all about age," he said.

Eclipse, at nine, not only was old but also would have to race with a colossal load of handicapping weight on his back, as dictated by the rules of the Union Course. Weight allotments were a fundamental nuance of racing in America and England, part of an effort by jockey clubs to make events as fair as possible. Horses were forced to carry more and more weight as they aged, the theory being that their burdens would offset their advantage over younger horses in experience, muscular development, and overall maturity. (One could argue that younger horses were strong, like human teenagers, and should carry the heavier burdens, but that was not the way it was done.)

Each racecourse operated with a "scale of weights" that assigned allotments by age — a certain amount for four-year-olds, more for five-year-olds, and a relative ton for nine-year-olds. Four-year-olds at the Union Course were assigned 108 pounds. Eclipse, at nine, would have to carry 126.

Johnson had deduced that the South could win, perhaps easily, by taking full advantage of that disparity. A brilliant young horse with fresh legs not only would make Eclipse seem that much older but would also have a huge weight advantage. Running an older horse such as Sir William would eliminate the advantage and level the conditions.

Slowly, precisely, Napoleon explained his thinking as the two men stood in the cold watching horses work out. Taylor began to smile.

This was brilliant! The weight issue was critical. And also, by selecting younger horses, Johnson was going with contenders on the way up. Sir William almost surely was on his way down from his racing peak, as was Muckle John. But John Richards, Washington, and Sir Henry were just getting started. They were clay that Johnson could fashion into masterpieces. Betsey Richards, at five, could also benefit from the weight strategy, because females received lighter weight assessments than males of the same age. She had raced and won several times at the four-mile distance, proving her talent and potential. Flying Childers, at six, was the oldest finalist and least likely to be chosen, but he had won at four miles, and Johnson wanted a consistent horse that could challenge the others in training. He liked Billy's little horse. He had a feeling it would improve.

The notion of focusing on Eclipse's age had occurred to Johnson when James Junkin Harrison visited Oakland in early January. Harrison showed Johnson a letter he had received from Van Ranst in which the New Yorker admitted having wanted to retire Eclipse after the National Course race. The old horse had accomplished enough, Van Ranst wrote, but Stevens and the other northerners had persuaded him to run the horse one more time.

Johnson was surprised Van Ranst had admitted that to a southerner with the Union Course race now on the horizon. The honest admission had helped Napoleon focus his thoughts. If Eclipse's owner was that concerned about the horse's age, the South should take advantage of it.

The names of Johnson's finalists spread quickly through the southern horse community in the coming weeks. At first, some horsemen did not understand the rationale. Sir Henry? Washington? John Richards? They were nice young horses, but they had never beaten the likes of Sir William. Johnson shrugged off the second-guessing, convinced he was right. The doubters would eventually see things his way.

By mid-February all five horses were under his supervision in Virginia. Racing Billy brought his two in from Raceland. The mare was already at Oakland; her owner, John Spann, a rice planter from South Carolina, had sent her up to be evaluated. A team of slaves belonging to Marmaduke Johnson brought Washington and Sir Henry from North Carolina.

There was no way to know what would happen in the coming months. The youngsters were brimming with potential, and Johnson hoped they would push one another and make the choice difficult. That was his goal: a final decision that kept him awake at night, a tough decision between fast horses. Given the variety and talents of his finalists and the improvement certain to occur, he was supremely confident that the horse he chose would challenge Eclipse as the northern horse had never been challenged before.

"This plan will work. It is foolproof," he said confidently to Taylor in the morning chill.

"Congratulations, sir. The plan is magnificent," Taylor said.

In mid-February the South's largest port city filled with rice and tobacco planters, socialites, and racing enthusiasts. It was Race Week in Charleston, one of America's oldest and finest racing occasions. Overseen by the South Carolina Jockey Club, the meeting was the first of the year on the racing calendar, the 1820s version of baseball's spring training, an annual sign that winter was almost over.

The meeting consisted of four days of events at the Washington Course, an elegant venue with wrought iron gates and a fine dining hall and grandstands. The course was located on the Ashley River on the outskirts of downtown, on land donated by William Washington, a cousin of George Washington who had led troops in the Battle of Cowpens during the Revolutionary War and had become an avid horseman.

Charleston, with a population of some 25,000, was America's sixth-largest city after New York, Philadelphia, Baltimore, Boston, and New Orleans. It was a complicated place, with entrenched southern manners and tastes but also flavored by the foreign ships that docked at the harbor. It was not unusual to hear strange tongues on the city's cobblestone streets or to see Europeans and Cubans conducting business with slaveholding rice planters.

Two of every five slaves emigrating from Africa to America came ashore in Charleston, and with the black population so high, many slaves felt empowered to dream of gaining their freedom. Just months earlier, in the summer of 1822, a former slave named Denmark Vesey (he had won his freedom in a lottery and worked as a carpenter) had organized an insurrection that would free thousands. But before it could take place, a slave informant tipped off the authorities, who swooped in and found daggers and bayonets. More than one hundred blacks were arrested, and almost three dozen, including Vesey, were hanged.

The tension from that episode still reverberated in early 1823, but as usual, all business in Charleston was put aside for Race Week. Only Mardi Gras in New Orleans surpassed it as an all-out party. Planters from the hills and low country outside Charleston left their rice and tobacco fields, gathered their families, and packed the city's hotels, inns, and rooming houses. The streets were crowded at night. Performances at the Concert Hall on Church Street were sold out, and other concerts and recitations drew crowds. A raffle of equine art was held at the Carolina Coffee House. Various dinners and balls presented the cream of society in all its finery and cordiality.

The horsemen of the jockey club typically put up large purses to attract the finest horses from North Carolina and Virginia, then sent out their own runners to try to knock off the visitors. A South Carolinian could boast for a year if he won an event during Race Week. The state's top horsemen included Wade Hampton, a revered soldier and U.S. congressman who owned three thousand slaves; James Richardson, a wealthy planter; and John Spann, who had sent the fine mare Betsey Richards to Johnson.

Johnson enjoyed the Charleston meeting. His fast horses had a history of breaking the hearts of locals. In February 1823 he brought two of his finalists, Flying Childers and Betsey Richards. He left the younger three back home in Virginia, overseen by Taylor. They were just starting their training and, Napoleon felt, might be set back by the travel, especially Washington and Sir Henry, who had just come from North Carolina. Although steamships had made transporting horses much easier, Johnson still thought it wise to have his younger finalists make just one more trip: north to New York in May.

Traveling with Racing Billy, the two horses, and a dozen slaves, Johnson reached Charleston several days before the meeting began.

Springlike weather greeted him, but when a nasty front arrived, the temperature dropped and a steady rain set in. Morning workouts continued on the muddy track at the Washington Course. Johnson and Billy monitored their horses and their likely opponents as slaves held umbrellas to shield them from the rain.

The rain ended by the opening of the meeting on Wednesday morning. Schools, courts, and businesses closed, and planters gave slaves the day off. The streets around the course were crowded with people, horses, and carriages. The crowd had the cosmopolitan air of Richmond or Washington, with planters in tailored clothes escorting wives and daughters wearing expensive frocks and bonnets. Carriages and liveries lined up along the course's inner railing. Outside the gates, slaves perched on tree branches to see the course. They cheered and bet as excitedly as those inside the gates.

Only two horses were entered in the four-mile event, both owned by South Carolinians. Spann was running his best colt, a colt named Sumpter, against a filly owned by Richardson. Johnson did not run Flying Childers or Betsey Richards; they were already known quantities at this distance. He felt he could hone their speed by running them at shorter distances.

Sumpter, a midsized bay with a long tail and quick feet, easily won two straight heats to take the purse, completing each heat in around eight minutes, impressive times given the lamentable condition of the course. After the race Johnson sought out Spann; Sumpter had shown him enough to convince him that he should consider the colt for New York. The horse was young enough (five) and could certainly push the other youngsters in training. Johnson offered $2,400, and Spann accepted. Sumpter switched barns that afternoon. The pool of finalists had grown by one.

An overnight rainstorm left the course even more waterlogged the next day. The biting cold caused some fans to stay home. "We have seldom experienced weather so low," one Charleston newspaper reported. But many of the savvy local fans came to the course to see Flying Childers run in the three-mile event. They knew he was under consideration for the Union Course race and were curious to see him. Like all southerners, they were already anticipating a victory in New York. Maybe this was the horse that would bring them glory.

Billy's horse was not usually in the spotlight. Flying Childers shared with Eclipse the burden of a famous name — a British horse with the same name had gained fame in the 1700s as the first great thoroughbred — but unlike America's Eclipse, this Flying Childers was inferior to his namesake. He was known for having consistently finished behind Sir Charles and Sir William whenever they raced. His frame was small, his step heavy. He just was not as naturally gifted, forced to work harder to cover the same ground as his larger rivals. But he did have a relentless, digging action, and a deep bottom. Johnson had worked wonders with lesser descendants of Sir Archie.

The other horses in the event were a six-year-old gelding owned by Richardson and a five-year-old mare owned by Spann. The three horses approached the start, ridden by slaves dressed in bright racing shirts. A drum tap sent them running. Flying Childers immediately took the lead, sloshing through puddles as his jockey's bright pink shirt and black cap — Billy's colors — flashed in front.

The local horses were no match for Flying Childers. He circled the mile-long oval three times to win the first heat without even being pressed, and then, after a half-hour break, won the second heat similarly. His time for both heats was around six minutes. Johnson and Racing Billy rode over to praise the horse after the second heat. He had looked quick, nimble — better than before. Johnson reached out and stroked his neck. Billy, who was enormously fond of the hard-working little horse, made a clucking noise. Flying Childers's ears pricked. He was, it seemed, pleased with himself.

More rain fell that evening as the temperature continued to drop. A schooner sailed into the harbor with ice on its mast. A slave on the run died of exposure on the wharf. The weather dampened enthusiasm for Race Week, but the races continued. Napoleon did not mind. He believed running in unfavorable conditions toughened a horse.

The next day the two-mile event was held, and again fans came out to see a horse in the running for the Union Course event. This time it was the hometown girl, Spann's dapper brown mare, Betsey Richards, now recognized as the South's fastest mare and South Carolina's best chance to represent the region in New York. A vision of femininity with her slender hips, level gaze, and distinctive dark coat, she was a consistent runner that won more than she lost. Local fans were excited. Who knew how fast she might go with Johnson overseeing her?

Racing Billy put up a common mare against her, and Richardson entered a colt. Betsey Richards virtually left them both at the start, finishing so far in front of Richardson's colt in the first heat that it was distanced and dropped from the race. From the stands, where fans watched from under umbrellas, Betsey Richards was a blur, her jockey's bright red shirt a flash of light on a dark canvas.

The second heat was similar to the first: Betsey Richards led the whole way, streaking through the gloom without a hitch in her gait. She was cool and steady. Fans applauded as she finished the second heat in exactly four minutes. She had not disappointed.

One event remained on the Race Week schedule: the Silver Plate Handicap, consisting of three-mile heats, with each horse assigned a weight handicap by the judges. Johnson entered both Betsey Richards and Flying Childers, wanting to see his finalists go head to head. Why not? Both had run so well.

The night before the race, the jockey club ball — the highlight of the social week — lasted until after midnight. Young women from the rice and cotton plantations danced with men in snug breeches, silk stockings, and buckled pumps while a band played polkas. A six-course dinner was served. The planters who ran the club made sure the evening went off smoothly. There was much talk about the next day's race. Everyone went to bed late but still rose on Saturday morning to see Johnson's finalists run. It was as if the Union Course race had come to Charleston.

The skies finally cleared that morning. The course was crowded at noon as the horses were presented to the judges and assigned weights. Flying Childers, age six, would carry 112 pounds. Betsey Richards was assigned 99 pounds, giving her a sizable advantage. South Carolina fans anticipated her victory.

Johnson and Racing Billy rode over to the course and positioned themselves on horseback along the inner railing near the finish. Johnson commented that he wanted both horses to run well. Billy naturally wanted Flying Childers to win but, like Johnson, he also wanted both to excel. He knew that Betsey Richards just might represent the South in New York.

"What is your best guess for what the day shall hold, Billy?" Johnson asked.

Billy smiled. "A victory by Flying Childers, of course. But an especially fine showing by the mare will be a result I also can tolerate."

Three horses were presented to the judges; at the last minute Richardson had entered the gelding that had finished a distant third in the three-mile event several days earlier. He was assigned 107 pounds and given no chance by most fans. At the trumpeter's toot, the horses dashed away. They leaned into the first turn, and Betsey Richards jumped in front by a body length. Running gracefully and with seemingly minimal effort, she led through the first lap. Flying Childers, digging hard, was close behind.

The mare maintained the lead through the second lap and early part of the final lap, taking one long-legged stride for every two taken by the tough little horse right behind her. She seemed in control, although Flying Childers's jockey appeared confident that he could eventually pass her. Sure enough, Flying Childers slowly began to gain ground. His head dropped, his compact frame tensed, and his legs dug even deeper into the grass. He closed to within several feet of the mare coming up the back straightaway and then drew even as they leaned into the final turn. Betsey Richards was on the inside, in the better position for the sprint to the finish. But Flying Childers had more momentum. He nosed in front with one hundred yards to go. The crowd urged Betsey Richards on, but Flying Childers had more left. He moved ahead in the stretch and came home two lengths in front.

The crowd was quiet. Most of the fans were disappointed, having wanted to see their hometown mare win the heat. The few who had backed Flying Childers with their wallets exulted. Billy beamed as he rode over to take a look at the horse between heats. Flying Childers had never run better. What a great rally!

After the break the horses were presented again to the judges and sent running. The slave riding Flying Childers tried a different tactic this time. He took the early lead and made sure he stayed ahead of Betsey Richards through the first two laps. The mare lagged three or four lengths behind but ran easily. Finally, with a half-mile left, Betsey Richards's jockey asked her to lengthen her stride and challenge for the lead. She closed on the backstretch, pulling within a body length as she rounded the final turn and headed for the finish. The spectators stood, pulled from their seats by the drama. Could she do it?

She could not. Flying Childers responded to the challenge, digging in again and increasing his pace. Betsey Richards never drew closer than a length, and in fact Flying Childers began to move farther ahead again as they reached the finish.

The disappointed fans applauded as the horses were caught by grooms and led back to the judges. Flying Childers had won in straight heats, a fine victory considering he was carrying thirteen more pounds than the mare. Betsey Richards had run well and shown admirable heart with her late challenge, but the result was disappointing.

Johnson and Billy went to see both horses back at the barn after the race. They cooled out nicely and were given baths and meals. Billy was a little more thrilled than Napoleon by Flying Childers's magnificent run, for he had won the purse. The horse was really coming on, Billy said. Johnson agreed.

Alvan Fisher, an artist and racing fan from Massachusetts, who was wintering in Charleston, attended all the races during the meeting. He soon wrote to one of his patrons in New York:

> Old Eclipse's bottom and speed is to be tried by one of two horses that recently ran here. I witnessed the running of both. Sumpter ran the four-mile heats with considerable speed with the course muddy in spots. He certainly is a fast horse, but I should bet on Eclipse (if they raced). The other horse is called Flying Childers — a very fast horse, but I doubt he can run with the pride of New York. He is a short horse but runs very clean. The report here is one of them, or another in Virginia, will run against Eclipse for the $20,000.

Johnson was pleased overall as he departed from Charleston. He had come with two finalists and was leaving with three. Sumpter, Flying Childers, and Betsey Richards had all shown they were worthy of having been selected. Privately, though, he was mildly disappointed about the final race; he had hoped Betsey Richards would win. The better she fared, the greater the likelihood that she might run in New York. Johnson could not help wishing for it, envisioning the massive weight advantage she would enjoy. But it was only February. There was still time for her to come on. And back in Virginia she would take on those talented youngsters. That would be nothing if not interesting.

Johnson was convinced he was on the right track.

While Johnson was in South Carolina, Taylor started training the younger horses. He moved them to Newmarket and ran them together every morning. It made for quite a sight. All three were fast and reckless. They snorted and gasped as they circled the course. Their slave jockeys were under orders to keep them together rather than let the training run disintegrate into a race. Sometimes the horses obeyed, but sometimes they ignored their jockeys and started racing like children who had boasted that no one could beat them. Their legs churned, their eyes opened wide. Taylor shook his head. He had his work cut out for him.

But boy, could they run.

Taylor had seen John Richards previously, in the workouts before Johnson picked the finalists. As he got to know the young horse better, Taylor acknowledged the keenness of Napoleon's insight. Others probably would think the horse could not be tamed, but Johnson had seen through the bluster and recognized the potential.

John Richards had a gargantuan stride covering at least thirty feet at full speed, and his lungs seemed limitless — he was never out of breath, even immediately after a session. He also had a mischievous shine in his eyes that suggested he knew precisely what he was doing when he disobeyed, that he was just being headstrong — a dangerous quality. But he could be taught.

He was bigger than the other youngsters, and he stood out when their training runs fell apart and they started racing for the hell of it. Other horsemen at Newmarket stopped to watch, awed by the group's overall fleetness. John Richards usually jumped ahead by a few yards, and neither Washington nor Sir Henry could catch him until their jockeys regained control with sharp tugs, ending the brief contest.

Such displays were a testament to John Richards's speed, but other factors would help determine if he would be a worthy challenger to Eclipse. The depth of his bottom and the firmness of his resolve remained unknown.

Watching Sir Henry and Washington during these morning runs, Taylor could see why Johnson had picked them, too. Sir Henry — or just Henry, as the stable help began calling him — was a broad-shouldered chestnut, still filling out. He was a babe, having been foaled so late in 1819 (June) that he would not turn four until after the Union Course event. Eclipse had sons his age. His callowness was apparent. He was more excitable than the other two young horses. Noises, shadows, and other animals spooked him. He also tended to ignore his jockey almost all the time.

Taylor was primarily concerned about Henry's mind; he needed to mature before he could take on a horse like Eclipse. But like John Richards, he had compelling physical attributes. His leg bones were long and elegant. His running action was flawless. And what a burst of speed! His full sprint lasted as long as his jockey would allow. There was no telling how long he could go.

Henry's owner, Lemuel Long, an aging North Carolina plantation owner and friend of Marmaduke Johnson's, had brought the immature horse along slowly, training him privately rather than having him compete in public. Henry had raced in front of fans only once, in October 1822, in a two-mile event at Newmarket. As it happened, his toughest opponent in a field of five that day was Marmaduke's Washington.

The two colts put on a memorable show. Henry won the first heat and led until the end of the second, but Washington caught him right at the finish. A dead heat was declared. Washington then narrowly won the third heat, forcing a rare fourth heat. With their endurance being tested, Washington took the early lead and held on to win the heat and the purse, but Henry pushed him to the end, finishing two yards behind. Fans told each other they surely had just seen the South's two best young runners.

The victory was Washington's third of 1822; unlike Long, Marmaduke believed in putting his young runners on the turf and seeing if they could win purses (and help him win bets). Marmaduke had bred Washington by mating one of his favorite mares, a daughter of Diomed, to Timoleon. That meant Diomed was Washington's maternal grandsire and paternal great-grandsire. Horsemen of later generations would never condone such close inbreeding, but it was a common practice at this time because of the popularity of Diomed and Sir Archie. In this case it had produced a runner of uncommon maturity. Washington was as relaxed as Sir Henry was nervous, wise beyond his years. He seldom nipped at strangers, jumped at shadows, or disobeyed. He was a young gentleman.

Johnson hurried back from Race Week in Charleston and joined Taylor at Newmarket to watch the three youngsters. On the first morning he ordered a three-mile run followed by a short break and then a two-mile run. It was the first time all six finalists were together on a course. Flying Childers, Betsey Richards, and Sumpter were not given a day off after their long trip.

All other activity at Newmarket ceased when the horses began to run. The shouts of stable boys and jockeys dwindled away. The other southerners who trained at the course wanted to see Johnson's choices in action. The six horses ran in a pack around the first turn and sprinted up the backstretch together. John Richards took the lead, which was fitting — the bullish youngster had moved ahead in Johnson's eyes. Competitiveness was a characteristic you couldn't teach. John Richards obviously had it; he didn't want another horse running in front of him at any time.

But the others were close behind and, with any urging, probably could catch and pass the front-runner. Johnson wanted things that way — up in the air, subject to change. The horses completed the three-mile run in close proximity, then came back minutes later for a two-mile run. Sir Henry took the lead this time, running along the inner railing with John Richards right on his outside shoulder and the other four close behind. Sumpter, the newcomer, lagged slightly to the rear.

Johnson watched approvingly. He and Taylor would sit down that afternoon and formulate a training program for the coming months, a schedule of workouts and trials of varying lengths. The distances would get longer and longer. Horses in training under Johnson were in for a rough time. They might run eight miles one day, ten the next, and twelve a day later. Napoleon could be brutal. Trials — private races of three or four miles — were held on Sundays. That was a day of rest for everyone else, but there would be no rest for these horses. A horse that rested too much might get to the Union Course and lose to Eclipse. Napoleon was not about to let that happen.

7

Don't Spit Your Tobacco Juice

WHO WOULD RIDE at the Union Course? Which southern jockey would wear Johnson's sky blue colors? Would Samuel Purdy wear Van Ranst's maroon shirt again?

A few decades later the public would have been obsessing over those questions. By the end of the 1800s, jockeys would be bright lights in America's sports firmament, their names widely known beyond their sport, their skill and maneuverings deemed crucial to the outcome of a race. They were stars, pure and simple.

But in 1823 jockeys were almost invisible, far less well known than the horses they rode and the horsemen who hired them. Purdy had brought home winners for three decades, but he was still known mostly to horsemen and longtime fans; many northerners knew of him only as a businessman and politician. Jockeys were seldom mentioned in published accounts of races, their impact considered minimal compared to other factors, such as pedigrees and training and the trainer's race-day strategies. Sometimes it almost seemed as if the riders did not participate, that the horses ran alone.

Granted, jockeys did not have as much influence on races in the era of four-mile heats as they would decades later, when shorter events became the norm. Pedigrees, stamina, and training tactics were indeed more important when horses had to race a dozen or more miles to win, as opposed to one or two. A jockey occasionally won a four-mile heat with a slick maneuver or lost through utter incompetence, but it took the decline of heroic-era distance racing for the riders to become consistently important.

The enduring power of southern planters, who had ruled the turf since the Colonial era, also helped limit the perception that jockeys mattered. As breeders, the planters wanted to maximize the value of their fastest horses, and they knew that value would remain high as long as the horses received full credit for winning. For that reason the owners downplayed the influence of riders, at least publicly. And they could get away with it because so many of the southern riders were slaves.

Experienced horsemen such as Johnson and Van Ranst already grasped what later generations would accept as one of their sport's first commandments: a horse that was more talented and in better condition than its opponent could still lose if its jockey erred, and an inferior horse with a shrewd jockey could win. The rider could be that important. Johnson had several he favored, and Van Ranst had used Purdy for years.

The Union Course event would represent a turning point, beginning the transformation of jockeys from unknowns to mainstream sports celebrities. Although they would not be fully recognized and respected until after the Civil War, they attracted so much attention in May 1823 that the public realized it could never again discount the importance of riders.

In the months before the event, however, Johnson and Van Ranst contemplated their riding choices alone, without outside influences. No one offered them opinions or suggestions. Fans cared about the horses being considered, but they shrugged about jockeys. What difference did those guys make?

A lot, as it turned out.

Horsemen on both sides assumed Purdy would ride Eclipse at the Union Course. He had been the North's best jockey forever, it seemed, and had ridden Eclipse exclusively in races since the horse's much-discussed comeback from two years at stud. Why tinker with such a successful arrangement?

Although Purdy was forty-nine years old now and hardly a vision of athleticism — his back was stiff and stooped, his dark hair gray at the temples, his belly bulging — he still had thick-fingered, strong hands and an unerring knack for controlling and navigating a horse. Riders half his age might be in better shape, but they could not match his instinct for knowing when to make a move or how to protect a lead. "His skill and elegance in riding have long been the theme of admiration," Van Ranst later wrote of him.

He had been raised in the late 1700s on a farm in Westchester County, New York, where he worked with horses and developed a talent for communicating with them and getting them to do what he wanted. Racing was not a popular activity in the North at the time, but Purdy tried it and liked it. He had a competitive streak that surprisingly surfaced, and the chance to prove his horsemanship in front of cheering fans was exciting.

Most northern jockeys were, like him, wiry white farm boys, tense little working-class toughs weighing about one hundred pounds, even with their boots on. They were unschooled, taciturn, and often vicious, willing to do whatever it took to win. Northern racing was a hardscrabble free-for-all; you could do almost anything as long as the judges did not catch you. It was not unusual to see a jockey reach over and slug a rival rider during a stretch run or spit tobacco juice at him or whip an opposing horse in the eyes as it was about to pass him.

The jockeys' work was strictly on the side, on days off from their field and mill jobs; northern racing was so limited they competed in only a few events a year and certainly didn't get rich doing it, garnering just a small cut of whatever pittance their horse earned. Some horsemen even balked at that, refusing to hand over a dime. A jockey knew from the outset that his day could end in a fistfight over a few coins.

Purdy, from the beginning, was an anomaly. Most northern jockeys were accorded little respect by others, but Purdy was smart and classy, a cut above the stereotype. He did not hit opponents or spit at them, preferring to win honestly. He was respectful of the trainers who employed him and in turn was treated with respect.

He started competing at northern courses as a teenager but soon ventured south, where better racing beckoned. He roamed the South every spring and fall, following the circuit of meetings, hopping on and off horses, and bringing home his share of winners. It was an unpredictable, physically demanding life. Purdy was knocked to the grass more than a few times and learned to use his elbows. Most of his opponents were cunning young slaves who competed fiercely, knowing that failure could mean a return to the punishing grimness of the fields.

Sometimes he traveled with Van Ranst, and he became closely associated with him; on many days they were the only northerners among crowds of southern planters and race fans. Purdy rode Van Ranst's horses and those of planters such as Napoleon, who hired him because they trusted him to give his best effort. (Not every jockey did.) He also traveled alone at times, riding for days on dusty roads between meetings and sleeping in the open air if he could not find a bed or wanted to save his pennies.

As a white rider he was an even greater anomaly in the South, where slave jockeys were the norm. Accustomed to dominating riders they literally owned, planters cut a variety of deals with Purdy. Sometimes he took a fee to ride in a race regardless of how he fared, though he found it hard to get his money after losing. Sometimes he took a percentage of the stakes if he won. He continued to ride for smaller purses in New York and Pennsylvania, but southern racing offered more challenge, excitement, and money, and he seldom missed a swing through the circuit. He eventually made it to almost every known racing venue in America, from backwoods Tennessee tracks (where the judges really let anything go) to Virginia's fashionable Newmarket.

But the southern sojourns became an annoyance as he grew older, married, and started to raise a family in Manhattan. While continuing to ride as often as possible, Purdy decided to try making money another way. Though not formally educated, he was forthright and capable at a variety of tasks, from architectural design to carpentry. With exquisite timing, he started a home-building business just as New York was swelling with thousands of newcomers who had jobs and needed places to live. Purdy immediately attracted more work than he could handle. Business boomed, and he added crews of workers who fanned out across the city, putting up houses.

Few New Yorkers knew Purdy as a jockey before the 1820s — northern racing was that irrelevant — but many knew him as a businessman. His success led several banks and insurance companies to put him on their boards. Finding himself comfortable in that realm, he ventured into the maze of local politics and was twice elected tax assessor of his city ward. In 1823 he was considering running for alderman, a post in which he would be one of New York's top decision makers.

Purdy lived with his wife and three children in a spacious home near the Bowery in lower Manhattan. Because of his many family, business, and political obligations, he no longer traveled south. He was too busy, and his body ached from all those years of riding and traveling. Sometimes it was hard to believe that this distinguished man of stature and responsibility had lived the strenuous life of a jockey.

But he could still ride.

Van Ranst had used him for the National Course race even though he was all but retired and resembled a businessman or politician more than a jockey. The old wizard believed Purdy was still the North's best rider, and certainly the likeliest to ride capably in front of hooting southerners.

It had turned out not to matter one whit — a monkey could have guided Eclipse to victory after Sir Charles broke down — but while Purdy's riding had not factored in the outcome, the *New York Evening Post* proudly reported that "Purdy [showed] the sportsmen of the South a new style in the rider."

That was not necessarily true — southerners had witnessed plenty of fine riding over the years — but the rare appearance of a jockey's name in a newspaper underlined what the confident (but not as nuanced about racing) northern fans believed was yet another advantage for their side in the upcoming Union Course event. Even though the jockeys never seemed to be the deciding factor in a race, the North, for what it was worth, had a good one.

Johnson had many jockeys to choose from for the Union Course event, but his best options, he believed, were Charles Stewart, the young slave, and a small white Virginian named John Walden. Both stood out as consistent winners. Walden, a twenty-six-year-old farm boy from southwest Virginia, had more experience. But Stewart, who had joined Johnson's stable at age twelve in 1820, had more natural ability. He weighed less than one hundred pounds and had an instinct for race strategy that could not be taught. Napoleon used numerous riders, black and white, and Stewart had quickly risen to the top. Though only fifteen, he was already winning races worth hundreds of dollars.

The use of slave jockeys dated to the Colonial era, when planters seeking to emulate the English gentry rode for pleasure and in fox hunts but deemed riding in races beneath them. The task fell to their help, and dark-skinned riders became commonplace at otherwise segregated southern courses. Wearing their masters' colors, they competed equally against the few whites, such as Walden, most of whom came from farms.

The typical slave jockey was a short, emaciated youngster who had literally been starved to minimize the weight he put on the horse. But as wrenching as that regimen surely was, he was happy for the chance to ride. Getting plucked from the masses and put on a horse was a rare privilege and offered an exciting break from a dreadful existence.

Most of the slave jockeys still had to work the fields, especially during harvest season, and were taxed perilously close to their physical limits by riding all morning and picking crops all afternoon in a half-starved state. But the best riders were given what amounted to royal treatment in their world, living in better quarters and earning some pay. When Johnson dispatched Stewart to North Carolina to ride in a meeting there in 1822, he knew he was offering the slave an escape to freedom — the jockey traveled alone — but he also knew Stewart would ride dutifully and return to Oakland, for his life there was good.

Slave jockeys operated in total obscurity for the most part, their names seldom known beyond the barns and stables in which they worked. Though horsemen respected some of them, recognizing them publicly was out of the question. Southern whites refused to attribute superior qualities of any kind to the lowly workers they bought and sold as chattel.

A few did become famous. A slave called Simon was a well-known jockey in the early 1800s. According to the historian Edward

Hotaling, Simon arrived in Charleston at age ten in 1800, having come from Africa on a ship with his parents. He never grew taller than five feet, but he exhibited such riding skill that he gained the favor of the best horsemen in South Carolina and Tennessee, where he participated in a legendary series of races against horses owned by Andrew Jackson, the future president.

In the fall of 1811, Jackson's best horse ran against a three-year-old filly named Haynie's Maria, sired by Diomed and owned by Jesse Haynie of Sumner County, Tennessee. Simon rode Maria, and Jackson, according to Hotaling, issued a good-natured warning to the jockey before the race.

"Now, Simon," he said, "when my horse comes up and is about to pass you, don't spit your tobacco juice in his eyes and in the eyes of his rider, as you sometimes do."

The cocky Simon replied, "Well, Gin'ral, I've rode a good deal agin' your horses, but none were even near enough to catch my spit."

Simon's horse won, and Jackson vowed to beat Maria. After failing with a colt named Dungannon, Jackson bought a four-mile star from Napoleon and tried again, but Maria and Simon prevailed. Jackson's fury registered on his face after the race, as Simon impudently noted.

"Gin'ral, you was always ugly, but now you're a show," he said to the future president. "I could make a fortune by showing you as you now look, if I had you in a cage where you could not hurt the people who came to look at you."

Jackson tried and failed again with a young mare belonging to a friend. A rematch ended with the same result. After yet another defeat in which Jackson lost a $1,000 bet on a horse named Western Light, the general tried and failed a third time with his friend's mare. The famously competitive general was so frustrated that he sold his horses. Simon and Maria had driven him out of the sport

Years later, when an interviewer asked Jackson if there was anything in his life that he had undertaken and failed to accomplish, he replied, "Nothing that I can remember except Haynie's Maria."

Now, with the Union Course event looming and a slave jockey near the top of his stable, Johnson had much to consider. Racial politics, unavoidably, were an issue. Southerners were used to seeing slaves ride, but Johnson wondered how northerners would react. A hostile response might intimidate a slave as young as Stewart. As well, it was rumored that southerners were going to wager more money collectively on this race than on any in history — tens of thousands of dollars. Johnson worried about having so much money riding on a slave. He believed in Stewart, but he knew that many southerners would prefer to see a white rider represent them in such an important and expensive race.

As with his horse selection, Johnson did not have to make a call until the day of the race, minutes before the start. He was glad he had all that time. Picking a jockey was, in some ways, his toughest decision.

As was his custom with an important race on the horizon, Purdy rode out to Harlem Lane several times in January to take Eclipse on cold, snowy training runs. He wanted to maintain their close relationship.

Purdy instinctively knew how to get along with horses. He ran his hands along their flanks before he got on, soothing them physically while speaking in a confident, familiar voice. And he kept talking once he was on their backs. He had learned that skittish or obstinate horses were more likely to follow orders and respond to the shock of a whipping or spurring if they liked and respected the man responsible.

Eclipse already liked and respected him, Purdy figured, even though he was not around the horse as much as Van Ranst. They had been through a lot together. Purdy had helped retrain Eclipse for racing during the long, hard summer of 1821, riding him through the lush countryside around Van Ranst's Long Island estate. Then, of course, they had shared the triumphs over Lady Lightfoot, Sir Walter, and Sir Charles.

After each victory, Purdy had jumped off Eclipse feeling certain he had never ridden a better horse — quite a statement after his more than three decades on the turf. But he was awed by the sheer power he felt underneath him. When Eclipse surged, it felt as if a whole team of horses were pulling him.

Recently Purdy had made a point of staying in touch with Eclipse between races; under the guise of maintaining their relationship, he really just wanted to spend a few more mornings around the old horse. Eclipse, he knew, would not be racing much longer, and Purdy enjoyed the excellence the horse exuded. Eclipse looked at him with such intelligence and was such a fine runner. Maybe other northerners did not know enough to appreciate a horse like this, but Purdy did.

Purdy's visits always began in the stall, where he patted Eclipse and clucked at him, then took him out for long runs in the snow. Van Ranst said little but looked on approvingly. The jockey just assumed he would be on the horse at the Union Course in May. Although he and Van Ranst had not traveled together through the South in years, Purdy kept a riding shirt in Van Ranst's colors in his closet, and he believed his experience would offset his age and physical limitations.

He had no idea that Van Ranst was starting to have second thoughts. The old wizard kept them to himself at first, saying nothing when the jockey was around. But one need only look at Purdy, Van Ranst thought, to know that the man's best riding days were behind him. He had to weigh close to 130 pounds, not a pretty sight on a five-foot frame, and he hunched over disturbingly as he walked, the years of riding having taken an obvious toll.

Purdy, at forty-nine, was exactly as old as America itself. Van Ranst could not help wondering if such an ancient rider would be able to fend off what was certain to be the toughest challenge the South had ever presented. Van Ranst kept envisioning an old jockey on old Eclipse being trounced by a young southern horse with an equally young, energetic jockey. He had no doubt Johnson's horse and rider would be youthful, and the more he thought about it, the more he saw Purdy's age as a key disadvantage. The North needed its own source of vitality, and since it could not come from a different horse, it had to come from a different jockey.

Van Ranst's options included a young lightweight named Billy Crafts and a shrewd veteran, John Buckley, who was retired but still able. Both had won races on fine horses and, Van Ranst believed, would skillfully represent the North. And both were younger than Purdy. A younger jockey would be stronger, better able to control Eclipse, better equipped to react to whatever the South threw at them.

As February turned to March, Van Ranst told no one about his misgivings — not even John Cox Stevens, who surely would have an opinion, probably to the contrary. Eclipse is still my horse, Van Ranst thought, and a decision like this should be mine, too. Why rush into it when the race is still three months away? Purdy would be upset to hear that Van Ranst was questioning his ability. And if he wound up using Purdy, he would have caused problems for no reason.

Van Ranst elected to sit back and let Eclipse's training unfold at Harlem Lane. As the months came and went, the old wizard studiously avoided discussing Purdy with anyone. But he thought constantly about the possible change of riders. Was it a good idea? Was it sheer foolishness? He debated the issue endlessly in his head. All he knew was that the question of who would ride Eclipse in May was not nearly as simple, or as settled, as everyone thought.

8

What a Heat!

A S FEBRUARY TURNED TO MARCH, Johnson put his six finalists through the hardest training they had ever experienced,
with no letup. They ran every day but Sunday, covering
miles and miles. Then on Sundays they raced.

Their routine had the look of a nocturnal military drill. Johnson
rose before dawn every day and took a carriage ride to Newmarket.
Slave stable boys and jockeys had already been there for an hour under Arthur Taylor's command, rushing around the lantern-lit stables
as they prepared the horses to run. The diminutive jockeys, dressed
in breeches and bright shirts, waited for their orders. The stable boys,
wearing olive, braided and saddled the horses

Johnson carefully matched certain jockeys with certain horses,
searching for pairs that worked well together. Slaves who were strong
but impatient went on the older horses, which tended to be obedient.
The more experienced riders boarded the youngsters. The best white
jockey, Walden, the farm boy, was paired with Henry, the most immature finalist.

Training began at first light, a deadline unfailingly met. The horses
ran in the rain. They did not stop even when a freak late-winter
sleet storm struck one morning. It was here, in the bustle of the
Newmarket dawn, that Johnson would make his decisions. Although
fans focused on how horses fared in races held before the public,
Johnson felt he could learn more about them in training and trials.

He could not control races, which included the horses of other men, but here he could exert total control, manipulating horses and jockeys and creating the exact situations he wanted — situations from which he could learn.

It was no secret that he favored the three youngsters — the bullish, competitive John Richards, fleet but immature Henry, and elegant Washington. Southern race fans craved a look at them, but Johnson had other ideas. His plan called for each to race in public only once before the Union Course event. Just one glimpse for the fans before May!

How the horses fared in those events would matter; you could not replicate some aspects of a race — the crowds, the noise — in morning training sessions, and Johnson needed to see how the horses responded in those conditions. Young horses in particular could lose concentration in front of a crowd. But their performance in Johnson's training camp would matter just as much.

He varied their routines. The toughest were the "bottom-building" days, which consisted first of marathon runs lasting anywhere from eight to twelve miles, and then a break followed by a second, shorter run at a faster pace. Johnson watched closely, searching for signs of excessive fatigue as the horses circled Newmarket's course again and again. Then there were "speed-building" days, consisting of four or five sprints lasting from one to three miles. "Chase days" were for developing competitiveness: a horse was started far behind a pack of opponents and urged to catch up.

Inevitably, the horses began to distinguish themselves in various ways. The older horses, Flying Childers and Betsey Richards, initially had a little more bottom than the youngsters and fared better in ten-mile runs, as was to be expected, for they had previously trained and raced at the four-mile distance. But the youngsters, especially John Richards and Henry, had more natural speed, making them the better potential candidates. You could build up a horse's stamina — Johnson was working on that with the youngsters — but speed was a rarer quality, difficult if not impossible to train into an animal. A horse either had it or did not.

Sundays were set aside for taking an overall measure of the horses' progress. Instead of training, they engaged in trials of varying distances, usually from two to four miles. Most of the trials took place at Newmarket, but on one Sunday in early March Johnson, just to break up the routine, brought them all to Oakland to race on his distinctive straightaway track.

It would be a four-mile event — two miles up, a turnaround, and two miles back. The morning skies were clear over Oakland, the temperature chilly. Johnson's wife and children rose early and came out to watch, joining their father, Arthur Taylor, and Racing Billy on the wooden stand by the finish. Jockeys were put on each horse and aligned for a start. Every jockey was a slave except Walden, who rode Henry. The riders wore bright shirts and caps of different colors to distinguish them. The shirts were tucked neatly into their breeches.

Walden, though inelegant and uneducated, like most white jockeys, had a quietly confident demeanor and a knack for calming highstrung horses. Henry, of all the finalists, needed his soothing presence: the young North Carolina horse often reared before training sessions, unable to contain his excitement, and was occasionally distracted by birds and butterflies as he ran. He needed to grow up. Johnson believed he could benefit from Walden's influence.

Napoleon ordered the riders to spread out across Oakland's grass course — it was just wide enough — and sent them running with a shout. Henry jumped in front, as he often did, and moved ahead by a couple of lengths in the first hundred yards; there was no doubt the young horse was the quickest of the six. But John Richards, with Charles Stewart riding, was right behind him. None of the others dropped too far back.

As he guided Henry, Walden gripped the reins so tightly that the leather cut the skin on his calloused palm. Johnson had given Walden specific instructions. Henry needed to be taught to focus on the task immediately at hand, as opposed to looking around while he ran. He also needed to learn to take it easy and conserve his energy when his jockey told him to, as opposed to running hell-bent until he tired. Eclipse would destroy him if he ran like that.

Racing across Oakland's grass that Sunday morning, Walden hoped Henry was ready for such schooling; until now the horse had shown only intermittent interest in doing what he was told. He was headstrong, for sure. But his quickness, a quality horsemen called "turn of foot," gave him enormous potential.

Passing the one-mile mark and bearing down on the turnaround at the end of the straightaway, Walden gave a hard tug on the reins, asking Henry to ease up. The horse fought back, lowering his head and flexing his neck muscles, as if to say "Forget it!" When Walden tried again as they neared the turnaround, Henry again demurred. The horse reached the turnaround and quickly reversed direction, still leading John Richards by two lengths. Flying Childers, Betsey Richards, and Washington were another three lengths back, running together. Sumpter brought up the rear, fading out of contention.

Walden tugged on the reins a third time to try to slow Henry down; the jockey was not concerned about winning, just about getting the horse to do his bidding. Henry again ignored the tug. Then he began to slow down. He had not learned his lesson. He had run too hard for too long and was out of steam. His stride shortened and his ribs heaved. John Richards closed in on him from behind, with Stewart using a whip for encouragement. Henry's lead shrank to one length as they passed the midway point of the return trip. One mile to go.

But it was clear that Henry would not be able to sprint to the finish. John Richards had more bottom. The muscular, square-shouldered colt sprang forward on low-slung haunches, almost like a frog hopping across a pond — a huge, strong frog. The lead changed hands with a half-mile to go. John Richards passed Henry and pulled ahead. There was no catching him now. John Richards hated to have any horse running in front of him. He had barely tolerated letting Henry hold the lead for this long. But John Richards's willingness to go against his own wishes indicated that he could be controlled and thus was a better candidate for the Union Course. Johnson was thrilled to see it.

Henry faded badly in the final yards. His breathing became strained. Washington passed him and finished second, five lengths behind John Richards. Betsey Richards also passed Henry and went on to finish third. Henry and Flying Childers, the little veteran digger, arrived together at the finish well behind the winner but safely in front of Sumpter. Coming to a standstill, Sumpter's jockey shouted that the horse had injured his right foreleg. Johnson hurried over to take a look.

Walden, meanwhile, brought Henry to a halt and shook his head. The trial had not gone well.

When Congress adjourned in March, John Randolph hurried from Washington to Petersburg to check up on the finalists. He was intensely passionate about the turf (he would leave 130 horses in his will), and it could be argued that his interest in the Union Course race was unsurpassed. Johnson was in charge of the southern side, but Randolph was its spiritual centerpiece. He had contributed to the $20,000 stakes, made a private bet of $1,000 with a northern friend, and was desperate to see the South win and reestablish its superiority. He had bred and raced horses for years, and while he was disappointed that he had not produced a finalist, he really cared only about seeing a southern horse defeat Eclipse.

Born to a privileged family in southern Virginia just before the Revolutionary War, Randolph had enjoyed racing as a boy and even rode in quarter-mile sprints before leaving the family plantation to attend the College of New Jersey, which later became Princeton. Upon inheriting the plantation, he built a training track, filled his library with breeding books, and maintained a sizable stable. An original thinker in Congress as well as in other spheres, he was less dazzled by Diomed's pedigree than other southerners were, and that opinion, held stubbornly, fatefully undermined his stable's quality. Although his horses competed regularly across the South, they seldom attained the heights Randolph envisioned.

His shrill, passionate orations had caromed through Congress since his election to the House in 1799, and now, at fifty, still a bachelor, he was one of the South's most prominent statesmen. He was tired from the congressional session when he reached Petersburg in March, but he quickly revived as he conferred with Johnson about the race. Napoleon was so honored by the visit that he spent the night with Randolph in a tiny garret room at the Chesterfield County courthouse. Randolph slept soundly for the first time in months, as he wrote in a diary: "The windows clattered, and William R. Johnson got up several times to try to put a stop to the noise by thrusting a glove between the loose sashes. I heard the noise; I even heard him; but it did not disturb me. I enjoyed a sweet nap of eight hours, during which, he said, he never heard me breathe. My feelings the next day were as new and delightful as of those of any bride the day after her nuptials."

When Randolph asked about the finalists, Johnson offered insights he had shared with few others. Although he still had more than two months to pick a horse, he was leaning toward John Richards. Randolph expressed surprise. Racing Billy's strapping bay had never publicly competed in a four-mile event. The horse's entire career thus far consisted of just two events: a two-mile race at Newmarket the previous spring, which he won (defeating Washington), and a three-mile event at a small track in Greensville County, Virginia, the previous fall, in which he was defeated by Sir Charles before the National Course debacle.

Like any horseman or fan analyzing the situation, Randolph wondered why Napoleon had so much faith in a horse that had raced so little. But Johnson explained that John Richards was excelling in training and trials and that he could not recall a more competitive animal. John Richards consistently won the Sunday trials between the finalists and he was responding to the demanding training regimen like a champion: he was blooming instead of wilting, his appetite increasing, his coat taking on a shine. On chase days, when he was asked to make up ground on the others, he raced with such fierceness and determination that you would think he believed he had to catch up to earn his dinner.

Any layman could stand by the rail during a morning training session and tell John Richards was the best of the six, Johnson explained. But things might be different if Henry ever grew up.

Spring slowly came to southern Virginia. The grass on the race courses turned green, and leaves unfurled on previously bare tree limbs. Johnson no longer needed a heavy winter coat for his early morning visits to Newmarket.

A steady stream of planters and horsemen came to watch the training sessions, claiming to offer support and assistance but mainly just wanting to see the horses run. Anticipation of the Union Course race was like a drumbeat growing louder across the South. People were intensely curious about Johnson's training camp, but the newspapers never wrote about it. Even the rumor mill was quiet. What was happening? Who was the favorite to represent the South?

Johnson was aware of the speculation and pleased to hear it circulating. Secrecy worked in his favor, he thought. It was good to keep the northerners in the dark, too. If they did not know about these young horses he was training, they would be that much more overconfident and likely to bet larger amounts.

Johnson's general assessment of the finalists changed little through March and early April. John Richards continued to stand out. Henry began to heed Walden's orders occasionally instead of never, a sign that he might be starting to mature and grasp what Johnson wanted. Washington was quiet and consistent. Flying Childers and Betsey Richards ran hard and close to the leaders every day.

The sixth horse, Sumpter, was eliminated after injuring his leg in the trial at Oakland. Although the injury was relatively minor, Sumpter missed enough training time to ensure that he would not be in prime racing condition in May. He had not been in great shape as it was. Johnson regretted having purchased him in Charleston.

Napoleon had to decide when to race the horses in public. There were not many opportunities. Nottoway, a small country track west of Petersburg, was the only Virginia course that held races in April. The Newmarket meeting was in early May, three weeks before the Union Course race. The other major Virginia tracks such as Tree Hill held their meetings too late for Johnson to use.

Johnson's first priority was to see John Richards race somewhere other than in training. Racing Billy's young bay almost looked too good to be true in the morning sessions, and he had won the most trials of any of the finalists. His bottom was increasingly deep after weeks of long-distance runs. Only Henry had more natural speed. And John Richards was consistent. He always ran hard, even on the rare days when he was obviously tired and needing a break.

After weighing his options, Johnson decided to run him in a three-mile sweepstakes at Nottoway. The meeting was a full month before the Union Course event, giving the horse plenty of time to rest up. Nottoway also had a four-mile event, but Johnson elected not to run John Richards in that, even though the colt had never raced at the heroic distance. A three-mile race now would serve as the proper steppingstone for the four-mile Union Course event in May.

When Johnson heard that only two relatively untested Nottoway County horses — a four-year-old colt named Tyro and an older male named John Stanley — had been entered against John Richards, he brought along Flying Childers to ensure that his youngster would be tested. The little digger had been game throughout the training camp, seldom winning but always competing. He would give John Richards a healthy run for the $300 purse.

The race day was sunny, warm, and windy. Nottoway's clientele consisted mostly of farmers and hunters, with a few planters mixed in; this was not Charleston or Washington. But they loved their racing, and they pressed together around the course, which was laid out on an open field in the middle of a forest. Newspapers had reported that Johnson was coming with two horses under consideration for the Union Course event against the North. The lone small stand near the finish was packed.

Johnson and Racing Billy watched on horseback, positioned near the finish. Racing Billy's pride was palpable. One of his horses figured to win today, and he had to admit he hoped it was John Richards. Encouraged by Johnson's faith in the young horse, he dreamed about owning the animal that represented the South in New York.

Johnson also hoped John Richards would perform well. He was more than a little nervous, having known horses that trained better than they raced, losing focus when surrounded by cheering fans. John Richards had not faltered in either of his public races the previous year, but young horses were like young people, often changing from year to year, or even from month to month. Who knew what might happen?

As the horses were being aligned at the start, Johnson rode over to Charles Stewart. The slave jockey was aboard John Richards, wearing a shirt and cap in Johnson's sky blue. The slave riding Flying Childers wore Racing Billy's pink, so fans could easily tell them apart.

Johnson had little to say; Stewart was already familiar with the horse, having ridden him all winter and spring. This was not an animal you had to encourage to run. Just get the most out of him, Johnson advised.

The start at Nottoway consisted simply of a judge shouting "Go!" The spectators cheered and John Richards jumped in front. He took a lead of three lengths over Flying Childers, with Tyro and John Stanley well back as all four horses reached a sprint. They circled the mile oval in those positions and started on their second lap. Johnson focused on John Richards. What a blessing for a horse to have such a stride, he thought. He was not a natural, effortless runner like Henry, but he was just so powerful, springing up and across the grass with every leap. Poor little Flying Childers had to take three times as many steps to keep pace, it seemed.

John Richards steadily moved farther ahead. As the horses passed in front of Johnson and Racing Billy near the end of the second lap, Johnson motioned for Flying Childers's jockey to make a better race of it. That was why the horse was here, after all. As expected, the Nottoway horses were not in the picture, unable to keep pace.

The jockey unleashed an immediate assault, encouraging Flying Childers by whipping him and digging into his hide with his boot spurs. Some horses balked at such treatment, but Flying Childers was an old hand, trusting and obedient. His response was to run harder. Stamina was not a problem for him. He closed to within four lengths of John Richards on the first turn of the final lap, then cut the lead to two lengths on the backstretch.

Stewart sat motionless, seemingly oblivious to the challenge. Then the slave turned to survey the field and saw a horse bearing down on him. He quickly turned back and whipped John Richards once, twice, three times. The young horse, plainly approving of the signal to run faster, dropped his head and jumped even farther than usual for one, three, five strides. He obviously had plenty left. All those morning sessions had made a difference. His lead grew again as the horses rounded the final turn. He breezed to the finish five lengths in front.

Grooms immediately grabbed both horses and led them to the stable in the woods behind the course. Johnson and Racing Billy rode over to watch. As grooms bathed and walked the horses, following Arthur Taylor's orders, Racing Billy noted that John Richards had proved that Johnson's faith in him was not misplaced. Johnson nodded. It had been an encouraging heat.

All four horses returned for the second heat, which unfolded differently. The Nottoway jockeys on Tyro and John Stanley asked for more at the start, flailing their horses with whips and spurs. The two ran evenly with the finalists for the first lap, and Tyro even took the lead at the start of the second lap. The Nottoway fans applauded, surprised to see one of their own in front. Stewart, a cool head even at fifteen, was unmoved. He knew he had the better horse. He sat happily behind the others, waiting for the right moment to strike. On the backstretch of the second lap he gave the signal to John Richards, a staccato burst of whipping. The horse accelerated, passing Tyro in five strides. Both Nottoway horses were left behind.

But John Richards was not alone. Flying Childers had moved right with him, forming what amounted to a shadow, a step behind and just off the leader's outside shoulder. The horses began the third and final lap in those positions, running close enough for their jockeys to reach out and shake hands if they wanted.

The final lap was a thriller. Flying Childers was every bit the equal of John Richards on this day. They traded the lead back and forth, never separated by more than a length. Flying Childers was ahead on the first turn, then John Richards passed him on the backstretch, only to see Flying Childers regain the lead on the second turn. They were dead even as they sprinted for the finish, both jockeys using whips and spurs, both horses digging hard into the thick grass.

Johnson and Racing Billy, watching from near the finish, were surprised to see such a close heat. John Richards seemed to be racing at top speed, but he could not shake the older, smaller horse. Flying Childers moved slightly ahead with one hundred yards to go. But Stewart never stopped flailing away, and John Richards pulled even with fifty yards to go.

The horses took their final strides together, in what looked like military lockstep, and crossed the finish in what appeared to be a dead heat. Spectators applauded. Johnson and Billy looked at each other without smiling. From their vantage point near the finish, they had not been able to tell who was ahead. Would there be a third heat?

The judges huddled for more than a minute before announcing that John Richards had reached the finish slightly ahead. It was a debatable decision. Some fans who had bet on Flying Childers made known their opinion of the ruling, shouting angrily at the judges. It did not matter. The event was over. John Richards had won the heat and the purse. Anyone who had bet on Flying Childers had to shut up and pay up.

Johnson and Racing Billy pocketed the $300 and stopped briefly at the barn before taking Johnson's carriage back to Oakland. Both horses seemed fine. John Richards, as usual, was barely out of breath. Taylor and the stable boys would jog the horses back to Newmarket later that day.

During the carriage ride, Johnson confessed that he was mildly disappointed. Even though John Richards had won, the horse had struggled in the second heat against a horse that he knew Eclipse could handle. John Richards would have to do better to win in New York. After watching the horse train for so long at such a high level, Johnson had expected more.

On the other hand, the race was still a month away, and John Richards was still a work in progress. He would not race again before May 27, but he would continue to train strenuously, and, Johnson hoped, that would make a difference. He remained optimistic. John Richards was a much better runner than he had been in January. There was still reason to believe he would be ready for Eclipse in another month.

In early May fans gathered in southern Virginia for the finest occasion in American racing — Newmarket's spring meeting.

Run by a jockey club of influential planters that included Johnson, Racing Billy, and James Junkin Harrison, the track was a jewel perched on the south bank of the Appomattox River just outside Petersburg. It was named for the English track where King Charles II had sanctioned the first modern races in 1660. The royal connection seemed appropriate. Newmarket attracted the cream of local society and horsemen from across America. It was said that the track "did not exist so much for the masses as the classes." A colorful flower garden bloomed by the clubhouse. Gravel walkways led to the stables and outbuildings in the woods adjacent to the course. The dining room served elegant meals. The living quarters were spotless. Women watched races from their carriages on Hare's Hill, an embankment overlooking the first turn named for Otway Hare, the club president.

Races at the spring meeting offered purses of up to $1,000, which helped attract the country's best horsemen and their fastest horses. Johnson, with his private training stable on the grounds, had the grass course to himself at other times of the year, but he had to share space in the spring. The barns were full for weeks before the meeting, and the mornings were busy with planters issuing training orders as slaves scrubbed and rode the horses.

As the meeting approached, the grounds were more lively than ever before. A number of top horses trained every day, including the respected older runners Sir William and Lady Lightfoot as well as Johnson's finalists. Southerners pointed out that the North could only dream of staging a week of races with so many fine horses. Their loyalty was heating up with the Union Course race just weeks away.

The four-mile event was the week's traditional highlight, a supreme test that had been won by many of the South's best horses over the years. Johnson elected to enter Henry, putting his youngest finalist on the spot. Henry barely knew what it was like to compete in front of spectators, his entire career thus far having consisted of one short race, which he lost. Now he was going to run in this race? To many observers it seemed an outrageous gamble.

Johnson, however, thought the move was perfectly sensible. He believed Henry had benefited more than any of the other finalists from the recent months of hard training. The colt had been so immature and incorrigible in the beginning that sometimes he seemed a lost cause. But he had started to exhibit a new maturity in April. He no longer halted running to chase after birds.

More important, he had begun to obey Walden. Johnson and the jockey had spent hours discussing Henry and how to get the horse to grow up. And one morning it became clear their work was starting to

pay off. On a bottom-building day consisting of an eight-mile training run followed by a two-mile sprint, Johnson gave Walden bizarre
instructions: push the horse hard for three miles, then ease up for
three, then push again, then just coast to the finish. Walden smiled
when given the orders. With his short, raggedy snipped hair, crooked
teeth, and wide-set eyes, he gave the appearance of being rough
around the edges, but he was far more insightful than he appeared.
He knew that the absurd-sounding orders were strictly experimen-
tal — a test for Henry.

That morning Henry showed the full extent of his potential for the
first time. He shot ahead of the others in the first three miles, his en-
viable quickness on display. When Walden yanked hard on the reins,
Henry briefly balked, obviously dismayed, but he obeyed, coasting for
the next three miles as the other finalists passed him. He snorted and
kicked at the air, frustrated at being forced to fall behind, but he allowed it to happen. Walden's heart soared. Last place never felt so
good. The quiet farm boy knew his boss would be excited.

Henry burst forward when Walden gave him the go-ahead to start
running again, but just as the horse reached top speed, the jockey
yanked on the reins again. Henry was confused and perturbed, but
again he did not fight. He jogged to the finish, ending well behind
the others. Johnson saw great possibilities in him for the first time.
What a fearsome runner he could be if he consistently followed orders like this.

Walden was smiling broadly when he met with Johnson after the
run. He commented that their crazy horse was starting to figure
things out. Johnson nodded, also smiling. As a reward, they let
Henry loose in the ensuing two-mile sprint. Henry came home in
front, two lengths ahead of John Richards.

Now, in early May, it was time for the horse to run in public.
Strangely, none of the other planters chose to take him on in the four-
mile event, instead shifting their horses to other races in hopes of
winning one of those large purses. Johnson was amazed; it was not as
if Henry had a great record that should frighten anyone away. But it
was imperative that the horse be tested, so Johnson entered Betsey
Richards. She also had benefited from the months of hard training. Although she was not quite the equal of John Richards, she

was a strong, long-winded runner. If she raced as she had at Charleston in February, she might even beat Henry.

To flesh out the field, Racing Billy entered a lesser mare named Spring Tail. Maybe she would clutter up the course and give the other two a hard time. It was worth a try, Billy figured.

The four-mile race, held on the first day of the meeting, was the closest thing in southern Virginia to a secular holiday. Fans gathered beneath sunny skies at the elegant course. The dining hall was booked, the grandstands filled, the roads around the track jammed with carriages.

Johnson spent the morning at the barn, discussing strategy with Walden. He wanted to make sure Henry followed orders in the frenzied, exciting setting. It was hard to predict how the horse would react, given how little he had raced.

Napoleon still considered John Richards the favorite to carry the South's flag at the Union Course. Although Henry was coming along, John Richards was more dependable. And another factor was working against Henry: even though he would still be three years old on May 27, he would have to race as a four-year-old because the Union Course, like most American tracks, used May 1 as the date for determining a horse's racing age. That meant he would have to carry more handicapping weight than a three-year-old would, making him a less attractive candidate, especially given Johnson's determination to make weight and age the decisive variables in the race.

Still, Johnson was not about to dismiss Henry just because of that. He had pushed the young horse especially hard, and Henry had responded, improving dramatically. Racing against Betsey Richards in the Newmarket four-mile event would give him a chance to show what he could do.

The horses warmed up on the course, moved to the start, and halted. Their jockeys waited for the starter to blow a trumpet in the brief silence that enveloped the course. Johnson, watching on horseback from his usual perch near the finish, studied Henry. The horse was agitated, his eyes wet and wide as he took in the scene. Was he mature enough to handle this? Johnson wondered.

When the trumpet blast sounded, Betsey Richards bolted to the lead, leaving Henry and Walden behind. The mare, ridden by a slave dressed in the red silks of her South Carolina owner, pushed well ahead in the first hundred yards, sprinting as if she had only a short distance to run and could go all out. Her eyes flashed and her muscles rippled as she leapt forward again and again. She was five lengths ahead of Henry and ten lengths in front of Spring Tail as she circled the oval the first time.

Johnson focused on Henry as the horses ran in front of him and began the second lap. What an excellent test for Henry, he thought. Betsey Richards was really moving. Napoleon had not discussed with Walden the possibility that Henry would fall far behind, but he was sure Walden knew what to do. Keep Henry reined in. Let him know who was boss. Save him for a charge later in the heat.

Sure enough, Walden gripped the reins tightly and tugged at Henry to keep him from breaking free and chasing after the speedy mare. Betsey Richards maintained a good lead as she continued her seemingly mad dash around the oval. As the second lap ended, several fans holding watches looked at their dials and announced that she was on a record pace, having covered the first two miles in well under four minutes. An audible buzz rolled through the stands and up Hare's Hill.

Spring Tail, unable to keep up, was in the distance, out of contention. Henry was seven lengths behind, a sizable margin. Rounding the first turn of the third lap, Walden decided he needed to start moving. He had hoped to wait until the last lap, but he knew that would be too late with Betsey Richards going so fast. She had run this distance before. She had the stamina to go hard until the end.

Walden whipped Henry and dug his spurs deep into the horse's hide. Henry began to run harder. He did not mind the punishment — he relished the chance to sprint. Ears pinned back, eyes flashing, he resembled a boy who had been told to put down his schoolwork, go outside, and play. All that was missing was a smile.

None of the finalists, not even John Richards, could match Henry at top speed. He closed on Betsey Richards even as she continued to hurtle ahead. The lead shrank to six lengths, then four, then two as the horses rounded the second turn. Betsey Richards continued to sprint along the inside railing. Henry caught her as they came through the finishing lane and started the final lap. Fans marveled at the young bay as he glided across the grass, his running motion as smooth and strong as a steamship on a canal. He nosed ahead on the turn as Walden continued to whip him.

Henry was a length in front as they came up the backstretch of the final lap. The mare continued to run hard even though she had yielded the lead. She refused to let Henry pull away as they rounded the second turn. In fact, she began to regain the ground she had lost, creeping closer with every step.

Had Henry's charge robbed him of a finishing kick? The fans in the stands stood up to get a better view of the finish. Henry and Betsey Richards came out of the turn and raced toward them, moving as if they were just starting the heat, not finishing it. Henry's eyes shone, his competitive gears engaged. He knew the mare was right behind him. He was determined not to let her pass.

Walden was not the least bit worried. Having ridden Henry all spring, he knew when the horse had something left. Even with the whip stinging his flanks, Henry was not running at his top speed. He had more to give if needed. Sure enough, Betsey Richards could get no closer. Henry held the lead through the final yards and reached the finish a length in front.

Slaves raced from the sidelines, corralled the horses, and led them away to Johnson's stable. The fans exhaled and sat down. What a heat! Johnson waved at Walden, who dismounted and went off in search of shade. There was no need to talk; Henry's performance said it all.

Then the judges announced the winning time — 7 minutes 54 seconds — and a new round of applause rippled through the crowd. The fans had just witnessed the fastest four-mile heat ever run at Newmarket. Johnson's jaw dropped. It took a lot to surprise him after all these years on the turf, but Henry had surpassed all expectations. Racing Billy slapped Napoleon on the back.

They left their horses by the railing and walked to the stable in the woods behind the course. Henry and Betsey Richards were being bathed to calm them before the excitement of the next heat. Johnson knelt and rubbed their legs, searching for soreness, then rose and looked into their eyes, which were clear. Both horses seemed fine. Johnson shook his head again, still amazed. Who could have predicted that Henry and Betsey Richards would run so well?

Twenty minutes later the three horses were back on the grass course. Racing Billy had decided to run Spring Tail again even though she had finished fifty yards behind the leaders. It was unlikely this heat would go any better for her. Neither Henry nor Betsey Richards appeared fatigued.

Johnson and Walden conferred before the heat began. Walden, on Henry, looked down at Napoleon, who held the reins. The horse seemed more keyed up than before the first heat. He stomped with his back legs and cocked his head sharply when a fan shouted his name. Johnson, noting the horse's mood, suggested a change in tactics. Let him run early, he told the jockey, take advantage of his enthusiasm. But do not wear him out. Remember, this is a second heat, more about bottom than speed. Save as much as possible for the end. Walden nodded and rode away.

The judges called for the start. The horses were aligned and sent running by the trumpeter. Henry took off at a faster pace than in the first heat. Encouraged by Walden, the horse churned across the grass. He was five yards ahead of Betsey Richards by the backstretch of the first lap.

Betsey Richards easily could have become dispirited, but she continued to run hard. The distance between the horses did not increase as they finished the first lap and began the second. Walden tugged lightly on the reins a few times to keep Henry under control. The two horses settled into a rhythm. They circled the course twice more without a change in position. Henry was five lengths ahead.

The pace was fast. A fan standing near Johnson, eyes glued to a watch, announced that Henry had run the first three miles in less than six minutes. That was exceptionally fast for a first heat, astounding for a second heat. Johnson worried that it was too fast, that Walden was not exercising sufficient control, that Henry would tire and lose the heat. Napoleon was supposed to be neutral, but deep down he wanted Henry to win, believing that the young colt, for all his problems, had the potential to beat Eclipse.

Betsey Richards made a gallant run on the final lap. Her bottom was deep, which was why Johnson had made her a finalist in the first place. Her breathing was labored now, but she ran through it. She cut the lead to two lengths coming up the backstretch and less than one length rounding the final turn. She charged right up to Henry's outside shoulder, almost close enough for Henry to eyeball her.

As the fans stood, drawn from their seats by the drama, Walden barely moved on Henry, seemingly unaware of the challenge. But that was a ruse. Walden knew exactly what was happening. He had ridden high-quality horses for more than a decade at southern tracks. He could feel a rival coming up on him, and he knew what to do aboard a horse as gifted as Henry. He abruptly responded coming out of the turn, unleashing a wicked assault on Henry's flanks, daring the horse to pick up his pace. Henry flinched, lengthened his stride, and accelerated.

Johnson's heart soared as he watched. The young horse still had something left!

Betsey Richards continued to push, but Henry drove on just as furiously, repulsing the challenge with his eyes firmly locked on the finish looming ahead. Betsey Richards could draw no closer. Henry sprinted through the stretch and reached the finish a length in front.

Johnson smiled broadly at Racing Billy, then turned and waved at Walden as the jockey dismounted. Walden and Henry made a fine team, Napoleon thought.

A buzz rolled through the crowd and grew louder when the judges announced Henry's time for the second heat: 7 minutes 58 seconds, just 4 seconds slower than the first. In the span of an hour, the colt had run the two fastest four-mile heats ever seen at Newmarket.

Johnson was delighted, although he realized his decision had just become tougher. John Richards still would probably give the South its best chance of winning at the Union Course — but now he was not as sure as he had been that morning. It would be foolish to ignore the warning Henry had just served. If the colt's first attempt at the heroic distance had turned out this memorably, imagine how fast he might go when he tried again.

9

Every Angle Covered

NEW YORK CITY VIBRATED with horse-racing excitement. Newspapers regularly updated readers on the performances of the southern candidates for the Union Course event. Eclipse's chances were endlessly analyzed in bars and taverns. Interest in the race was "extending and accumulating for many months," a New York civil engineer, Charles Haynes Haswell, wrote in a memoir published later. It seemed decades before, not just two years, that racing had been banned in New York.

But unlike the southern buildup to the race, which had thrilling finishes, shouting crowds, and conflicting opinions — a drama that reached into the very soul of the region — the North had only a single horse exercising in solitude. Eclipse trained by himself throughout the snowy northern winter and chilly early spring. He did not take part in races or parade before fans. Almost no northerners even went out to watch him train at Harlem Lane. His fans were not concerned about his conditioning. He was going to win. Did he not always win?

He grew a thick winter coat, ate abundantly, and exercised without being pushed to top speed. With Van Ranst in charge, the scene was serene, with none of the bustle and military precision that marked the South's training camp. A few other horses were stabled at the barn adjoining the Harlem course; they went for early runs as their handlers drifted in and out. Eclipse slept late and worked out in midmorning, when Van Ranst arrived.

Unlike Napoleon, who had other horsemen around him offering support and ideas, Van Ranst operated alone. John Cox Stevens was knowledgeable and passionate enough about horses and racing to help, but he was distracted by preparations for the race and virtually out of contact. New York had few other trainers, and none who had raced in the South since the 1700s, as Van Ranst had. His expertise far exceeded that of anyone who could advise him. He was the lone strategist for the North and did not even employ an assistant. He dictated when and how Eclipse trained, adjusting to the weather and the horse's mood. Eventually he would decide on the jockey.

The old wizard usually spent the winter overseeing his breeding business at his Long Island estate, but in 1823, with the Union Course race approaching, he stayed at his house on Cliff Street in Manhattan so he could keep an eye on Eclipse. Almost every day he rose late and took a carriage through the noise and crush of Manhattan's streets and into the silence of the Harlem countryside. The racecourse was little more than rows of wooden sticks stuck in a field to indicate where the horses should run. The barn was cramped and chilly. Van Ranst employed a couple of grooms and exercise jockeys, who arrived early, fed Eclipse, changed his stall, and waited around for the boss.

The old wizard's visit always started with a trip to the horse's stall, where he patted Eclipse, rubbed his hide with both hands, and spoke in gentle tones. The horse made a nickering noise and rubbed his nose across the old wizard's thick winter coat. They were happy to see each other. Van Ranst then ordered the grooms to ready Eclipse for a run. His long tail was braided, a riding cloth and saddle draped over his back. Outside, Van Ranst spoke to the exercise jockey. He had several in a rotation. They all wore white breeches and maroon shirts and caps, not that anyone else was around to be impressed.

Van Ranst's orders varied. On some days Eclipse circled the track four or five times at a pace Van Ranst carefully controlled. He stood by the finish and used hand signals to tell the jockey to speed up or slow down over the next mile. Top speed was never that fast. On other days Eclipse sprinted harder for one or two laps, a quick, hard burst of speed to maintain the firmness of his lungs.

His training was so different from that of Johnson's horses that it almost seemed they were being prepared for different events. Eclipse would not race, even in private, before the Union Course event. Van Ranst did not believe the old horse would benefit from that and, in fact, would suffer. If he was going to race at his best in May, Van Ranst figured, he needed to be as fresh as possible.

The regimen seemed to sit well with Eclipse as winter gave way to spring. He was given a haircut in April, his winter coat coming off in ragged clumps. He looked terrific, his muscles toned, his eyes bright. The light training seemingly had preserved his strength, although on some days his sagging hide was evident.

Van Ranst seemed as serene as the Harlem Lane scene, though he brooded as the months passed, watching Eclipse with a mixture of pride and concern. He knew this was the last time around for the horse; the old wizard could get emotional about that, for he knew he would never have another horse anywhere near this gifted. He fervently wanted Eclipse to win, but the South was making a massive effort to defeat him. Van Ranst had southern friends who regularly reported Johnson's plans to him. He knew that Napoleon was going to unprecedented lengths; the time and energy he was investing were daunting, as was his determination to win.

Would the race be too much for Eclipse? Van Ranst slept poorly, coming back again and again to his concern about having pushed the horse too far. Stevens and the other financial backers were more concerned with the business aspects of the race, attracting fans, getting them to and from the course. Van Ranst respected those concerns and the men who held them; he was proud to be part of a fraternity of such influential men. But as the only serious horseman among them, he had doubts he could not seem to quell. The fight of Eclipse's life was nearing, and Van Ranst alone wondered if the horse had enough left to fight back.

As the sun set over Manhattan one night in early April, lights blazed inside John Cox Stevens's mansion on Washington Square. Servants polished the brass fittings on the front door. Cooks finished preparing a meal. Uniformed coachmen stood on the cobblestone street outside the front gate, waiting for a parade of carriages to deliver the evening's guests.

Stevens had called a NYAIBH planning meeting. The gathering, which would include some of New York's brightest, wealthiest men, had much to discuss, with the Union Course race now just six weeks away. How much was each man contributing to the $20,000 stakes? What could they do, individually and collectively, to promote the event?

As much as average New Yorkers were ready to root for Eclipse, they were still not as emotionally invested in the event as southerners. They did not believe their regional identity depended on the performance of a horse, nor did they care about sires, pedigrees, or horsemanship. A race was not their idea of a referendum on regional superiority.

The men gathering in Stevens's living room intended to do something about that. They included Michael Burnham, publisher of the *New York Evening Post*; Stephen Price, owner of the Park Theater; William Niblo, owner of the Bank Coffee House; and Van Ranst. Like Johnson in the South, they were in charge of their side of the challenge, but they saw the race mainly as an opportunity to promote the turf, the Union Course, their businesses, and their city. Their goal was to infuse the North with the South's passion. The more they could turn the event into a spectacle, the more they would benefit. Winning was important but, in the end, almost secondary — to all except Van Ranst.

The forward-thinking New York entrepreneurs were not alone in looking to take advantage of a situation. Their city was a profiteer's haven in 1823. Its population had quadrupled since the end of the Revolutionary War as the new waffle-iron street grid (adopted in 1811) rapidly expanded northward from lower Manhattan's watery edges. Expensive homes and stores lined Broadway, the main thoroughfare. Banks and insurance companies populated the area around Wall Street. Building companies such as Samuel Purdy's could not put new homes up fast enough.

Although crime had also increased and the city sometimes strained to provide basic services, a cosmopolitan society was evolving. The classes mingled, but an urban gentry was emerging. New Yorkers wanted to attend theaters and clubs, eat fine meals, read newspapers. The men gathering at Stevens's mansion wanted to add horse racing to those interests, and believed the time was right to instill that habit. New Yorkers were asking each other questions as the race neared. Who was going to the Union Course to see the race in person? How would they get to Jamaica? How much were they going to bet on Eclipse? What about the hundreds of southerners rumored to be coming for the race — where would they stay? What would they do when they were not at the course?

Stevens, the group's leader by acclaim, had called the meeting to address those questions and all others pertaining to the race. He had negotiated the race's terms and conditions back in November and then pledged the largest percentage of the $20,000 stakes. At thirty-eight, he was a stately and determined figure with a high forehead, pointed nose, bushy eyebrows, and piercing brown eyes — and an enthusiasm for sports unmatched by anyone in New York.

He was the eldest son of one of America's pioneers of steam navigation, Colonel John Stevens, who had fought alongside George Washington during the Revolutionary War and then amassed a fortune developing screw-powered steamboats and operating ferry lines between New York and New Jersey. His four sons had helped their father in business, and they still devoted time and energy to developing steam travel. Colonel Stevens was now focusing on locomotives, but his son John's real passion was sports. He was a fixture around New York Harbor, building sloops, starting sailing clubs, and racing wealthy boaters from Philadelphia and Boston. He was also serious about the turf. He owned a stable of runners and had lobbied legislators in New Jersey, where he had a residence, to repeal the state's ban on racing. He owned a 170-acre racing compound near the Union Course, where two private trainers would later develop some of America's most successful horses.

Married to the equally wealthy daughter of another steam travel pioneer (they split their time between a Manhattan mansion and an estate on the Hudson River), Stevens was an indefatigable industrialist who did not operate on a small scale. No one else in New York — or anywhere for that matter — would have had the imagination, money, and energy to build a new racecourse in a state where the sport had been illegal, and then make the racing surface out of dirt — a radical plan. Stevens had dreamed up the project, bankrolled it almost entirely, and personally overseen the costly, vast, and meticulous undertaking. He had spent weeks at the site and even got down on his knees to smooth some of the dirt. He was sure that horses would run faster on dirt and fans would flock to see the speedier sport. He was determined to make the Union Course a popular attraction and earn back his investment.

He wanted Eclipse to win, but if the horse lost in front of a massive crowd, he would have a hard time calling the day a failure.

To the sound of hooves clop-clopping on cobblestone streets, a succession of elegant coaches arrived at Stevens's mansion.

Each of the men who stepped down to the street and passed through the front door could help the race in his own way, beyond contributing to the stakes. Niblo could get people talking at his coffee house. Price was a master at staging events for large crowds. Stevens could help fans by arranging for special ferries across the East River between Manhattan and Brooklyn.

But none could match the potential impact of Burnham, whose *Evening Post* was the most popular of the city's fleet of newspapers, which also included the *Spectator, American, Commercial Gazette,* and *Statesman.*

Published six days a week out of an office on Williams Street, the *Evening Post* was edited by William Coleman, a New Englander and staunch Federalist who printed news, political commentary, and satirical odes by respected writers. Burnham was the businessman, the salesman, the promoter. NYAIBH had cannily courted him and other New York news editors and publishers during and after the 1821 state government vote to legalize racing. Papers that disagreed vehemently on politics and social issues were unified in their support of the twice-yearly Union Course races. NYAIBH's advertisements were prominently placed, and race results were given in detail. The reporting was resolutely positive, suggesting it was time to dismiss outdated but persistent notions about racing's negative effect on society.

The steady drumbeat of positive news items had helped legitimize the turf among New Yorkers and bring it into their daily conversation. People who otherwise would not have known about Eclipse became his fans. The *Evening Post* was especially supportive of both the horse and his sport. It printed accounts of races in Virginia and South Carolina as well as of those at the Union Course and published letters of challenge between horse owners that led to grudge matches, hoping the correspondence would increase interest.

In January 1823 James Junkin Harrison issued a new challenge to Van Ranst that ran in the *Evening Post*. Still smarting from the Sir Charles debacle, Harrison proposed to race another horse against Eclipse's two-year-old sister (which Van Ranst owned) for $5,000 a side. Van Ranst turned him down, replying in a letter in the *Evening Post* that the sister was not ready to race. Several other challenges also were published that winter and spring. A man from Vermont offered to put up $5,000 and race his horse against any horse Harrison selected. Harrison turned that down. A dog owner from New York offered to bet $100 that his dog could lick "any hound from Virginia." It was as if the North–South races had engaged the nation's competitive gears, encouraging people to invent ways to put their money on the line. The *Evening Post* was the forum.

Seated in Stevens's parlor, the men listened to Burnham's plans for promoting the race. He planned to publish articles about Eclipse and the southern horses being prepared for the race, as well as reports on the Union Course, which was being renovated. He was sure his competitors would do the same, he said. But the most effective promotional tool, he said, were advertisements, which would begin running in mid-April and continue through the race. His paper was filled every day with ads for everything from ferry lines to saloons to cows. Several subscribers had already reserved extra space for the month leading up to the race. Ferry operators in particular wanted to advertise their services to the thousands who would cross the East River going to and from Jamaica. NYAIBH would run a daily ad listing the races and entry fees for the rest of the Union Course meeting. The ads and articles would amount to a daily reminder to thousands of readers that the race was approaching.

After Burnham finished, Price spoke. He was an attorney who had owned and run the Park Theater either solely or in partnership for nearly twenty years. Unmarried and wealthier than everyone in the room except Stevens, he lived in an extravagant home at the corner of

Broadway and Leonard Street, a prime intersection. He was more interested in show horses than racing; later in 1823 he would take over an equestrian company and station it for several weeks at the Broadway Circus before sending it on the road to perform. But no American had ever made the theater more profitable than Price, and few knew more about giving the public what it wanted.

His advice for putting on a show for thousands of spectators included selling as many tickets as possible in advance at various locations around Manhattan; chaos could ensue if every fan had to buy a ticket on the day of the race, he warned. He also suggested widening the entry gates at the Union Course so more than one line could get through; hiring bands, jugglers, and other entertainers to liven up the atmosphere; and staging more than one turf event per day to make the days longer and more exciting.

Then it was Niblo's turn. Like Burnham and Price, the thirty-four-year-old coffee house owner was not a horseman, but he was an effective promoter known for working every conceivable angle. His business was located in the rear of a bank building at the corner of Pine and Williams, across the street from the *Evening Post*. It was a popular place, offering food and entertainment as well as coffee, and was a trendy setting for parties.

His contributions to the race would include operating a private transportation service (Niblo's Express, consisting of carriage and ferry rides); catering the meals NYAIBH would serve to the horsemen and judges in tents by the course; and raising a flag over the Bank Coffee House to signal the winner. He also encouraged the horsemen he knew to patronize the Bank as the race neared. He wanted it to be the gathering place for everyone who enjoyed the turf, including the southerners coming to New York. (In 1829 Niblo would open a massive theater and entertainment complex on Broadway known as Niblo's Garden, which became a landmark, with seating for three thousand.)

Eclipse's financial backers, having covered every angle, began to gather their belongings, thinking the meeting was over. Then Van Ranst cleared his throat. The others looked at him and realized their mistake. They had forgotten about Eclipse! Oh, yes, the horse!

Everyone sat back down. Van Ranst updated them on the horse's months of training. Eclipse had done well since his return from the National Course. He looked fit and ready to run.

Van Ranst did not mention that he had some reservations and almost wished Eclipse were being bred to mares this spring instead of having to take up a final, difficult challenge. The old man could not bring himself to say that in front of these men. They were not serious horse people, and they would not understand.

Then Stevens, the most horse-oriented of the others, asked about jockeys. Who would ride in May? Would it be Purdy, as everyone expected?

Van Ranst paused and then spilled the secret he had harbored all winter. Purdy was almost fifty. Perhaps young Billy Crafts or the retired veteran John Buckley would do a better job.

The room went silent.

Burnham, Price, and Niblo were hardly turf experts, but they knew Purdy was a good man and an accomplished rider who had won at the National Course. From a business perspective, they wondered if it made sense to tinker with success. Stevens was openly concerned. He asked if it was wise to try a different jockey, after Purdy had brought them such joy in November.

Van Ranst smiled somewhat defensively and launched into the argument he had made so many times in his head. Purdy was old. Eclipse was old. The southern horse and jockey would be much younger. Johnson, the southern strategist, was a shrewd manager who surely would see an advantage he could exploit. Something had to be done.

The men listened without commenting. Van Ranst, as the horseman, supposedly knew best. It was his job to have Eclipse ready to race. Their job was to make the event successful.

Van Ranst finished his explanation and smiled thinly. An uneasy feeling lingered in the air. The old wizard nervously fingered his white goatee and rubbed a fidgety hand across his jacket front. He cleared his throat. Still no one spoke.

Finally, Stevens pushed back his chair and stood, commenting a little too loudly that the meeting had gone well. The others followed his example. They all shook hands and briefly made small talk before leaving.

The meeting had indeed gone well — for the most part. But when the door closed for the last time and Stevens was left alone, he wondered if he had gravely erred by turning the training of the horse entirely over to Van Ranst. Replace Purdy? What was the old wizard thinking?

Van Ranst fumed for days. He stalked back and forth across the Harlem Lane barn, barking at his stable boys and jockeys. He slept poorly. His pride was hurt. That moment at the end of the meeting had embarrassed him to the core. He could sense the doubts of the others in their silent response to his idea about replacing Purdy. They were not sure, not sure at all. They thought they knew better.

But had they raced horses for more than a quarter-century, as he had? No. Had they traipsed from racecourse to racecourse all over the South? No. Did they know how to win purses? No. He, the only horseman in the room that night, had trained Eclipse since the horse was five. He had prepared the horse to win at the National Course. His opinion deserved respect.

A chain of events soon brought the situation to a head. Purdy, who had continued to visit Harlem Lane all winter to take Eclipse on training runs, contacted Van Ranst in late April to arrange a meeting. He went to Harlem Lane unaware he was about to be ambushed, for Van Ranst was waiting with an attitude. The old wizard had never committed himself to using another jockey, but the memory of the NYAIBH meeting, and the silence that greeted his remark, had stirred him to action.

The two men shook hands outside the barn and stood in a slanting morning sun, their breath visible in the early spring chill. They had known each for years, and Purdy did not believe any secrets lay between them. He was wrong. Van Ranst began to speak, saying he regretted having failed to raise the issue before now, but he believed another jockey might serve Eclipse better in the upcoming challenge.

Purdy smiled at first, believing that his friend was joking. But then he realized the old wizard was serious. Incredulous, he glared, eyes narrowing to slits, and asked if any northern jockey had a longer record of success. Van Ranst admitted no northerner could come close to matching Purdy's record, but added that that was not the point.

The stable boys and exercise riders hung back in the shadow of the barn, afraid to step in.

Was it not true, Van Ranst asked, that Purdy's children might soon bear children of their own? Purdy raised his eyebrows. So his age was the issue? He asked if Van Ranst had gone mad, pointing out he was no older than when he rode Eclipse to his greatest triumph at the National Course.

Van Ranst raised his right hand to stop Purdy from continuing. Sir Charles was injured that day, he said. This challenger will be younger, healthier, and far more formidable. Purdy stared hard at the old wizard and virtually spit his reply. The entire North would suffer if Van Ranst picked another jockey. Eclipse would experience defeat for the first time, and their side would lose money.

The comments infuriated Van Ranst. He felt he was back at Stevens's house, where his knowledge had been doubted. That settles it, Van Ranst said. Crafts will ride. The youngster has won many purses.

Purdy stepped back, eyes fixed on the old man. He could barely believe this was happening. He pointed out that he had not competed in the races Crafts had won. Van Ranst shrugged. He saw the larger picture. No one else did. This was the right move and he knew it.

Purdy did not respond. His disappointment was profound, but what could he say? He turned abruptly and walked to his carriage. He thought about leaving behind the maroon riding shirt he had put on that morning as a show of support for Van Ranst, but something kept him from ripping it off and throwing it on the ground. He figured he would never wear it again, but he would not disparage Eclipse in that way. Even though he was so angry he was already conjuring (and enjoying) visions of failure for Van Ranst and the North, he still had respect for the horse. He kept his shirt on.

10

A Hairline Fracture

MARMADUKE JOHNSON WAS VISITING his son at Oakland during the Newmarket meeting. He had come from North Carolina to see his finalist, the even-tempered, hard-running Washington, compete in one of the races. Napoleon had kept Washington out of the public spotlight until now because the colt had accomplished so much as a three-year-old in 1822, winning three races — more than Henry and John Richards combined. He was a known quantity. Johnson had elected just to train him rather than race him, hoping to improve his performance by the spring. Unfortunately, Washington had not trained as well as Johnson had hoped, finishing mostly in the middle of the pack in trials and workouts. His running action was smooth, but his burst of speed was unexceptional. He seldom ran poorly, but he seldom stood out. He was, in a word, dull.

After watching Henry's astounding performance in the four-mile event at Newmarket, Marmaduke asked his son where Washington stood among the finalists. Napoleon replied that the horse was still in the running but needed to improve. Marmaduke, who had observed races since the 1780s, had to agree. Washington was obviously capable, but he had never run the way Henry just had.

Napoleon, seeking to give his father's horse the best possible chance to shine, entered Washington in the sweepstakes event at Newmarket. The race, consisting of two-mile heats, had drawn a large field, including Sir William, the fine eight-year-old that Napoleon had bypassed. Washington would have a chance to show what he could do. Sir William, a squatty bay, was a tough and seemingly indestructible opponent, easily the most decorated southern horse other than those that had already lost to Eclipse. Some horsemen still could not believe Napoleon had excluded him from the pool of finalists. Sir William had spent the past winter on the turf in Georgia and the Carolinas, racing every week and usually winning. The *American Turf Register* later said of him, "Few horses ever won more races or did more hard service." Two days before the Newmarket sweepstakes, he had run in the meeting's three-mile event, winning the first heat before narrowly losing the next two.

The second-guessing by horsemen and fans did not bother Napoleon. He remained convinced that the South's best chances lay with a significantly younger horse. As much as he respected Sir William, he did not believe an eight-year-old could deliver the magical performance needed to beat Eclipse. Something special was going to have to happen for the South to win at the Union Course, and Sir William was just too old.

In any case, it was too late now. As worthy as Sir William was — that he could compete in a sweepstakes just forty-eight hours after a three-mile event indicated his strength — his sole contribution to the southern effort would be his square-off with Washington.

Newmarket was crowded for the sweepstakes. It was the last race of the meeting, and with temperatures warm and skies blue, fans filled the stands, surrounded the course, and lined Hare's Hill with their carriages. Though Johnson was a towering racing figure, his judgment was on trial. It would be interesting to see how Washington fared against the older horse that had been turned down. The fans who traded bets before the race had differing opinions.

Sir William and Washington were among the five horses presented to the judges before the start. A white jockey from the Carolinas rode Sir William. One of Johnson's youngest slaves rode Washington. Johnson had instructed the boy to be bold, for a two-mile heat was almost a sprint. Napoleon was curious to see if Washington had the speed to hold up.

A trumpeter sent the horses running. Washington took the lead, moving three lengths ahead on the backstretch of the first lap. He ran smoothly and easily, seemingly nowhere near top speed. His jockey's sky blue shirt bobbed ahead of the pack. The fans waited for Sir William to charge. Those that had bet on the older horse offered encouraging cheers as he passed the finish the first time, still trailing by three lengths.

But he never made a run.

Washington, seemingly buoyed by the lack of a challenge, picked up the pace on the backstretch of the second lap. His legs thrashed, his head lowered. The jockey relaxed, sitting down rather than continuing to stand in the stirrups and hover over the horse's neck. The rider did not need to do anything — Washington was in command. The colt moved farther ahead on the second turn and swerved into the sprint to the finish. He was six lengths ahead when he passed the judges. Sir William finished third.

Napoleon and Marmaduke watched from the front row of the stands, Napoleon having eschewed his usual vantage point — on horseback, near the finish — to accompany his father. They exchanged smiles after the race. Washington had destroyed Sir William. All that hard training finally was paying off. Maybe Washington would rank with Henry and John Richards, after all.

The second heat changed their mood. Sir William's jockey changed tactics, taking the lead with a blazing early pace. Washington fell ten lengths behind in the first half-mile, and his young jockey was slow to respond. The horse did not begin to gain ground until the second lap, and by then Sir William had too much momentum. Sir William won the heat by five lengths.

The horses took a half-hour break before coming back for the deciding third heat. Napoleon left his father and sought out Washington's jockey, who was sitting in the shade behind a barn by the course, trying to relax. Johnson lectured the frightened dark-skinned boy. Do not fall so far behind again, he warned. Be ready to run at the start. The slave stood at attention and nodded.

Back at the course, bettors continued to back both horses, the split reflecting the closeness of the competition. The upcoming heat would be Sir William's sixth in forty-eight hours, a grueling test of his stamina. But his supporters doubted he would falter.

Fans cheered the horses' return to the track and applauded when the trumpet sounded. Washington took the early lead, his jockey's ears still burning from Johnson's lecture. The youngster led by three lengths for most of the first trip around the oval. But Sir William did not lag behind. He raced with an ominous ease, seemingly almost jogging. It was clear he had plenty left. Then he began to charge as he approached the finish for the first time. His jockey kicked and whipped him. He caught the younger horse on the first turn and moved ahead by one length, then two. Washington did not fight back, at least not at first. Johnson watched silently, his disappointment growing.

Washington finally made a run on the second turn and closed to within a length as the horses turned for home. But Sir William easily dismissed the rally. The older horse pulled away nearing the finish as Washington fell back, beaten and discouraged. Sir William reached the finish four lengths in front.

Marmaduke waited until dinner that evening to express his disappointment. He admired Sir William, he said, but believed Washington had not been ridden skillfully. Napoleon could not argue. The Carolinian riding Sir William had bested the young slave on Washington, taking command of the race with that move at the start of the second heat. Napoleon, seeking to salve his father's wounds, pointed out that Washington had run hard throughout a long afternoon against a tough opponent and that the race had been of the highest quality, with the time of the final heat faster than that of the first heat.

Marmaduke was not comforted. He knew Washington had needed to win. He knew his son liked John Richards and Henry more, and he could not blame him. Washington had not improved enough. John Richards and Henry had shown more potential. Even Betsey Richards, the mare, had performed better than Washington. It would take a major change of form for his horse to get to run in New York.

After Newmarket, Johnson wasted little time before heading north. The Union Course race was in two weeks. He had to get going.

His traveling party was a sprawl of humans, including Arthur Taylor, two dozen stable boys, grooms, and jockeys, and almost a dozen horses: the five finalists, a few extra runners, and Johnson's personal walking horse. First they had to get from Petersburg to Bristol, Pennsylvania, a resort town on the Delaware northeast of Philadelphia, where Johnson's close friend Bela Badger lived on an eight-hundred-acre estate with a racecourse. Johnson planned to train the horses there for a week and then continue on to Jamaica for the race. At some point he would pick a challenger.

The trip to Bristol was a marvel in itself, a spectacular feat of coordination. No American horseman had ever tried to move so much humanity and horseflesh so far — 299 miles from point to point — in so little time. A decade earlier the trip would have required a week of horses footing it on dusty roads, exhausting them. Johnson never would have taken on a race involving such a trip. Southern horsemen were spoiled.

But the miracle of steam travel had changed everything. Johnson split the party into two groups. Flying Childers, John Richards, several of the extra horses, and half the grooms and jockeys set out first, with Taylor in charge. At the Petersburg dock they boarded a private steamboat equipped with stalls to keep the horses separated. Dozens of race fans came out to watch the spectacle. It took more than an hour just to load and arrange the animals.

The creaking wooden ship sputtered down the James River from Petersburg to Norfolk, where the horses were taken off and put up overnight at a stable. The next morning they boarded another private boat that carried them along the edge of Maryland's Eastern Shore and into Delaware Bay. They spent the night at Wilmington and changed ships again to a ferry that took them up the Delaware River, past Philadelphia, and into Bristol.

The second group, which included Betsey Richards, Henry, Washington, grooms, jockeys, and Napoleon himself, left a day after the first group and followed the same route. On each ship Napoleon retreated to private quarters. He was the only one served food and drink. He opened a window, put his head outside, and stared at the water as the breeze ruffled his flowing white hair. He reflected on what had happened since January. His horses had benefited from the hard training — some more than others. It was good that he still did not know which would challenge Eclipse; a tough decision meant several horses were running well. Napoleon still liked John Richards, but he could see going with Henry or even Betsey Richards. He also had to pick a jockey. John Walden, the white boy, had impressed him by helping to calm Henry. It would be hard to turn him down in favor of the young slave Charles Stewart.

The trip to Bristol went smoothly. Neither traveling party encountered bad weather, rough water, or blown engines, the banes of steamboat travel. Everyone was in Bristol by May 15. Napoleon was delighted. He was ninety miles from the Union Course with twelve days to continue training his horses.

Bristol was a vacation spot. Wealthy families from America and Europe had summered there for years, drawn to the luxurious Bath Springs and elegant hotels such as the George the Second. Napoleon's host, Badger, was a prominent man in the town, a fifty-five-year-old farmer whose Fairview Race Course bustled during the summer despite Pennsylvania's ban on racing.

Badger could not pass himself off as a real southerner — he was originally from Connecticut and still lived north of the Mason-Dixon Line — but he was effectively a southern horseman, a close ally of Johnson's with a record of racing well-bred stock throughout Virginia, Maryland, and the Carolinas. He and Johnson co-owned horses and spoke often about breeding and racing.

Badger had lived on his riverside estate since the early 1800s. The rich meadowland property contained Fairview, a fishery said to be the finest on the Delaware River, and a racing stable. A steady stream of boats and carriages passed through the property carrying vacationers to the Bath Springs. Badger normally paid little attention to the traffic, but he was on his pier to meet Johnson and his horses as their ferry arrived. He hailed Napoleon as the winner of the upcoming Union Course event, which had the whole country engrossed. Johnson laughed and stepped off the ferry to shake hands. He had not seen Badger that winter; the Pennsylvanian usually came south looking for horses to buy, but he had postponed his trip because Napoleon was coming his way for once.

At dinner that evening Badger eagerly asked what had happened since January. Johnson reviewed the months of training sessions, trials, and races and explained that he had not picked a challenger yet. Badger nodded. That morning he had watched Taylor supervise John Richards and Flying Childers as they galloped lightly on their first day at Fairview. The horses were impressive, Badger said. Napoleon explained that he had become infatuated with John Richards early on and still favored him, but that Henry was coming on and Betsey Richards also was running well. Badger nodded again. He was looking forward to watching Henry, Betsey Richards, and Washington in action and perhaps helping Johnson pick a challenger.

Johnson had great respect for Badger and welcomed his friend's input. The months of training in Virginia had been for elevating the speed and stamina of the finalists, and the recent races at Nottoway and Newmarket had been for letting the southern fans see the possibilities, but through it all Napoleon had expected that only now, at Fairview, with Badger by his side, would he decide which horse should represent the South.

Once it was known that Napoleon and his finalists were at Badger's, carriage drivers and boat captains leaving the property were grilled as they continued on their routes. Had they seen the horses? Had they learned the identity of Johnson's challenger? No. The Fairview training was shrouded in secrecy. Outsiders were not allowed to watch, and the trial results were not made public. Johnson, Badger, Taylor, and Johnson's jockeys and grooms were the sole witnesses to the drama that unfolded.

The course was a grassy oval etched out of a lush riverside field. Set between foothills, it was subject to steady winds. A single wooden stand marked the finish. The finalists were tested daily at standard heat distances — two, three, and four miles. No more bottom-building days. No more sacrificing winning for the sake of getting a horse to take instruction. It was time to answer the essential question: which horse was the best runner?

The military precision of the Virginia camp was re-created at Fairview. The stable boys and jockeys, most of whom were slaves, slept in Badger's outbuildings and rose before dawn to prepare the horses to run. The animals were roused from slumber, given water, and walked in circles to loosen up their legs. They would not get to eat until after they ran. Taylor, as always, oversaw every move, shouting and directing. Johnson and Badger arrived after dawn, which came earlier now.

For three days the horses ran and ran. Charles Stewart rode John Richards; Walden was on Henry. Those two horses dominated. John Richards tended to nose in front at the end, his natural competitiveness tipping the scales in his favor. But it was clear that Henry's performance at Newmarket had not been a fluke; he was more mature now and as quick as ever.

The others? Betsey Richards was always in contention. Flying Childers had stamina but not enough natural speed. Washington lagged behind. Napoleon, Badger, and Taylor assessed the group every day as the horses were bathed following their workouts. Sometimes the decision appeared easy. John Richards had beaten Flying Childers and Washington in public races. Betsey Richards was a step slower. The only horse that compared, Henry, was not even four years old. John Richards was more mature — he was the choice, right? Right?

But then on Sunday, May 18, nine days before the race, Johnson's meticulous plan suddenly was turned upside down. John Richards was coming up the backside, bathed in sunshine, when he suddenly developed a hitch in his gait. Stewart, who quickly brought the horse to a halt, could not recall the animal taking a bad step or stepping on a rock. But John Richards was plainly favoring his left hind leg.

Johnson, Taylor, and Badger raced over from their vantage point near the finish. Slaves followed them, and everyone crowded around John Richards. A groom held the young horse steady. When Johnson ran his hand up and down the leg, John Richards did not react — a hopeful sign. But Napoleon's heart sank when he grabbed the horse's hoof and knelt for a closer look. He motioned to Badger and Taylor to kneel beside him. Any horsemen could see the problem — a fracture on the hoof, an injury known as a "quarter crack," as in a quarter-inch wide.

Johnson rose from the ground and told the grooms to take John Richards back to the barn for a bath. The three horsemen stood silently for a few moments, trying to fathom what had just happened.

John Richards probably could resume training in several weeks and surely would race again; a quarter-crack was a common injury, usually just a temporary setback. But the timing was disastrous. There was no chance that he would be ready to run at the Union Course in nine days.

Napoleon was staggered. He had nurtured John Richards for five months and believed the horse was ready to beat Eclipse. But now he was out, no longer even an option. It was that simple. Another horse would have to run.

Johnson was morose at dinner that night. His plan had sailed along without a hitch since January, but now he wondered if he had pushed John Richards too hard. Had he overtaxed the horse and indirectly caused the injury himself? Or had the horse just taken a bad step? Johnson barely slept that night. He could not help wondering if his best chance to win in New York had just gone down with an injury. John Richards loathed losing, an admirable quality. John Richards would have competed fiercely against Eclipse. The southern fans would have loved it.

The next day brought another setback. Washington virtually quit in the daily trial, finishing two hundred yards behind the pack. The horse did not seem the least bit interested in running. It was a performance with rebellious undertones. Washington seemed to have gotten tired of being pushed so hard and decided not to cooperate. He did not respond to his jockey and stubbornly refused to pick up his pace.

Johnson, already depressed about John Richards, was troubled by Washington's nonchalance. Although the trainer had decided against using Washington in New York anyway, it was unsettling to see a well-bred, talented, successful runner just give up. It made Napoleon wonder if he had pushed all the finalists too hard. Would there be more problems in the days before the race? Would the South be able to present a worthy challenger?

Badger tried to revive his friend's spirits. He suggested Johnson should be happy that he had devised such a meticulous, comprehensive plan. Yes, the losses of John Richards and Washington were disappointing, but did they not highlight the whole reason Johnson had prepared five horses? Both Henry and Betsey Richards were capable of beating Eclipse. There would be no reprise of the embarrassment Harrison had foisted on the South at the National Course.

Johnson felt somewhat better. Badger was right. He still had three healthy horses that could run four miles. Eclipse would not win by forfeit. There was that good news, at least.

Racing Billy Wynne caught up with the group in Bristol that night. When Johnson told him about John Richards, he was bitterly disappointed. His horse had seemed entrenched as Johnson's choice when the horses left Virginia. Billy said he wished Flying Childers, not John Richards, had suffered the injury; he had envisioned John Richards trouncing Eclipse before thousands of sullen northerners. Johnson smiled, for he, too, had pictured John Richards winning.

The next morning, his last at Fairview, Napoleon called for a final trial between the three remaining finalists. He saw little risk. The Union Course race was still six days away, and the horses would have time to recover. Why not let them run? An injury was always possible, but it was probably safe to assume the South had used up its supply of bad luck in the past few days.

As Johnson, Badger, Racing Billy, and Taylor watched, the three horses were brought together at the start and sent running. Johnson focused on Henry and Betsey Richards, for he was sure now that one of them would represent the South. Flying Childers would be chosen only if injuries knocked out the other two.

Johnson began to feel better as he watched the trial. He probably favored Henry over Betsey Richards, but both horses looked fit and ready as they sailed across the grass. Henry had come so far. He and Walden had become a team, a horse and jockey in tune. Walden commanded and Henry obeyed. Their Newmarket performance was already the stuff of legend. Imagine if they reprised it at the Union Course! The thought was exciting enough that Johnson almost laughed out loud. But he could not forget Betsey Richards, who had raced evenly with Henry at Newmarket. Johnson had learned not to underestimate her.

Either horse would make a fine challenger, Johnson thought. Each would race with a huge weight advantage over Eclipse, Henry because of his age and Betsey Richards because of her sex. And each had been sired by Sir Archie, so Johnson's favorite stallion would be recognized.

Given the swelling public interest in the race, it was hard to believe so little was known about the drama of the South's final preparations. (Carriage drivers leaving Badger's property continued to offer outdated information to those seeking news: "It appears Johnson is going to start John Richards!") Most people assumed he would have a challenger ready — such was his reputation.

The success of Napoleon's preparations became evident as the remaining finalists circled Fairview's oval course. Henry built a ten-yard lead, his running motion smooth, his balance perfect, his head cocked slightly to the right. He was a horse at his peak. Badger leaned over and shouted congratulations to Johnson for having successfully readied the southern side. Napoleon nodded. A breeze ruffled the grass as Henry, with Walden aboard, passed them and headed into a second lap. Johnson smiled. Thousands of southerners were coming north at that very moment, counting on him to restore their dignity and replenish their pockets. Johnson wished they could see this — a North Carolina horse, trained in Virginia, racing brilliantly in Pennsylvania before heading off to New York. What a roar would sound!

Johnson felt relieved. The worrisome developments of the past few days were behind him. A short trip to New York and a few days of light training remained, but he had done his job. He had formed a plan, searched "the world," identified five horses, and trained several to the point that they could win. His confidence was restored. He would present a challenger southerners could back with pride, something more than just a worthy opponent to Eclipse. He would present a horse that could win.

11

Nothing Is Heard
but the Race

S UDDENLY, WITHOUT ADVERTISEMENT, Eclipse was paraded through the streets of Manhattan on a sunny weekday afternoon two weeks before the race. Shouts of recognition and encouragement greeted him for miles as he grandly pranced down the city's dirt roads, interrupting traffic with his head held high, seemingly basking in the kingly moment.

Shopkeepers heard the commotion, rushed to their doors, and smiled at the sight of the North's famous horse as they wiped their hands on their aprons. Children ran after him and gingerly touched his flanks, awed to be in his presence. Hundreds of men and women stopped in their tracks and applauded, knowing they would later tell everyone they knew that they had seen the great horse in the flesh that day.

A quartet of stable boys dressed in Van Ranst's maroon colors guided Eclipse with lead ropes to keep him from bolting. Two boys walked in front of the horse and two walked behind him. The procession rumbled along as it might for a presidential candidate on the stump, gradually becoming louder and larger as followers were caught up in Eclipse's thrall. Much as the fabled Pied Piper of Hamelin had entranced a German town centuries earlier, Eclipse now held New York spellbound.

The horse was merely being moved from Harlem Lane to Long Island to complete his training for the race. He would stable at John Cox Stevens's verdant estate, less than a mile from the Union Course. Stephen Price had suggested to Van Ranst that he make a show out of the normally routine business of transferring the horse. It would generate excitement, the theater owner said. People would love seeing Eclipse.

Van Ranst brought up the rear of the impromptu parade, hiding from view in his shadowy single-horse carriage, which rattled along well behind Eclipse. Idly fingering his white goatee, he listened in astonishment to the hours of uninterrupted applause, barely believing that a horse — his horse, no less — could cause such a fuss in New York.

The old wizard had been lost in a fog for months, holed up while he trained the horse. In his preoccupation, he had become isolated from the public, out of touch. He knew that people were aware of Eclipse and the race, but he had no idea the horse had become this popular or the race this important. It was almost enough to make an old horseman dizzy. Racing had been anathema to most northerners until recently. Now, it seemed, they could hardly wait for Eclipse to race again and sink the South back into a depression.

It was all very exciting; if the horse's fans had constituted little more than a platoon before, they were an entire army now. But that unnerved Van Ranst, brooder that he was. He already feared that the public did not understand the gravity of the challenge Eclipse faced. These people are just as unwitting as I was until this afternoon, he thought. They have no inkling of the danger that lies ahead. While they sing and dance around Eclipse, they think only of victory, not about the brilliant competitor Johnson is preparing.

For about the thousandth time since the race was arranged, Van Ranst wished he had stuck to his belief that Eclipse should be servicing mares now rather than performing for the racing public. He loved the horse, had faith in him, but the pressure to win was becoming a crushing weight. Sweat formed on the old wizard's forehead as he sat in his carriage.

Reaching lower Manhattan as the sun began to set, he elected to stable Eclipse for the night at a livery; he would cross the East River and continue on to Jamaica the next day. He slept at home on Cliff Street that night, then resumed the trip at dawn. Eclipse was walked to an east side dock and put on a public ferry for the short ride over to Brooklyn. Shouts and applause continued to greet him. The ferry customers who shared the ride with him could hardly believe their good fortune.

At the dock in Brooklyn, the horse disembarked and was walked the eight miles to Jamaica, the crowds slowly diminishing as he ventured deeper into the countryside. He arrived in fine shape. He had been moved between Van Ranst's various barns many times and had traveled to Washington the year before. This time his trip ended at Stevens's sprawling compound on Jamaica Bay, which included a mansion, cottages, a row of barns, and a grass training track. Stevens had offered to put Van Ranst up in one of the cottages. Although he had his own estate in Dutchess County, he wanted to be close to Eclipse until the race.

Almost within sight of the Union Course, Van Ranst reflected on the stunning trip from Harlem Lane. His horse had been cheered nonstop, acclaimed as a champion by thousands. But Van Ranst knew he was in a position as dire as it was unconditional. Thousands of northern dollars would be staked on the race. Excuses for failure would not be tolerated. Eclipse had to win. It was that simple.

A week before the race, the great migration began. Thousands of southerners left home and headed for New York, traveling on horseback and by steamship and stagecoach. Some came with their families, some came with slaves, some came alone. They cascaded together over roads, down waterways, and through towns, crowding all available routes to New York, their pockets filled with money for backing Johnson's horse.

At most a few thousand southerners had been expected to travel to the Union Course when the race was first announced in November; surely the long, expensive trip would discourage most fans from coming. But that conservative estimate had grossly miscalculated the passions of the horsemen and racing fans of Virginia, Maryland, the Carolinas, and Georgia. They were intensely proud of their record of producing America's fastest thoroughbreds and were willing to travel far to see a claim to their throne debunked.

What better place to shoot down the North than New York itself! They sang about the South and its horses and heroes as their steamships churned north. They shook hands in public coaches and compared the amounts they would bet. They convened in taverns and raised toasts. Southerners crawled over Maryland, Delaware, and Pennsylvania on their way to the big city. In the end some 20,000 — almost equal to the entire population of Delaware (24,057 in the 1820 census) — would make it to New York, crowding the city's streets for a week before the race.

Fine Manhattan hotels such as the Clarion and the Grand filled with southerners. Business soared at restaurants, taverns, and theaters. Racing fans from New England, Tennessee, and Kentucky were also expected for the race — no serious supporter of the sport wanted to miss it — but it was southerners, with their manners, tastes, and distinctive accents, that overwhelmed the city.

Meanwhile New Yorkers, to their great surprise, also found their hearts beating faster as the race approached. Months of newspaper articles and advertisements had familiarized them with the horses and their owners and attendants. The southerners swarming their city stirred local pride. These impudent folks expected to win! "The knowing ones of the Pedee, Santee, and Roanoke [southern rivers] are here with their little niggers and appear to be up to a thing or two," the *New York American* reported, lest anyone doubt the sectional tensions underlying the event.

New Yorkers who had never cared about the turf found themselves rooting hard for Eclipse and making plans to travel to the Union Course. John Pintard, the secretary of the Mutual Insurance Company and a recent founder of the New-York Historical Society, surveyed the scene from his Wall Street apartment and wrote a letter to his daughter, who lived in New Orleans: "New York is overflowing with visitors from all quarters to attend the race. The stakes are deposited. The preparations are immense. Had I a friend under whose care I could place [his mother and aunt, whom he took care of], it would gratify me [to attend], but as this is impossible, we do not even talk about what engrosses all conversation else-where."

Southerners and northerners mingled throughout the city for days, walking the streets in groups. There were handshakes, but just as many hard-edged taunts. The southerners resented northerners for thinking they knew anything about racing. The northerners felt in-herently superior with their economy based on honest trade rather than the sweat of what the newspaper had called "little niggers." The Bank Coffee House filled every night with horsemen and rowdy rac-ing fans from both sides. They all expected to win and loved belittling the other side. Eclipse? Wait until he took on a real horse. The south-ern finalists? What had any of them done?

The constant bickering persuaded more and more people on both sides to make sure they were at the Union Course when the starter's drum sounded Tuesday. Decades before the nation's sporting age be-gan, America's first sports spectacle was at hand. Many of the south-erners in town already had tickets for the race, but with a simi-larly competitive spirit now infusing Eclipse's backers, twice as many northerners as southerners would eventually pack the course.

The event dominated all talk in the city. The papers were filled with advertisements for carriage, ferry, and steamship services. Fans headed to the race had to cross the East River and make the eight-mile journey to Jamaica, just as Eclipse had recently done. They were urged to plan ahead. One ferry service pledged to continuously rotate "three large boats so passengers with horses and carriages may not meet with any delay in crossing." Another pledged to take "a route much shorter than any other on the river," running four large barges. William Niblo offered to transport his customers in a private boat. Hundreds of carriages were reserved for the second part of the trip, over the dirt roads connecting Brooklyn and Jamaica.

"The race will make more noise than Newmarket or Epsom," the *New York Spectator* wrote.

Strangers are pouring in from all quarters. We have white hats and sallow faces from the South; rosy cheeks and cunning fizzes from the East; Johnny Raws from the North, and a few of the knowing ones from the West. Nothing is heard but the race. It is impossible to say how the thing will go. The southerners are full of money and ready to bet any sum against Eclipse. Northerners are ready to pony up anything on behalf of their favorite sorrel. There is much speculation.

Religious, political, and patriotic ceremonies had previously attracted the largest crowds of Americans. Mobs angry about taxes had often gathered during the Colonial era. George Whitefield, a charismatic Anglican evangelist from England, drew as many as thirty thousand people to his sermons before the Revolutionary War. Thousands in Philadelphia and elsewhere cheered readings of the Declaration of Independence in 1776. Parades honoring the Declaration's signing, the ratification of the Constitution, and George Washington's birthday were always popular.

It had been unthinkable until now that a horse race could attract a similar-sized crowd. Races seldom attracted more than a few thousand fans. The crowd of six thousand that gathered to see Eclipse and Sir Charles at the National Course was easily the largest anyone could recall. It had seemed silly to expect any more than twice as many people at the Union Course six months later. When the NYAIBH renovated the course for the race — widening the entrance, adding an extra gate for carriages, erecting three new stands along the finish, and putting up a board fence around the course to keep people under control — it thought twenty thousand fans at most would attend. But that many southerners alone would pass through the gates on race day.

Large sports crowds had been common in earlier societies and civilizations. The ancient Olympics in Greece, which began in 776 B.C. and were held every four years until A.D. 393, drew forty thousand spectators at their peak; chariot and horse races were among the major attractions. The ancient Romans had the Circus Maximus, a chariot-racing venue, which held two hundred thousand spectators and often filled for races between the Blues and the Greens, intense rivals. Races consisted of seven laps around a narrow oval, a distance of about five miles, and the crowd could be heard for miles. Romans were also fans of gladiatorial contests in which thousands of competitors fought to the death. By the second century A.D. the Roman world had more than fifty arenas and amphitheaters for such contests, including the famed Colosseum, built in A.D. 80 and still standing almost twenty centuries later. It held sixty thousand spectators.

Large crowds gathered in medieval England for tournaments of mock warfare in which knights jousted and fought on horseback with blunted swords. The popularity of such events waned with the rise of gunpowder and firearms, but real blood remained a lure: a crowd flocked to the execution of Charles I in 1649. The return of the monarchy in 1660 marked the beginning of horse racing's popularity. Crowds labeled "vast and unruly" were seen at Epsom by the mid-1700s. Classic races such as the Epsom Derby and the St. Leger were inaugurated in the late 1700s and soon attracted many thousands. Charles Dickens wrote it seemed "all of London turned out" for the Derby.

Why had America not experienced the roar of a great sports crowd before 1823? The main reason was that spectator sports were not popular. But also there had not been a metropolis like Rome or London to provide and tolerate the crush of humanity. The slowness and difficulty of travel kept fans from journeying far, and communication systems were so primitive that it was hard to spread the news of an upcoming event.

But all that was changing.

New York City's population in 1823 was more than 120,000, larger than the populations of such states as Rhode Island, Mississippi, Missouri, and Illinois. Having that many people within easy traveling distance of the Union Course made it possible for a great crowd to gather. New York also had the facilities to receive, house, and transport the hordes. Had 60,000 people tried to gather anywhere else in America, thousands would have had been stranded with no place to sleep or eat. Only New York had enough beds and food for so many people and enough horses, boats, and carriages to move them. Though filled to capacity by race day, the city could manage.

Steamship travel also helped the spectacle unfold. Until that time southerners never could have traveled north in such numbers. A horse-drawn coach ride from Petersburg to New York took three days, and with few public lines operating, no more than several hun-

dred people could travel at any time. Now thousands had traveled by
ship, covering the distance in a fraction of the time once needed.

But the main reason the Union Course race became America's first
major sports event was the fundamental allure of a contest that people on both sides had become emotionally invested in. Just as sports
spectacles in ancient Greece, Rome, and England served as substi-
tutes for real war, with rivals battling symbolically rather than with
weapons and blood, the Union Course race pitted one American region against another, one way of life against the other. Slaveholders
against slave opponents. Planters against industrialists. Each saw its
side as superior and saw the race as a chance to emphasize that superiority. It was the sporting equivalent of a civil war and, as it turned
out, one of the first shots of the real battle between North and South
that unfolded more than three decades later.

"It is useless to disguise the fact. All heads are occupied and all
tongues eloquent about the races," the *New York American* wrote.

> Local feelings and attachments are highly excited. Eclipse is in every
> mouth, and hopes and fears hang upon the issue, such as in this coun-
> try, at least, never waited upon brute beasts before. The bustle and the
> crowd in the city are incredible. And it is not alone the crowds assem-
> bling here, and which will gather on the course, that feel an interest in
> the results of the race; the theme has long occupied the press, and
> thanks be to it, the intelligence of this contest has been conveyed to the
> uttermost corners of our land. The canoes which are navigating the
> head waters of the Missouri and the rafts which are descending the St.
> Lawrence will alike bear those whose bosoms will beat with hope and
> fear along with the thousands of fluttering hearts on the Union Course.

Eclipse resumed training at Stevens's estate with Van Ranst watching
carefully. He was joined by Billy Crafts, Purdy's twenty-six-year-old
replacement. Van Ranst had suggested that the rider come stay at the
compound, ride Eclipse every day, and bond with the horse. Eclipse
was very intelligent, the old wizard told him, almost human in some
respects. He would race better for a rider he liked and trusted.

The training routine was the same as it had been at Harlem Lane.

Eclipse ran alone, his rhythmic grunting the only noise in the quiet scene. The horse's temper was short, his mood sour, his animal instincts flaring; he seemed to know a fight was approaching. Van Ranst varied the speed and distance of his runs. On some days he jogged five miles; on others he ran harder but circled the oval just twice. Big, dark, and angry, he was ready for the race now, Van Ranst believed. The old wizard was just trying to keep him fresh and fit.

Though Crafts rode Eclipse every day, he spent most of his time in his cottage. Pale, slender, and sullen, he was not very good company. He had won purses for a decade on New York tracks, but his success had come mostly on lesser horses in smaller events. Staggered by the invitation to ride Eclipse in such an important race, he had barely croaked a positive reply when Van Ranst extended the offer at Harlem Lane. He was excited by the opportunity, but it scared him. He had never been on a stage so grand or raced on or against horses so gifted. He was not sure he belonged here.

Van Ranst spoke at length with him about tactics. Eclipse was famous for being a front-runner, he said. The horse was so dominant he had barely experienced the sensation of running behind a competitor, and Van Ranst did not want him to do so now. He hoped Eclipse would race on the lead, but he was worried about the speed of the challenger. Van Ranst emphasized to Crafts the importance of being ready to adjust to unexpected circumstances. There was no telling what might happen.

Van Ranst felt fairly positive about Crafts as the days passed and he watched the young rider work. Crafts was quiet, but he had a nice way with the horse. His hands flashed quickly as he worked the reins, he changed speeds subtly. The only problem, as Van Ranst saw it, was his small size. He was well under one hundred pounds and lacked Purdy's strength. At times he almost seemed to lose control of the horse. Van Ranst lectured him about that. It was critical to hold on tight. Eclipse was a mighty animal who could send you flying if you lost your grip.

Crafts listened and nodded, seldom replying. He quickly tired of the old man's lectures; he just wanted to ride. And he was pretty good, he thought. But he had never ridden a horse anywhere near this caliber. Eclipse was just so big and strong, such an awesome specimen. When Crafts asked him to accelerate, he sped up with such a burst that he almost surged out from under the jockey. Crafts held on, but he felt like a sailor slipping around the wet deck of a boat in rough waters. He was not in control.

His fears mounted as the race neared, but he kept them to himself. Van Ranst would have been mortified to hear them. Day after day he got on Eclipse and made it through the training runs, but sometimes he was holding on for dear life, hands gripping the bridle, legs wrapped tightly around Eclipse's flanks. He had seldom fallen off a horse, but he feared it might happen now.

It was not a problem in these private training sessions, but the race would be another story. Please, Crafts thought, do not let me fall or lose control of Eclipse in front of thousands of fans at the Union Course.

Five days before the race, Johnson and his party of southern horses and horsemen embarked on the last leg of their journey. They left Bristol early one morning, traveling by foot and by carriage, and reached Manhattan late the next day. The ousted finalists, John Richards and Washington, were left behind at Badger's estate. The three remaining finalists traveled with Johnson, accompanied by Taylor, Badger, Racing Billy, and all the jockeys and stable hands who had come from Virginia. They brought along a couple of other horses that might run in other races at the Union Course.

New Yorkers were anxious to see the famous southerner and his animals. Earlier that week the *Evening Post* had erroneously reported that Henry had completed his winning four-mile heats at Newmarket in six minutes apiece — a physical impossibility, as anyone familiar with the turf knew. The correct times were around eight minutes. But New Yorkers were unschooled in the sport, and a mild panic ensued. Who was this miracle horse Johnson was bringing? An animal that flew instead of galloped? How could poor Eclipse beat such a freak?

"This [six minutes] is less time than a horse has ever been known to run before, either in Great Britain or this country, and, we must say, ever will run again," the *Evening Post* wrote. "It is a thing incredible to anyone the least bit conversant with the speed of horses. No stud book or racing calendar ever contained a record of such a performance."

The paper ran a correction two days later, attributing the better information to "a gentleman acquainted with the facts" of the Virginia race. You could almost hear relief sweeping across the city. Few readers recognized that even amended, Henry's winning times were spectacular, foretelling potential trouble for Eclipse.

Johnson and his horses passed through New York and continued on to Jamaica without the hullabaloo that had accompanied Eclipse's royal procession. A few New Yorkers recognized the white-haired Johnson. One taunted him, suggesting that it did not matter which horse he picked because Eclipse could beat them all. Johnson managed to smile, but he burned inside. These people need a whipping, he thought.

Upon reaching Jamaica, Johnson and Badger checked into their rooms at a small inn near the course. The horses were put up in a stable just down the road; it had barns and a half-mile training track.

On Sunday morning, two days before the race, Johnson took the finalists to the Union Course. Most northerners planning to run horses during the meeting had them stabled at barns near the course. It was their custom to meet in the mornings to train on the dirt oval.

Napoleon made a grand entrance, perched high in the saddle, white hair flowing down his neck, as he led the jogging finalists. He resembled a general taking an army into battle, lacking only a flag to trumpet his allegiance. The northern horsemen fell silent, intimidated by his dramatic aura. He motioned to Taylor to get the horses running. Taylor, also on horseback, barked commands to the stable boys and jockeys, their dark skin equally startling to some northerners.

The horses, which had never raced on dirt, started separately. Flying Childers set off first, legs churning as he ran counterclockwise. Betsey Richards went after him, quickly reaching a fine speed with her balanced running action. Finally Henry, with Walden aboard, began to canter, taking measured strides, holding back.

The northern horsemen studied the southern animals. Like everyone on both sides of the race, they were anxious to know which of the three would challenge Eclipse. Would it be Henry, as many expected?

Would it be Betsey Richards, the elegant mare? Would the mysteriously absent John Richards make a last-minute dash to the starting post?

The New York papers were obsessed with the issue, writing as if the fate of the nation depended on it. "An impenetrable mystery overshadows this great subject. Clouds and darkness hang upon it. Expectation is all agog," the *New York American* wrote. "We have mentioned Henry as if he was the antagonist, but this is not known. All doubts will be resolved when the riders mount, and not before. Betsey Richards could be the choice. We have heard something of her having exhibited more bottom at the Newmarket race, although Henry beat her. It will doubtless be one of those two."

As the three finalists trained on Sunday morning, Johnson knew the northern horsemen were observing them and also carefully watching him, looking for clues that would give away the challenger's identity. None were forthcoming. The horses were treated similarly, as if each were being prepared to race. Johnson had turned inward on the subject in the past few days, refraining from discussing it even with Badger and Racing Billy. He was making up his mind.

To be sociable, he rode over and greeted the northern horsemen, knowing they were afraid to approach him. The men took turns shaking his hand and complimenting him on the condition of his horses, each of which galloped a few circuits around the course. Johnson agreed. They were fine animals, indeed.

Unable to contain their curiosity, the northerners asked if he had made up his mind. Napoleon smiled and shrugged. He had until Tuesday. The public would know his answer when it was time to present a horse to the judges. Those were the conditions, remember.

For months some New Yorkers had strangely insisted that the Union Course race would never come off, believing that the southerners, for all their talk, were afraid they could not beat Eclipse. The race would end with a forfeit, they said, just like the National Course event. Johnson's presence at the Union Course quashed that ill-advised rumor. Thousands of southerners were flooding into New York for the event, and now three fit, fast southern horses were training on the course. There would be no forfeit.

Johnson was entranced by the dirt course, which he had heard so much about. After he spoke to the northern horsemen and sent his horses back to the barn down the road, he dismounted and walked the course by himself, lost in concentration, his eyes focused on the ground in front of him. He had many questions. Were there rocks or undulations that could throw a horse off stride? How deeply into the dirt did the horses dig? Would there be a problem if it rained?

He was impressed with the course as he walked it. The dirt was smooth, rocks few. He had heard Stevens's claim that horses would run faster on this oval than on any other, and Johnson now agreed. A race on this surface would be about speed more than stamina, and that should help the southern side on Tuesday. Eclipse had stamina, but the challenger should have more speed. At the same time, Eclipse was accustomed to the surface, having run on it and won numerous times. Napoleon could not decide which side would benefit more from the dirt track. He finally decided to call it even; neither side had a clear-cut advantage.

Oddly, after carefully counting his steps all the way around the oval, he believed it was slightly more than a mile in length. That would not do. If you added up the extra distance in a heat encompassing four trips around the oval, the horses would be running a lot farther than four miles. That clearly benefited Eclipse, whose bottom was legendary. Johnson pledged to bring up the issue with the judges. He guessed that the northerners knew full well that the course was longer than four miles and were hoping to get away with having slightly longer heats.

Ha, Johnson thought, smiling to himself. It would take more than this trick to outfox a man called Napoleon.

12

———⟨⟨∘/∘/∘⟩⟩———

I Have Decided
on Our Challenger

O N MONDAY MORNING under a low gray sky, as the horses were in the midst of their usual training runs and horsemen chatted and commented near the finish, the mood inside the Union Course abruptly changed. Someone shouted, heads turned, and all conversation stopped. The jockeys pulled up their horses.

Eclipse cantered majestically onto the dirt, stepping high. A portly exercise rider guided the northern star, holding the reins tight. (Crafts had decided to remain in his cottage to rest up for the next day.) Van Ranst followed on foot, having ridden over in a carriage. The other northern horsemen shouted excitedly, like children at play, as Eclipse broke into a counterclockwise jog. The white jockeys and stable boys employed by the other northerners applauded the sight of their horse on the track. He would beat those southerners!

Van Ranst had kept Eclipse sequestered at the Stevens compound until now, seeing no need to bring him to the course when he had a fine training track available right by his barn. The horse certainly did not need any introduction to the dirt surface. But now, with the race just a day away, Van Ranst thought Eclipse could use a run on the dirt to remind him of the feel. The old wizard was also curious to see the southern candidates; he had heard about their coming to the course, and he wanted to take a look.

As it happened, Johnson was there, having arrived earlier with his horses, again with a ceremonial flourish. Henry, Betsey Richards, and Flying Childers had circled the oval once, twice, three times, jogging lightly. The northern horsemen had watched carefully, trying to discern which was favored. Henry had a nifty turn of foot, no doubt. The mare had a natural elegance. Either surely would give Eclipse a test. But which would it be?

Suddenly their opponent had stolen the show, occupying all eyes. Johnson, who had not seen Eclipse since the National Course race six months before, watched silently, having forgotten how big he was and what a forbidding aura he had. The horse jogged with an intimidating ease, body language casual, steps huge. Napoleon saw that he was in fine shape and obviously ready to run.

But he was nine, Johnson thought, noting the sagging flesh line at the horse's jaw.

As Van Ranst walked over to greet the northern horsemen, Johnson rode over to say hello. The old wizard and Napoleon shook hands. They had known each other since the early 1800s, having crossed paths many times in the South. They spoke briefly now. Van Ranst gazed at Johnson's finalists, just finishing, and praised their looks and conditioning; he wanted to know which would race tomorrow but knew better than to ask. Napoleon then complimented Van Ranst on Eclipse's looks. It was going to be one hell of a race, Johnson said.

An awkward silence ensued. The two horsemen surely could have discussed their months of preparation, but this was hardly the time. Both had deep secrets to keep — Johnson's about his selection of a challenger, Van Ranst's about his new jockey. They did not want to talk now. Anyway, Napoleon needed to get his horses back to the barn, and Van Ranst wanted to watch Eclipse jog. They went their separate ways.

Napoleon sent the finalists back to the barn ahead of him. He wanted to be alone. After months of training and endless deliberations, he had decided on a challenger.

Henry would represent the South.

Johnson had made up his mind tentatively during the trip from Fairview to Jamaica and had confirmed his opinion during his walk around the dirt oval the day before. It would be a speed race, so Henry would have an advantage. But before he told his inner circle, he wanted a little time to think about it.

Just a month earlier, Johnson had not considered Henry a serious possibility; the horse was talented but seemingly determined to disobey at all costs. But he had undergone a dramatic change. Walden had worked wonders with him, nurturing him with whispers and pats and getting him to obey without sacrificing any natural speed.

Even though Napoleon had leaned toward John Richards for much of the past four months, he now believed Henry was the best candidate. Henry's performance at Newmarket had borne the mark of greatness. Though very young, the horse had the potential to blaze past Eclipse. It was possible the great northern horse would never know what hit him.

Other factors also made Henry the right choice. Johnson had long considered the weight issue potentially decisive, and Henry, as a four-year-old, would carry just 108 pounds, as opposed to 126 for Eclipse. What an advantage! Betsey Richards would not have to carry much more of a handicap, but every pound mattered, and Henry was faster than Betsey Richards. Henry's selection also made it easy for Johnson to pick a jockey. Walden and the horse had formed a bond. The white boy was the obvious choice. Johnson was relieved that he did not have to put the young slave Charles Stewart in the spotlight with thousands of southern dollars on the line. Stewart was gifted, but in Napoleon's opinion, not sufficiently seasoned for this moment. Walden was solid. Walden would come through.

The only drawbacks to choosing Henry were the possibility that he might lose concentration in front of a crowd and the rule that required him to carry the four-year-old weight handicap even though he was still three. Johnson was no longer worried about a mental lapse, so the first concern was minimal. But the second concern had nagged at him for weeks. He hated that Henry had to carry more weight than his age dictated. Johnson knew a rule was a rule, but was it not wrong to ask such a young horse to carry a heavier handicap?

Johnson had often been able to persuade judges to bend a rule in his favor, and he thought he might be able to do so now if he argued his side convincingly enough. He would speak to the judges that afternoon. Maybe he could save a pound or two.

In any case, Johnson's mind was made up. It was time to announce his decision to his entourage of southerners. He left the course and rode back to the barn. Taylor was overseeing the bathing and midday feeding of the horses. Badger and Racing Billy were sitting in the shade. The grooms and jockeys were hard at work.

Napoleon motioned for everyone to gather around. "I have decided on our challenger," he said in a commanding tone. The workers immediately put down their buckets of feed and water and rushed to stand close to their master so they could hear. Badger, Taylor, and Racing Billy elbowed through the workers and stood next to Johnson.

Napoleon cleared his throat, smiled, and waited, loving the suspense. "Henry shall run for us," he finally said in a rumbling voice, "and Henry shall win for us."

A loose cheer went up. It was a popular choice. The inner circle and the barn help had grown to appreciate Henry's spectacular natural talent. The grooms and jockeys had been debating their master's choice for months while they cleaned the barns and worked with the horses. (They argued and shouted when no whites were around, then fell silent in white company.) A few had even bet on which horse he would pick. Henry had become the obvious front-runner after John Richards went down, but those who cared for Betsey Richards had thought Johnson might be swayed in the end by the attractive female. They now owed money to Henry's backers.

Badger, Taylor, and Billy crowded around Johnson, slapping him on the back as they ran through Henry's assets. The youngster raced with an unmatched explosive quality, and now that he had learned to follow orders, he would challenge Eclipse with youth, speed, and intelligence, a combination of qualities the northern horse had never confronted in a rival.

"Henry is a marvelous choice," Badger said, "and certain to be a formidable challenger. My forecast is that his name will be known to millions by the end of the week as the vanquisher of the great Eclipse."

Of all those listening when Johnson announced his choice, Walden was the most affected by the selection, for now he knew he would ride in the race the next day. Johnson surely would speak to him about it within minutes. The idea so thrilled him he could actually feel a tingle. Just a country boy, he could hardly believe the turn his life had taken. He would represent the entire South in a race in New York before a sea of people.

The choice was no surprise, of course, given the events of the past month. Henry's Newmarket race had elevated his chances, and then his main competitor, John Richards, had gone down with an injury. After that Walden had pretty much known he would end up riding.

Johnson approached him outside the barn. Walden smiled. He felt a kinship with the famous trainer after all their discussions about Henry. Napoleon shook his hand and told him he would be wearing the colors the next day. Walden nodded and responded that it would be the highest honor he had ever known. Johnson tossed him a sky blue shirt and cap. Catching them, Walden smiled at Charles Stewart, who was standing nearby, watching intently. The two jockeys had become close, having spent all spring together. Stewart had never really expected to ride in the great race; he would get a mount in another race at the meeting, and that was enough for him, a thrill in itself.

Napoleon wanted to discuss tactics with Walden. With a horse as fleet and excitable as Henry, he said, you never want to discourage him from running, especially early in a race. Walden should let Henry loose from the beginning but also make sure the horse did not completely exhaust himself and leave nothing for the end of the heat and the rest of the race. Johnson was confident Sir Archie's influence would help there. Henry had enough bottom. His speed was the factor that could decide the race. An aggressive approach would show the North that the South had come to win. Eclipse, Johnson figured, probably had never trailed another horse in a race. It was possible he might fall behind and become discouraged. Johnson had seen that happen.

Walden listened carefully and nodded, his confidence growing by the second. Months of training had primed Henry for this moment. It did not matter that Eclipse was unbeaten. The northern horse had never faced a challenge like this. Henry would start furiously tomorrow, his first steps leaving no doubt about his intentions. He was there to bury the North.

Walden could hardly wait. He could not remember ever having been more excited.

The Union Course meeting was scheduled to start Monday afternoon at one o'clock with a sweepstakes for three-year-olds. Fans were lined up at the entrance by midmorning. Some of the racing-mad southerners who had come to New York were ready to see horses run. New Yorkers skipped work, caught up in the excitement. Some fans planned to stay overnight around the course — why travel all the way back to the city when they would just have to return the next day? They had either booked rooms at inns and boarding houses or planned to pitch a tent.

The NYAIBH was expecting four or five thousand fans on Monday, a good-sized crowd in any other context but minuscule compared to the numbers coming on Tuesday.

Entry fees had been widely advertised. Fans entering by foot or on horseback paid fifty cents. A one-horse wagon cost a dollar, regardless of how many people were inside; a fancy coach had to pay a dollar and a half. Men hired by the NYAIBH worked the entrance and took in the money.

The scene outside the gate was loud and chaotic. In front of a row of booths and tents, men — opportunists all — hawked roasted chickens and pigs, alcoholic drinks, ferry tickets, and carriage rentals. Fancy tables were set up inside some tents, and cooks prepared meals of beef and fish. Some of the booths were still being put together. The sound of carpenters hammering nails blended with the sound of a brass band practicing in a nearby field.

A crowd grew amid the swirl of smoke, smells, and shouts. Northerners and southerners waited together in the entrance line and then, once inside the gates, raced to stand where they had the best view of the course. They talked of that day's sweepstakes, but mainly about the great race the next day. Bets were discussed and, in a few cases, arranged, even though the southern horse had not yet been identified.

Publicly the NYAIBH did not support gambling. A great many Americans still disapproved of horse racing because of the rampant wagering involved. Dice tables, card tables, and shuffleboard courts often appeared at courses along with the betting on horses, enabling more gambling to take place before and after races. The temptations were many and, it was widely believed, too great, causing people to throw away hard-earned money earmarked for necessities — paying bills, for instance.

With the turf often faulted by politicians and religious leaders for promoting immorality, course managers had no choice but to maintain an appearance of cleanliness, even though they knew gambling was commonplace. The only way the NYAIBH had obtained a racing license in 1821 was by pledging to rid the premises of dice and card games. The association had written in its bylaws that sheriffs would patrol the course and "remove all tables at which money can be won or lost." As the North–South race neared, the New York newspapers, ever supportive, predicted that a healthy atmosphere would prevail: "A sufficient number of peace officers, together with the sheriffs of Kings and Queens [counties], will attend and prevent all gambling and other improper proceedings."

But while gaming tables and shuffleboard courts were banished, tens of thousands of dollars would be bet on the race — almost surely more than had ever been wagered in one place in America. One southerner supposedly wanted to put five hundred slaves on the line. A few others were rumored to be ready to bet their entire estates. New Yorkers surely would take up these dares. Bettors would put up money, goods, land, whatever they could. An ad in Monday's *New York American* read, "Gentlemen who bet (and lose) their boots on the Union Course race are informed that new ones can be purchased good, fashionable, and cheap at No. 2 Bowery." Even the shoes on men's feet would be on the line.

Bankers in both regions were concerned. The wealthy men backing the $20,000-a-side stakes could afford to lose, but many others who planned to bet surely could not. Some would put up more than they had. And the losing region would experience an immediate drain of many thousands of dollars, enough to send debt soaring and interest rates spiraling. What banker would not worry?

Was there any chance that common sense would prevail? None. Americans had gambled since the 1600s on horse races, lotteries, cockfights, dice games — just about anything, it seemed, other than whether the sun would rise in the East. (And someone somewhere surely had won money on that.) The first colonists had exhibited a gambling instinct just by leaving England for America — exploring a new world involved risk-taking, opportunism, and high expectations, the same elements found in betting — and their descendants had faithfully carried on the tradition.

The thirteen original colonies had held lotteries to help fund the building of churches, libraries, and government buildings and to start such colleges as Harvard, Yale, and William and Mary. The practice was so accepted that participating was deemed a civic obligation. George Washington, Ben Franklin, and John Hancock were among the many public figures who attached their names to private lotteries benefiting various projects. Anyone could organize a lottery on behalf of any cause, including oneself. In 1768 the prominent Virginia horse breeder William Byrd III staged a lottery to save his finances after gambling away an inherited fortune. His lottery failed, and he later committed suicide.

Lotteries were still popular in 1823. Congress had just voted to hold one to help fund the landscaping of Washington. (It would prove a disaster when organizers fled with the money, leaving winners unpaid.)

Betting on horses had a similar, though less upstanding, tradition in America. The money never benefited churches or universities, but the practice was just as popular. Only the wealthy could breed and race horses, but anyone, even slaves, could bet on them. It was a raw and unregulated practice, a roiling brew of loose arrangements between distrustful men. Colonists put up coffee, sugar, tobacco, and clothes to back their horses in quarter-mile races in the early 1700s. The transition to thoroughbreds and oval-course racing brought out high society and raised the stakes. George Washington wrote in his diary about gambling in Annapolis in the 1760s. Andrew Jackson put thousands on the line in the early 1800s.

In 1823 many Americans still derived an unquenchable thrill from putting up money and then rooting for a horse. Politicians usually refrained because so many voters were offended, but some did not care. John Randolph had made a side bet of $1,000 on Sir Charles at the National Course race in November, while a New York friend bet on Eclipse. They had agreed to transfer the bet to the Union Course race rather than quibble over paying off after the controversial forfeit and substitute race. Now Randolph was among the southerners in New York, having traveled by steamship from Washington. Randolph, of course, had contributed to the $20,000 stakes, and as the race neared, he seemed incapable of turning down additional wagers. He was stopped by a northern fan as he stepped off his ship in New York. "Fifty dollars on the famous proposition, sir: Eclipse against the world!" the northerner shouted.

"Fifty it is!" Randolph cried.

Preparations for the race seemed complete. The southern side had deposited $20,000 at the Global Bank. The North's $20,000 was at the Municipal Bank. John Cox Stevens's brother had imported a marine chronometer from England to make sure time was kept accurately at the course. The NYAIBH had picked a trio of judges from Maryland, Philadelphia, and Washington, all horsemen who were supposedly neutral on the North–South issue. Their job was to make sure that the handicap weights were met, the jockeys behaved, and the race unfolded fairly. The presiding judge was Charles Ridgely, a former governor of Maryland, who had once backed a major racing stable and bet $9,000 on a race.

Napoleon, after telling his insiders about Henry, returned to the Union Course with Badger and Racing Billy to watch the sweepstakes and enjoy the day. But Johnson, as always, had an ulterior motive. He arrived early and sought out Ridgely, whom he had known for years. It was still burning Johnson that Henry had to carry 108 pounds. Three-year-olds raced with 98 pounds at the Union Course, and many four-year-olds in the South raced with 105. Napoleon asked Ridgely if the weight allotments could be negotiated, because one of his finalists was a June foal and thus especially young and deserving of accommodation. At the very least, Napoleon said, the horse should carry no more than 105 pounds.

Ridgely was not buying. He pointed out that the Union Course's scale of weights had been in effect since the track opened in 1821. Then he recounted the history of the scale and why it was heavier than those at southern courses. Improving the North's horses had been the reason racing was resumed in New York in the first place, he said, and John Jay had suggested using heavier weights to make the horses sturdier and increase their usefulness away from the turf. Johnson nodded. He knew the history. And he saw that he was not going to get his way. America, unlike England, had no national jockey club to appeal to, no governing body that set rules and arbitrated disputes. Each club set its own rules, and the judges upheld them. Henry would have to race with 108 pounds.

Napoleon changed the subject. He had walked the course the day before, he said, and he believed it to be longer than a mile by at least fifteen feet. Would Ridgely check the distance and, if necessary, change the start and finish to make each lap exactly a mile? Napoleon did not explain that he wanted his young horse racing no farther than four miles to win a heat or that longer heats favored Eclipse.

Ridgely doubted that Johnson was right, for much study and sweat had gone into making sure the Union Course's dirt track was just right. But the judge said he would send a pair of horsemen out to walk the course, as Napoleon had done the day before. Remarkably, the horsemen returned with identical reports; the track was indeed longer than a mile.

Ridgely could only shake his head at Johnson's brilliance. How real and rare it was! The judge located Napoleon in the crowd and pledged to move the start thirty feet ahead, shortening the run to the first turn but ensuring that the heats would consist of exactly four miles.

Johnson nodded. He had known all along that he was right.

By one o'clock on Monday, some five thousand fans were at the Union Course. Four horses were presented to the judges for the first event of the meeting, a sweepstakes consisting of one-mile heats. Three of the horses were colts, the fourth a filly owned by Van Ranst. All were three-year-olds.

A colt named Prizefighter took the early lead in the first heat and held it, completing his lap around the oval in 1 minute 54 seconds and reaching the finish ahead of a colt named Knickerbocker. Van Ranst's filly was third. After a thirty-minute break, all four horses ran in the second heat and finished in the same order, so Prizefighter took the purse.

Johnson watched from a stand near the finish, his frustration simmering. The horses in the just-completed event had all carried 98 pounds. They were the same age as Henry. Why could he not carry 98 the next day? He could destroy Eclipse if he had a 28-pound handicap advantage. But Ridgely was not going to budge. There was no getting around it.

Seated nearby, Van Ranst had quietly watched his mare, a half-sister to Eclipse, run third in the sweepstakes. A few other northern trainers had tried to make small talk with him before the race, but he was short with them, lacking the necessary patience. Now he sat alone, dressed in a thick coat better suited to winter.

His thoughts turned to Tuesday's race. He had managed to keep from the public his plan to use Crafts rather than Purdy, but it was almost time to let the secret out. He knew it would cause a stir. He remembered that night at Stevens's mansion when the NYAIBH group had responded silently to his plan, not knowing what to say. Many in the crowd tomorrow would be similarly dubious. Purdy had never lost on Eclipse and, in fact, had never even been challenged. Why change now?

But Van Ranst, now that he had seen Johnson and the southern finalists, was surer than ever about his decision. Henry, the horse he figured Johnson would choose, was just a babe, but he was quite a specimen, full of vigor. Eclipse would have to be at his best to win, and he needed a jockey younger than forty-nine to coax the best out of him. The day might involve an entire afternoon of whipping and spurring. Crafts, though oddly quiet, was quick on the draw, a young and able rider. He could do the job.

Van Ranst knew he was in for a tough time the next day. He looked around and saw some northerners already betting on Eclipse, surely expecting Purdy to ride. What would they say when they saw Crafts? The old wizard tried not to dwell on it. He was hot. He stood to stretch his legs and took off his heavy coat. Purdy was a great jockey whose time had passed; his decision to change riders would eventually be celebrated. Van Ranst kept telling himself that.

Billy Crafts spent Monday holed up in his cottage at the Stevens estate, alternating between excitement and terror. What with the size of the crowd, the talents of the horses, and the dollars on the line, this was going to be an event unlike any he had experienced. When he had told Van Ranst he would ride, he had expected a typical Union Course event, manageable in scale and expectations. He had not expected anything like this.

He paced all afternoon, working up a sweat going back and forth on the hardwood floor. Several times he tried to nap but gave up after tossing and turning for an hour. His chances of sleeping that night were slim, he guessed. He had been alone, without anyone to talk to, for two weeks now, staring at the walls and stewing over the possibility that he would not be strong enough to control Eclipse.

He was going a little crazy with fear.

After the sweepstakes a surprise second race was announced. The NYAIBH had decided to stage a trotting event, since the sweepstakes was so brief. Five horses pulling one-man racing carriages were presented to the judges. They would compete in three-mile heats.

Trotting lacked the tradition of thoroughbred racing — it had not surfaced until after the Revolutionary War — and it was a distinctly American endeavor (the British had never picked it up), a popular attraction at county fairs. Cheers resounded and small bets were arranged as the horses set off around the Union Course.

A four-year-old mare from Philadelphia held the lead until the last turn of the first heat, when it abruptly pulled up and was passed. But it came back to win the next two heats and capture the purse. "Much amusement was afforded by this exhibition of speed and bottom," the *New York American* reported.

It was almost four o'clock by the time the race ended. On any other day, the course would have emptied after the final event. But this was not a typical day. The great match race was less than twenty-four hours away now, and many fans intended to stay in the area overnight. Some pitched tents in a nearby field. Others set off to find hot food and a roof for the night. A few made plans to sleep in their carriages. The area around the course was as crowded and noisy as a city street corner.

Gas lights, candles, and bonfires shone brilliantly as the sun set. A large tent inside the entrance to the course seemed almost ablaze. NYAIBH was using the tent as headquarters during the meeting, and on this night, the horsemen, judges, and officials for the great race would dine together inside. Such social affairs were a tradition on the southern turf, and the NYAIBH intended to meet that high standard. The omnipresent William Niblo would present a sumptuous meal.

Guests arrived at eight o'clock. Johnson, Badger, and Racing Billy were seated at one end of a long table, Van Ranst and Stevens at the other end. Ridgely sat in the middle beside William Van Ness, a New York judge who was president of the NYAIBH. Nathaniel Coles, the Long Islander who had bred Eclipse, also was present.

Cooks working in a temporary kitchen in another tent sent course after course to the table. The main course was lobster fresh from Long Island Sound, a culinary treat for southerners. Then the champagne began to flow. Van Ness rose and toasted the turf, prompting more toasts. Northerners and southerners hailed each other, their horses, and their sport.

A pale moon high in the clear sky shone on the horsemen as they left near midnight, woozy from the long night of celebrating. Stepping from the tent, Johnson, Van Ranst, and the others encountered a scene unlike any they had ever experienced in racing. Hundreds of fans, northerners and southerners alike, shadowy figures shouting wildly, called to them from the darkness just beyond the tent. Campfires burned in the distance.

"Hail to Johnson, Napoleon of the Turf and defender of southern honor!" the southern fans shouted when they saw him leaving the tent.

Johnson nodded and offered a raised hand in salute before stepping into his carriage with Badger and speeding away.

"To the keepers of Eclipse, unbeaten son of New York!" northerners cried when they saw the old wizard.

Van Ranst turned and squinted, trying to make out the faces. He had eaten little, for his nerves had upset his stomach. He wanted to thank the northern fans for their support but also warn them that a tough challenge lay ahead. He asked one of the other departing horsemen if those were New Yorkers shouting at him. The other horsemen shrugged. Van Ranst lingered at the foot of his carriage and then shrugged and ducked into the carriage, which sped away.

"Northern bottom shall soon be exposed as the colossal fraud it surely is," one southerner shouted as the carriage departed.

"You are challenged to say that over here, friend," a northerner replied.

A couple of fights broke out, as northerners and southerners relied on fists rather than horses to prove their superiority. A long, loud night in the fields lay ahead. Sheriffs roaming the area would earn their pay.

And then, finally, the day of the great match race would dawn.

13

Riders Up!

As the sun rose over Manhattan that Tuesday, thousands of people and hundreds of vehicles and horses filled the streets near the East River. John Pintard, secretary of the Mutual Insurance Company, left his Wall Street home and walked to the river to see if the crowd headed to the Union Course was as large as expected. It was even larger. Pintard, stunned, later wrote to his daughter in New Orleans:

> Fulton to Pearl streets was blocked with coaches, stages, double- and single-horse wagons, stages, barouches, and gigs, four and eight abreast, filled with ladies and dandies, high life and low life, waiting for two steam boats and two horse boats, incessantly plying across the river along with row boats of all sorts and sizes. Literally the [entire] city of New York — that is, the gay, idle, and curious — poured out its population on Long Island.

Southerners and northerners were crammed together in lines that snaked for blocks. They jostled, laughed, and taunted each other as they slowly edged toward the ferries. Some began betting. It was later estimated that more than $200,000 in side bets was wagered on the race, an amount that infuriated conservatives and rekindled calls to ban racing as a public scourge. Hundreds of private dramas were played out as strangers came together and agreed to put their money on the line against each other. There was nothing organized about it.

Men just shouted out their side, suggested odds, and negotiated with anyone who approached. If they could strike a deal, they shook hands and pledged to pay, win or lose.

A few of the day's largest bets were on the overall stakes: no money would change hands until one horse had won two heats. A few men, mostly southern tobacco planters, bet their entire estates and settled in for a long, nervous day of watching horses determine their future. But most bets were of the "rolling" variety: a bet on the first heat at negotiated odds, with the winnings then rolled into a new bet on the second heat at new odds, if they could be agreed upon, followed by, if needed, yet another bet on the third heat — again at new odds.

Throughout the morning leading up to the first heat, southerners sought underdog odds of two-to-one and three-to-one on the first heat, exploiting the popular northern belief that Eclipse was infallible.

"But the identity of our horse is not even known," said one planter waiting in line for the ferry as he tried to arrange a bet with a northerner in front of him.

The man just laughed. "You want two-to-one or three-to-one in your favor against a lone horse taking on 'the world'? You have lost your mind, sir," he said. "I will entertain only wagers set at even money odds."

Back and forth they went, northerners in high collars and stovepipe hats haggling with smug planters, many attended by slaves. The sight of the silent, dark-skinned servants made some northerners nervous, underscoring their differences with their rivals. Northerners sat back in their carriages and muttered, "Trust a Southerner with a penny, indeed; but with a man's life, for shame."

The ferry boats went across the river as quickly as possible, leaving the docks dangerously overloaded with people, horses, and carriages, and returned empty after depositing their cargo in Brooklyn. Load after load made the crossing, and the lines in the streets slowly dwindled as the morning wore on.

Pintard walked back to his apartment through a city that became empty and still as he moved away from the river. "All business seems to have been suspended in New York, and all feelings absorbed by the intense interest in the race," one Washington newspaper reported. An unofficial holiday — Great Match Race Day — had been declared in New York.

Josiah Quincy III, scion of one of New England's most important families, had bought a choice grandstand ticket from a Harvard classmate and was among the hordes headed for the course. A future mayor of Boston, Quincy later wrote a firsthand account of the day, which was published in 1883. Starting early in the morning and traveling with a group, he made it across the river on a ferry but then was stranded, as the traffic on the road from Brooklyn to Jamaica was almost at a standstill. An unbroken line of horses, carriages, and pedestrians covered the eight miles.

Quincy wrote:

> I could obtain no carriage to take me to the course, as every conveyance was engaged. Carriages of every description were driven rapidly, and were in very close connection; so much so that when one of them suddenly stopped, the poles of at least a dozen carriages broke through the panels of the carriage preceding them. The drivers were naturally much enraged at this accident, but it was a necessary consequence of the crush and hurry of the day, and no one could be blamed for it. The party I was with, seeing there was no chance of riding, was compelled to foot it. But after plodding some way, we had the luck to fall in with a returning carriage, which we chartered to take us to the course.

The hordes gradually made their way to the course, where the scene was Roman in scale. Tens of thousands of fans were on the grounds — far too many for the few entrance gates to accommodate. Individual lines for carriages, pedestrians, and horseback riders had formed at dawn and quickly stretched a quarter-mile down the road. Some fans held tickets, but many still needed to pay to get in. It soon took longer than an hour to get through the lines, which continually grew as more people arrived during the morning. The booths and tents selling food and drink were sold out long before noon.

Once inside the gates, fans on foot hurried to get close to the track's outer railing, where they could view the race. They were soon stacked two and three deep around the oval, a shouting, sweating mass. The crowd thickened as the morning wore on, the back of the pack eventually pressing against the board fence that circled the course. There was little room for late arrivals.

A horde also formed inside the oval, where carriages and spectators on horseback were directed so that animals would be separated from people on foot. By late morning, carriages and horses were lined up all the way around the inner railing. Just as many were still outside the gates, waiting to get in.

The three raised stands along the run to the finish were packed long before noon. Politicians and wealthy landowners sat in chairs arranged in rows. So many congressmen and senators had come up from Washington that a roll-call vote could have been taken. Congress had shut down for the race.

Although President Monroe had stayed in Washington, where he awaited news of the race (and, he hoped, a southern victory), Vice President Daniel Tompkins was in the stands, sitting with Aaron Burr, the former vice president who had killed Alexander Hamilton in a famous duel years earlier. New Yorkers to the core, Tompkins and Burr were ardent Eclipse fans. Southerners erupted in cheers at the sight of Andrew Jackson, smiling and waving as he made his way to his seat; a lifelong horseman and ally of Johnson's, he had interrupted his presidential campaign to attend the race. Southerners also applauded John Randolph as the Virginia congressman entered and sat down.

Although everyone who was anyone seemingly was at the course, thousands remained in New York, either stuck at work or unable to arrange the trip to Jamaica. Much effort had gone into making sure they would receive the news from the course as soon as possible. A courier had been hired to ride Flying Childers and carry the results to Brooklyn. (Johnson had agreed to let the horse be used this way.) At the Liberty Pole in Brooklyn, the courier would pass the results to a clerk who would raise one of two flags, white if Eclipse had prevailed and red if the South had won. The Bank Coffee House had planned a similar system. Vendors at the Fulton Market in Manhattan had taken out newspaper ads promoting their view of the Liberty Pole: "The interior of our establishment will be in perfect order for the accommodation of those ladies and gentlemen who feel interested in the great race of Eclipse. The market, being opposite the white flag that will be hoisted at Brooklyn at about two o'clock, affords a convenient place of expectation."

It was estimated that Flying Childers could make it from the course to the Liberty Pole in twenty-two minutes at top speed. People in the city would know the outcome of the race less than half an hour after it was over. And for those unable to monitor the various poles and flags, the *New York Evening Post* would print the results in that day's edition, scheduled to circulate by early evening. Never before had an American newspaper held up publication strictly for sports news. Historians would later view the *Evening Post* of May 27, 1823, as the country's first sports extra.

Napoleon and Badger had arranged to meet early in the morning and take a carriage to the stable. Although they had not gotten home from the NYAIBH dinner until after midnight, this was no day to sleep late.

Badger rose on time, dressed, and waited for Johnson in front of their inn as the sun came up. Five minutes passed. Ten. Badger finally went to Johnson's room and knocked on the door. No answer. Badger knocked again, but Johnson still did not reply. Badger pushed on the door, which creaked open. Napoleon was sprawled across the bed, eyes closed.

Badger rushed in, knelt at his friend's side, and asked what was wrong. Johnson did not reply, then rolled on his side to face Badger and vaguely motioned to his stomach. Badger did not have to guess what Napoleon was trying to say.

His stomach was on fire.

Badger rose and stood over the bed, wondering how to proceed. Johnson finally croaked a few words. Sweat covered his brow. His long white hair was matted against his pillow. He had been up since the middle of the night, becoming violently ill every few minutes. He feared he had eaten a spoiled lobster at the NYAIBH dinner.

Badger, who had sat beside Johnson all evening and eaten the same meal, supposed that was possible. But he wished that he, not

Johnson, had had the spoiled lobster. On this, of all days, Napoleon was needed at the racecourse, Badger said. Johnson looked up and smiled thinly, then groaned and rolled back on his side, grumbling a few words. He wanted a doctor. Badger hurried downstairs and woke the innkeeper, who knew a doctor who lived nearby. A rider was dispatched, and the doctor, hearing that the great southern horseman needed attention — on the morning of the great race, no less — came quickly. Badger led him up the stairs and into Johnson's room. The patient's pale complexion and ghastly expression left no doubt about the state of his stomach.

The doctor asked Johnson where the waves of pain started, how often they swelled. He asked if it was a lobster that had felled him, as Badger had suggested. Johnson nodded. The doctor stood up, exhaled, gathered his thoughts, and spoke. Johnson was not in danger, he said, even though he appeared so. He would be fine by evening, once all traces of the lobster were purged. But that process could take hours, and there was no way to hasten it. The cramps would not abate until nightfall.

Silence enveloped the room. An open window let in the morning sunlight along with the shouts of spectators descending on the Union Course. Johnson moaned and looked at Badger. Both understood what the doctor was saying. After all the months of planning, plotting, and anticipation, Johnson, incredibly, would miss the great match race. He was too sick to leave his bed, much less direct his horse that afternoon.

The thought made Johnson more ill than any spoiled lobster could. So much was on the line! Eclipse had to be beaten! The South's reputation was at stake, as was Sir Archie's. Johnson, in a feverish state, suddenly thought of the northern man who had chided him as he passed through Manhattan several days earlier, saying it did not matter which southern horse raced against Eclipse. What an impudent fool. These people had to be taught a lesson, and the moment had arrived to administer it. Henry was primed to blow past Eclipse that afternoon and settle the score.

He suddenly rose, resting on his elbows in the bed, rallying. His voice boomed. He did not care what the doctor said; he could not miss the race. He had thrown every ounce of his inspiration into it. Henry was going to win in a romp. These silly northerners would know by the end of the day that their racing did not compare. His eyes shone.

Badger, who halfway believed that Johnson walked on water, briefly wondered if the great trainer really could block out the pain and carry on. But then another wave of pain surged. Napoleon groaned, closed his eyes, and sank back onto the bed. He was going nowhere. Despondent, he motioned to Badger to come closer. His voice was little more than a whisper. It is going to be up to you and the others, he said. Go to them now. Taylor. Billy. Tell them of this sudden illness. Advise them that Henry is to race, Walden is to ride, and the South is to win.

Badger was near tears as his friend spoke. He pledged to return later that afternoon with news of a great victory. Johnson nodded and groaned, the pain swelling yet again. Badger ran down the stairs and out the front door to his carriage. He told the driver to hurry to the barn. He had important matters to discuss there.

The driver moved the horses along. Badger sat back, thinking about what he would tell the others. It was unfathomable that Napoleon would not be at the course to lead them. What would they do? He cursed out loud, shaking his head at the bad luck.

That morning Purdy rose at dawn. In the pale light he pulled his silk riding shirt out of a closet and fingered it, staring at the fine maroon cloth, wondering what to do. Should he wear it to the Union Course? Or should he just wad it up and throw it in a kiln on the way to Jamaica?

He had no good reason to wear it, of course, for he was not riding that day. He would have to buy a ticket like everyone else. Crafts, a jockey with a fraction of his talent, would guide Eclipse in the great challenge race — the thought broke Purdy's heart.

He had managed to carry on for the most part since Van Ranst had demoted him that morning at Harlem Lane. His work and political commitments left him little time to dwell on the snub. He had told his family about it but, ashamed to have been replaced, almost no one else. When anyone asked, he changed the subject. But it came back to him in the evenings and kept him awake at night, especially as the race neared. Everyone was so excited and he was left out.

He was furious with Van Ranst. How could his old friend have put the North's chances in such jeopardy? Purdy was sure that Crafts would struggle to control Eclipse. To direct this great horse, one needed strength, experience, and a close bond. Eclipse did not run for just anyone. He ran for riders he trusted — and he trusted Purdy. They had been through so much together in their races and training runs.

Purdy sat back on his bed, holding the maroon silks, deliberating. If he wore the shirt to the race, he might be called upon to ride if some disaster struck. Trainers sometimes changed jockeys from heat to heat for various reasons. This could easily be one of those occasions. But did Purdy want to provide such a safeguard for the North? That was the question.

Part of him wanted to see Van Ranst revealed as a fool for having bypassed him; the old wizard deserved such a comeuppance. If he wore business clothes to the race and Van Ranst could not turn to him, the North would crash and Van Ranst would be criticized in newspapers throughout the country. Purdy smiled at the idea.

But then he unbuttoned the shirt, put his arms through the sleeves, and pulled it around his shoulders. He would wear it to the race after all.

He just could not bring himself to abandon the North on such a day. More important, he could not abandon Eclipse. As much as he wanted to see Van Ranst embarrassed, he knew this was no time to put personal feelings first. He had to swallow his pride. If Eclipse was in danger of losing, Purdy wanted to be ready to step in and try to save the horse's honor, not to mention the stakes. Eclipse deserved that much. It would be a shame if one man's silly error doomed such a splendid animal.

Purdy slowly went through the rest of his familiar dressing ritual, pulling on his white riding breeches and tucking the bottoms into his black riding boots. In the early morning silence, with the rest of his family asleep, his mind drifted back to his long life in the saddle. He had been doing this since he was a boy in Westchester County. He had dressed to ride hundreds of times — this would be the last time, for sure. Deep down, he hoped it was not in vain, hoped he would get the chance to ride Eclipse.

He grabbed his maroon riding cap and black whip and stuffed them in the pocket of his overcoat, then grabbed a cap and tugged it low over his eyes. He strode toward the ferry docks, obscure amid the multitudes headed for the course. Hat tugged low, coat covering his clothes, he spoke to no one and went unnoticed while crossing the East River on a ferry and sitting in an open-air public carriage during the ride from Brooklyn to Jamaica.

He could have taken off his hat and coat and identified himself as Eclipse's longtime rider, but he wanted no part of such attention now. He would have to explain that he was not going to ride today because Van Ranst had picked another jockey, considering a forty-nine-year-old a liability in a race in which the North had staked so much. What a humiliation.

Purdy's mind churned during the bumpy carriage ride. The people around him laughed and shouted, but he sat low on a backward-facing bench, shoulders hunched, eyes fixed on the floor. He gave no outward sign of the angst inside him. He reached inside his coat and fingered his cap and whip. People would soon know about Van Ranst's decision to snub him, and he hoped they would beg for his return. As angry as he was, he would be ready if they did.

Taylor and Racing Billy were at the barn, chatting with Otway Hare, president of the Newmarket track in Virginia. Jockeys and stable boys hustled through their morning chores, walking the horses in circles to warm them up and rubbing their legs. Everything stopped when Badger arrived and asked everyone to gather around. Speaking in dull, numbed tones, he told the story of finding Johnson in a miserable state.

Napoleon will miss the race, he said.

Taylor and Billy stared hard at Badger, hoping he was pulling a fast one; he could not have delivered more stunning news. Walden's mouth dropped open. None of the other jockeys and grooms said a word. A horse whinnied in the background, cutting through the silence.

177

Then Billy smiled. This was a joke, surely. But Badger did not smile back. It was no joke — Johnson was face down in bed. A spoiled lobster had accomplished what the North could never do — defeat the great Napoleon.

The southerners eyed each other silently, contemplating the task before them: they would have to manage their side that afternoon. Johnson would be unable to make any decisions regarding tactics. It was a crushing setback. Johnson always knew what to tell a jockey when things went wrong and when to make a decisive adjustment. His instincts were unmatched.

When Racing Billy commented that the South's chances had been dealt a blow, everyone nodded. But then Billy turned more hopeful, suggesting that Johnson's hands still lay on the reins of the challenge. Napoleon had selected Henry, a horse trained to perfection. He had nominated Walden and discussed tactics. Perhaps his presence would not be required because of the brilliance he had already shown.

The others nodded, wondering if such optimism was sensible or ridiculous. The southerners resumed their morning routine, faces grim now, confidence shaken. A pall settled over their camp.

Van Ranst was up early, as first light filtered through his cottage windows. He had not slept well in months, especially since his argument with Purdy. He was glad the race was finally here. A longer wait might have killed him .

He rose, dressed, and walked over to see Eclipse. The horse was relaxing in his stall, having just eaten his last meal before the race. The stable boys rose when they saw the old wizard, who nodded at them and walked into the stall. He patted Eclipse and nuzzled the horse's nose against his chest. I hope I have done right by you, old man, he thought. Eclipse nickered, pleased as always to see this man who patted him every day.

Van Ranst lingered with the horse for a few extra moments, then stepped out of the stall and gave his orders to the stable boys. Take the horse out and walk him in a circle for a while, then take him to the track and let him jog around the oval a few times. He would need every ounce of his bottom that afternoon. But he should loosen up beforehand.

After that, Van Ranst said, bring him back to the stall and braid his tail. Thousands of people would see him today. It was imperative that he look the part of a champion.

The stable boys scrambled into action. Van Ranst thought about choking down a quick breakfast, then decided against it. His stomach was in knots.

The barn housing the southern horses was on the road from Brooklyn to the Union Course. Fans heading to the race rode and walked past it all morning. Many kept going, but hundreds stopped to look at the finalists.

Henry, Betsey Richards, and Flying Childers jogged lightly on the half-mile grass track by the barn. Johnson had, of course, still not revealed which one would run that day. Even in the final hours before the race, his surrogates kept his secret. With exercise jockeys guiding them, the horses were galloped as if they would be the one to compete. Each looked fit, fresh, and ready. Henry skipped lightly across the grass, his nimble feet a marvel. The long-legged mare cantered elegantly, her head raised, intrigued by the commotion. Flying Childers covered ground with choppy steps The dark-skinned grooms showed each horse the same amount of interest. No outsider could discern favoritism.

Crafts lay in bed through midmorning, drifting in and out of sleep. He could not help it: he dreaded what was about to happen. As excited as he was to take part in the race, he had an ominous feeling. He finally rose when he heard stable boys shouting and Eclipse jogging outside his window. It was time to get up. He could not hide in his cocoon any longer.

His riding outfit was draped on a chair by the window. Van Ranst had given him a maroon shirt and cap, white riding breeches, and black boots — fancy stuff. Crafts was used to wearing faded work shirts in the saddle. Northern jockeys did not dress up.

Slowly he pulled on the shirt, the breeches, the boots. They were crisp, heavy, new, itchy — and too big for him. Crafts felt weighted down, out of sorts, in the outfit. He wondered if he were in a dream. Was this really happening?

As he dressed, he watched Eclipse through the window. The horse was jogging lightly on the grassy course, but even now, the exercise rider was plainly tensed, muscles taut, as he gripped the horse's flanks, trying to keep some control and not fall. Crafts knew what the jockey was feeling: a mild sense of panic. Eclipse was such a strong horse.

He thought back over the past two weeks. He had ridden the horse every day, but they had failed to form a bond. Van Ranst had implored him to try, claiming that Eclipse ran better for a rider he trusted. But the horse showed little affection for Crafts, obeying orders in a mechanical way. Admittedly, Crafts had not tried all that hard to form a relationship. He just rode and went back to his cottage. That was all he had ever done with any horse. Keeping a distance had served him well until now. But Eclipse seemed to want more.

Feeling vaguely like a clown in his clothes, Crafts took a deep breath, opened the cottage door, and stepped into the sunshine.

He had never been so scared.

Walden paced as he watched the crowds passing the southern barn on their way to the course. He had slept well the night before in the little outbuilding he shared with the other jockeys and stable boys. He was not overly nervous, not fearful of what the day might hold. He was upbeat, expecting to win. Having Johnson on your side tended to have that effect.

At dawn he rose and donned the sky blue shirt, breeches, and cap Johnson had given him. The clothes fit snugly, as if a tailor had cut them to his measure. The jockey knew he had never looked better, never felt better. He strutted over to the barn and went in to pat Henry. The young horse had risen from the hay-covered floor. Even he knew it was time to get going.

Walden patted Henry and spoke to him. Henry nodded forcefully and nickered. The horse was especially animated whenever Walden was around. Soon the grooms took Henry away to dress and braid him and prepare him for his morning run. The jockey had nothing to do until the race.

Then Badger arrived with the stunning news about Johnson.

Walden was standing at the back of the pack when he heard that Johnson would miss the race. His eyes widened. He took comfort in Napoleon's presence, as did the others on the southern side. They always felt they had the upper hand as long as Johnson was around. But to Walden he was especially important. The jockey had become the trainer's eyes and ears aboard Henry, a physical extension of himself. Henry had been their special project. But now Walden would have to go it alone.

When Henry was led to the training track for his morning jog, Walden came down and stood by the railing to watch. He played a mind game with himself, seeing if he could remember every piece of advice Johnson had given him. Start fast. Hold the lead. Be ready for anything.

Johnson's second-in-command, Taylor, sensed Walden's nervousness, saw that he had become pensive after seeming almost ebullient the day before. As a former jockey, Taylor could understand the feeling. It was a familiar predicament for a jockey; when something goes wrong, you still have to ride.

Taylor sidled up to Walden along the railing of the training track. Walden asked if anything was going to change because Johnson was absent. Would another jockey ride? Would there be a shift in tactics? Taylor smiled. Nothing would change, he said. Walden was still the rider, and Henry was still to start quickly, as Johnson wanted. Taylor told the jockey to take the reins with Napoleon's words ringing in his ears. Go fast. Henry had proved he had the bottom to persist after a hard-running start. The South could win that gamble. Walden nodded.

The morning went on and on. It seemed the afternoon would never come. Walden watched the endless stream of fans on their way to the course. He thought he had seen it all, but nothing in his experience had prepared him for this. The people just kept coming and coming, a sea of humanity stretching as far as he could see. Soon, he thought, all those eyes would be focused on him. It was enough to bring a man to his knees.

Stevens joined Van Ranst at their compound just before noon. He had tended to other race-related matters through the morning, trying to see to it that the course could handle the crush of fans. No one had expected this many people, more than could even be estimated. Stevens was shocked but thrilled — win or lose, the event was going to be a success beyond anyone's wildest dreams.

But to make sure his allegiances were clear, he was determined to walk to the race with Eclipse and Van Ranst and be part of the horse's grand entrance.

The group started down the road at noon, an hour before the race was supposed to start. The course was less than a mile away, but Van Ranst wanted Eclipse to be able to go slowly. The procession moved at a leisurely pace. Eclipse led the way, guided by stable boys holding lead ropes. Van Ranst and Stevens walked together behind him. Crafts brought up the rear.

Surprisingly, they were alone at first; the compound was on the opposite side of the course from the road to Brooklyn, now crowded with fans. But people saw them and began to swarm around as they neared the course. Northern fans shouted support. Go, Eclipse!

Somewhere a brass band began to play.

Johnson lay in bed, eyes closed, listening to the shouts of fans, a brass band playing, the grinding noise of thousands of people squeezing into a small space. He could hear it all easily, even though the Union Course was a mile away.

He had vomited countless times during the morning, filling a bucket the innkeeper had provided before leaving for the course. It was past noon now, and the sickness finally seemed to be abating. He had not picked up the bucket in half an hour. Not that he felt like jumping out of bed and running to the course. He was still weak, drained, and miserable from hours of purging. He would not be able to rise for hours.

But as awful as he felt physically, his mental state was even worse. Missing the race was the most depressing moment of his life. In the six months he had spent preparing for this day, calibrating the southern side of the challenge to a perfect pitch, he had never felt ill even for a moment. He felt young, fresh, and sharp. He had never imagined that he might miss the race. The bad luck was astonishing. Badger, sitting beside him at the dinner, had not eaten a bad lobster. He guessed that no other guests had either. Just him. Now the South had to win without him. He closed his eyes. His illness could decide the race. He hated to think it, but it was true. Taylor, Badger, and Billy were all astute horsemen, but he surpassed them all. That was just a fact. If the events of the afternoon demanded a change in tactics or a sudden and dramatic decision, the South would not be at full strength.

Lying in bed, he felt another wave of nausea begin to rise. He reached for the bucket. Just thinking of the undermanned South had made him sick.

Maybe his absence would not matter. Maybe Henry would blow past Eclipse and win by a distance. It was certainly possible, given Henry's current form. Johnson hoped that happened, but he was worried.

The southern inner circle gathered at the barn shortly after noon and began the short walk to the course. Slaves walked Henry, two in front and two in back, each holding a guide rope. Henry pranced, head bobbing. Badger, Racing Billy, Taylor, and Walden followed close behind, their confidence coming back as they watched Henry. What a specimen of youthful energy! Hundreds of southern fans walked with them, a strutting army of boasting escorts, pride swelling uncontrollably.

"Northern dreams die now!" one man cried.

"It is Henry for the South . . . and defeat soon for the North!" shouted another.

At last the fans had an answer to the great question that had loomed over the event since its inception. Some raced ahead, breathlessly announcing to others that Henry would race for the South. The news spread fast. Southerners standing outside the entrance erupted when they saw their entry nearing the course, the very sight of Johnson's sky blue colors stirring them to cheer.

"Henry it is!" they roared. "Beware, Eclipse! The boast of the South is upon you!"

The course was completely overrun. Fans took up every seat in the stands and almost every inch of ground inside and outside the dirt oval. Hundreds sat in the trees beyond the fence. If the mob grew any larger it would knock down the fence.

The noise was enough to make a man cover his ears. As northerners and southerners greeted one another, issued challenges, and arranged bets, every conversation amounted to an exchange of shouts.

"Even money, taking Eclipse!"

"Two to one and no less, foolish man!"

"What say ye, sir?"

"Three to one . . . and no less!"

The crowd was so great it spilled onto the dirt racing surface. As the start time for the race neared, hundreds of fans stood where the horses would run, the horde stretching a quarter-mile on either side of the finish.

The judges tried to clear the track so the race could begin on time. They brought in temporary peace officers who had been hired to patrol the grounds, but their presence failed to get people off the track. Then sheriffs came through threatening to arrest anyone who did not move. Few budged. The fans stood on the dirt debating odds and wagers. They were not about to clear off.

The southern fans cheered when Henry made it through the crowd and reached the start. When the shouts died down, Ridgely, the lead judge, asked the southern horsemen for help. Would it be possible to rear Henry into the crowd and help disperse these people? Badger nodded. By all means.

Henry was walked into the throng, and then the grooms holding his shank startled him. Already excited, the chestnut reared. That succeeded in scattering some of the fans on the track. They jumped over the inner and outer railings. Just as this happened, Eclipse arrived at the judges' stand, to roars doubling those that had greeted Henry minutes earlier. There was no doubt which horse was on its home ground. The judges asked Van Ranst if the northern star also could be reared.

The sight of both horses climbing into the air at the same time elicited the loudest cheer yet. What a show this promised to be!

When the track was completely clear, the judges went to work.
Eclipse and Henry were presented and inspected. A coin was flipped
to determine their placements at the start of the first heat. The North
won and would choose position first. The jockeys were then weighed
on the track scale. The judges made sure each horse was carrying his
assigned weight: 126 pounds for Eclipse and 108 for Henry. Each
jockey weighed less, so pouches filled with lead pellets were heaped
on each horse until the correct totals were reached. Eclipse stood impassively as almost thirty pounds were laid across his back. Henry
needed only a pair of pouches, weighing less than ten pounds. His
spirits seemed high as he skipped away from the judges with his ears
pricked, a sign he was ready to run.

Then Ridgely shouted, "Riders up!" — the traditional signal that
the race was almost ready to begin.

The southern managers helped Walden up and onto Henry. Van
Ranst's stable boys helped Crafts onto Eclipse. At first, no one noticed that the jockey wasn't Purdy. Many in the crowd were unaware
of the significance of the change. But then the more knowing fans began to shout. Where is Purdy?

Purdy was hidden in the crowd near the finish. He had not said a
word. With his hat still pulled low and a coat covering his riding
clothes, he looked like any other fan.

In the final moments before the start, the fans continued to bet,
never thinking their horse might lose. The horses galloped leisurely
through the finishing lane, loosening up for a final time. Fans hastily
compared them. Both were chestnuts with coats that gleamed in the
sun, a testament to their superb condition. Eclipse was larger, measuring more than fifteen hands at his withers, with hard muscles in
his massive chest and shoulders, strong loins, a long waist, and a
pounding, rhythmic running style. His only evident blemish was that
pouch of flesh hanging from his jaw. Henry, just under fifteen hands,
was more compact, but he bounded eagerly on muscular haunches.
With his taut barrel chest, he looked as if he could run all afternoon.

A groom walked Eclipse across the dirt to the inner railing, the
northern side's choice of a starting spot. After Badger, Billy, and Tay-

lor conferred, Henry was placed twenty-five feet wide of his opponent, closer to the outer railing. The shouts reached a crescendo, and then the noise abruptly fell away as the horses pawed the dirt, seemingly knowing what was about to happen. Amazingly, the enormous crowd that had been buzzing all day went silent.

A drummer climbed the steps of the judges' stand and looked out at the crowd. The creaking of wooden boards was audible in the hush. He paused a moment and raised his right hand, clasping a stick, over his drum. When his hand came down, the starting tap echoed across the grounds. The great match race had begun.

14

Good God, Look!

FROM STARK SILENCE, the crowd erupted in noise. Fans bellowed the names of the horses and urged them to run. Some whistled, others rang cowbells. The sound, a hungry, full-throated din, was destined to become an American staple, but this was the first time it was heard in any of the twenty-four states. The horses paused, plainly taken aback. They had trained in solitude for months. The noise was a physical assault on their senses, jarring, confounding, frightening. Both horses worked through it. Walden and Crafts jabbed them savagely with boot spurs and whipped them across the shoulders and neck. The message was unmistakable: get going! Eclipse and Henry snapped out of their reverie and remembered what they were supposed to do. They began to run.

Henry broke faster. In his first steps he resembled a hunting arrow released from a bow, hurtling through space. His back hooves dug deeply into the sandy loam, finding traction and sending a dirt spray into the air behind him. He bared his teeth as a wild animal might and lowered his head, steely eyes focused ahead. The thrashing from Walden surely hurt, but he savored the chance to run. He sprang forward, then sprang even faster, seemingly almost taking flight.

Eclipse was left flat-footed at the start.

Walden's mood soared. What a response from Henry! Sprinting for the first turn at an angle, veering in gradually with every stride, the horse approached full speed just fifty yards into the race. Walden dug his spurs into the horse's flanks, hearing Johnson's voice in his head: "Be aggressive. Henry is young, fresh. Eclipse is accustomed to leading. Take that away from him. Make him experience doubt." Napoleon had drilled all that into Walden's head the day before, convinced it would work because of Henry's natural exuberance and the noise the immense crowd surely would make. Henry was bound to be excited, probably too excited. Why not make the most of what would surely be a spectacular starting burst?

Walden wished Johnson could see this. Henry was three lengths ahead as he reached the first turn and had already moved from the outside to the inner railing. He leaned into the turn, a sweeping arc a quarter-mile long. The southern fans along the turn exhorted him: "On, Henry! On, boy!" Walden tugged on the reins and shouted encouragement. Henry accelerated yet again, tantalizing the northern fans. If they had expected another Sir Charles, lame before taking a step, or another Lady Lightfoot, aged beyond her best days, they were in for a surprise.

Eclipse was facing a challenge unlike any he had ever encountered.

Crafts was stunned. He had expected to have the lead. Van Ranst had told him to trust Eclipse, told him that the great horse always moved first. But Henry had left him in the dust.

Eclipse recovered decently enough, breaking into an acceptable run. But he was a step behind Henry, then two steps behind, then three as he neared the first turn. Crafts's vision of the race — leading early and facing a serious late challenge — was already wrecked. He remembered Van Ranst telling him about having to adjust to unforeseen circumstances, but he had barely listened. He had grown tired of being lectured by the old man. But here, in all its grim certitude, was an unforeseen circumstance.

The distance between the horses was four lengths as Eclipse came out of the turn and ran up the backstretch, a quarter-mile straightaway sprint. Crafts now had a perfect view of Walden and Henry, directly in front of him. That horse was a runner, no doubt about it. His legs blurred as he moved. His feet were quick. And the man on his back was obviously capable. Walden had settled into a rhythm, hands on the reins with a firm, underlying pull that kept Henry under control without quelling the urge to run. Crafts could see the Virginian was not going to give away the lead with some foolish blunder. He and Eclipse would have to make up the deficit on their own.

Crafts tried to establish control of Eclipse on the straightaway, but his pull on the reins was inconsistent — tug, release, tug, release. That sent mixed messages to Eclipse: Run! But wait! Run! But wait! Eclipse responded accordingly, rallying and then slowing, rallying and then pulling back. The result was disastrous. Henry moved farther ahead on the second turn. Five lengths now separated the horses. Eclipse, to the astonishment of his fans, was getting blown away like a leaf in the wind.

"He is to be distanced!" one northern fan cried.

Crafts tried to stay calm, but he knew this was all wrong. Eclipse had never been so flatly outrun. He knew the southern fans were elated, the northern fans surprised, Van Ranst shocked. And he knew he was the only one who could do anything about it. There was no hiding now, no cottage to retreat to. All eyes were on him and the horse beneath him.

Crafts had no idea what to do.

Coming out of the second turn, the horses dashed past a keen observer at the front of the crowd along the inner railing. Cadwallader Colden was from a family of scholarly New York politicians and doctors, but he had disdained those fields. At forty-nine, he was a horse owner and breeder, belonged to the NYAIBH, and knew more about racing than most northerners. Wry and well educated, he would write the definitive eyewitness account of this race, published seven years later as a 2,200-word letter to the editor of the *American Turf Register and Sporting Magazine,* a then-new racing journal. He signed it "An Old Turfman," seeking anonymity, but his pseudonym fooled few.

Colden watched on horseback, accompanied by a friend, John Buckley, a diminutive former jockey who was now a trainer. Buckley, also on horseback, and Colden were positioned where the straightaway dash for the finish began. Colden had selected this spot because he believed it was the most telling juncture of a race, where horses either accelerated or faltered with the finish in sight.

189

As Henry raced past him the first time, Colden was impressed, later writing that the pace "was a killing one." Colden had seen hundreds of races over the years, for he, too, had traveled through the South, mostly as a spectator. But he had never seen a horse as fleet as this one. What balance, what drive, what a turn of foot! Colden got a close-up look as Henry went by, eyes fixed on some distant point, a fearsome racing mechanism.

Could he keep it up? Colden wondered. Walden seemed to be in control, but the pace was alarming. Henry had hurtled past Colden as if he were about to finish the fourth and last lap of the heat, not the first. The time of the lap had to be a record, he figured. Although timekeeping at American racecourses was shoddy, a few instances of amazing speed had become legendary. Timoleon had once run a mile in 100 seconds. A Virginia horse named Sir Hal had won a four-mile heat in 7 minutes 42 seconds. Henry was on such a pace, Colden believed.

Colden leaned forward and looked left, craning his neck over the railing to see Henry finish the lap well ahead of Eclipse. Buckley said something to him, but the shouts of the southern fans around them made it impossible to hear. What was the time of the lap? Colden, alas, had given his watch to a friend seated in a stand at the finish. The friend could precisely judge when the heats ended and better calculate accurate times. Colden cursed. He wanted to know the time. But he did not need a watch to know it was breathtakingly fast.

There was little change during the second and third laps. Henry remained ahead by anywhere from four to seven lengths. He looked fresh, eager, ready to go even faster whenever Walden gave him the go-ahead.

Eclipse, lagging behind, seemed almost tired, and clearly he was bothered by the steady spray of dirt, kicked up by the front-runner, hitting his face.

Southerners screamed Henry's name. They seemed to believe they had already won. Their joy irritated the horrified northerners, who had no reason to cheer.

Van Ranst watched silently as the noise swirled around him. He was seated in the front row of the stand closest to the finish. He could not believe this southern horse, which just ran and ran as if it would never tire. His worst nightmare was being played out. Eclipse looked old. He should be at stud, not matched against a brilliant horse that was young enough to be his son.

The first heat had been a disaster from the start. And Crafts was not helping. What was wrong with him?

Crafts's mind wandered into dangerous places during the second and third laps. Nothing in his experience had prepared him for this. Eclipse was not the confident horse Crafts had ridden at Stevens's estate. The animal, unaccustomed to trailing, unable to gain ground, dirt hitting his face, was tense and frustrated now. Henry easily fended off all of his challenges, seeming almost to mock him.

Crafts was in over his head. It was time to admit it — a bad time, but time nonetheless. He had known it as soon as Van Ranst offered him the ride. What was the old man thinking? Billy Crafts was a small-time rider. Purdy was the better choice for a pressure situation like this. Eclipse had never lost a heat, much less a race, and tens of thousands of northerners had come to the course expecting him to win. Now, the horse was growing desperate, his stride becoming choppy, his breathing hurried. Crafts had no answers. He was no savior.

His panic swelled until finally, on the back straightaway of the final lap, three-quarters of a mile from the finish, the weight of it shattered him. The distance to Henry was not shrinking, and Henry showed no signs of slowing as he bounded through the dirt as if each step were his first. Eclipse had to go faster. Crafts, panicking, kicked the horse's flanks with his spurs, then pulled out his whip and began to thrash. It was a violent attack. A few spectators along the rail actually gasped. No one had ever seen the great Eclipse treated so cruelly. Crafts continued his assault as they moved up the backstretch.

Champion that he was, Eclipse responded. His head lowered, his stride lengthened, and he began to gain ground on the final turn. His massive muscles strained against his hide. His eyes blazed with determination. The margin between the horses narrowed to four lengths, then three.

"Look! Here he comes!" northerners shouted.

Crafts was in a trance, whipping Eclipse as if he wanted to put the horse to death rather than win a heat. The jockey's mind was blank as he drew back his whip and flailed it across Eclipse's right side while continuing to dig in with his spurs. A gash opened on the horse's side, sending a rivulet of blood down his flank. Another cut, surely painful, opened on his testicle.

Eclipse inched even closer to Henry, narrowing the lead to a length and a half as he came out of the turn and pointed for the finish, a quarter-mile ahead. But just as it seemed he was ready to rally dramatically to win the heat, he abruptly threw up his tail and flicked it twice — a sign that he was either too distressed or too tired to keep going. He had had enough. He was not going to make a run.

It happened right in front of Colden and Buckley. The former jockey leaned over amid the noise and shouted, "Eclipse is done!"

Crafts kept up his assault, struggling just to stay upright as his right hand worked the whip and his left hand clung to the reins. He did not have the strength to hold and direct such a powerful horse with one hand while keeping his balance. When Eclipse's tail went up, shifting the horse's momentum, Crafts came untethered.

"Good God, look at Billy!" Buckley shouted as the jockey flopped around on the horse, barely holding on.

Just then Walden turned his head around to check on his rival. He obviously liked what he saw. He had not used his whip or spurs at any point and surely did not need them now, with Crafts on the verge of being unseated. He maintained his firm, steady pull on the reins and was otherwise motionless, in sharp contrast to the flailing, flopping Crafts.

Incredibly, Eclipse continued to gain ground. The fast early pace had finally caught up with Henry, and he was unable to mount a driving kick to the finish. Eclipse closed to within a single body length as they passed in front of the first of the three stands perched along the finish. The fans stood, drawn to their feet by the drama. Some northerners had their hands over their mouths, aghast; they had never thought about losing. Southerners, meanwhile, all but danced in place, eyes shining as they shouted.

Walden's heart soared as he passed the second and third stands and bore down on the finish, represented by the small cupola along the inner railing in which the judges stood, overlooking the track. Eclipse was as close as he had been since the first hundred yards, but it was too late. Henry was clearly in front as he passed the judges.

First heat to the South!

Southern cheers echoed across the course as northerners stood solemnly, barely believing what had happened. Some did not even know the name of the horse that had beaten the great Eclipse and taken their money.

The judges soon announced the time of the heat, recorded by chronometer. It showed that Henry had covered the four miles in 7 minutes 37½ seconds — faster than Sir Hal's record. The watches of several spectators, including Colden's friend near the finish, showed it slightly slower, around 7 minutes 40 seconds, but that still beat the record. Henry had just run the fastest four-mile heat in American history.

Fans attending their first race did not grasp the significance, but those experienced in the turf knew they had witnessed a special moment. The suggestion that the dirt track would speed up times had proved remarkably prescient. Eclipse had taken eight minutes to complete one heat against Sir Charles six months earlier. His time today was some twenty seconds faster, yet he had lost. As for Henry, well, what could you say? Seven minutes and thirty-seven and a half seconds! Not even Johnson had thought that possible.

Shouting with joy, Badger, Taylor, and Racing Billy left their seats in the stand closest to the finish, jumped onto the track, and jogged across the dirt to the finish. Walden met them there, having stopped Henry, turned around, and brought him back to the judges. The jockey sat atop the horse, smiling as he caught his breath. He shouted that the heat had unfolded just as Napoleon said it would. Badger and Racing Billy smiled and helped him dismount. Taylor, ever the realist, commented that things had indeed gone well, but that poor riding had also done in Eclipse. He predicted that the North would change riders before the next heat. Their boy had been unable to control his horse.

As the crowd buzzed, hundreds of fans spilled back onto the dirt by the finish to stretch their legs. Southerners demanded their winnings from northerners who had bet heavily on Eclipse.

"Here is your money, sir," one erect northerner said dolefully, handing over a fistful of bills and coins.

The planter with whom he had bet smiled wickedly. "The pleasure is mine, I am sure," he said.

After a pause, the southerner continued, "I am now suggesting new odds for the second heat: six to four with Henry favored."

The northerner ignored the proposal, his optimism dashed.

Colden left his place near the second turn and made his way through the crowd to the finish. He wanted to see the horses. "Henry was less distressed than I expected," he later wrote. Eclipse, on the other hand, was miserable, with a cut on his right flank and a deep incision on his right testicle. The blood from both injuries flowed down his hind legs, coloring his white right hind foot. Colden understood why the horse, normally so gallant, had given up near the end of the heat, flicking his tail in defeat. He had been physically violated.

All over the grounds, packs of incredulous northerners gathered with glum faces. They sorted through the possible explanations for Eclipse's downfall. Perhaps he really was too old for this. Certainly, the Eclipse they knew would never throw up his tail and admit defeat on the course. But in his defense, he had absorbed quite a beating from his jockey.

It was beyond their expertise to definitively lay blame on any one factor, but they agreed that the callow jockey had not helped matters.

Van Ranst was ashen, speechless. Clearly, his decision to replace Purdy was a colossal mistake. Anyone could see Crafts was overmatched. The little jockey did not have the strength to control Eclipse (he had almost fallen off!), and he lacked the guile and expertise to beat such a formidable opponent. He rode scared. And he had sent Eclipse conflicting signals throughout the heat, keeping the horse from running at top speed until it was too late. That had cost the North the heat, Van Ranst was sure.

In fact, Crafts had erred repeatedly — getting beaten at the start, sending mixed messages, almost falling off, and, worst of all, abusing

Eclipse with his whip and spurs. Why, it was indecent to do that to such a splendid animal, Van Ranst thought.

The old wizard, alone in his misery, heard his name called and snapped out of his reverie. The voice belonged to Stevens, who was beckoning from the track, just below him. His presence was requested at an emergency meeting, Stevens shouted. Could he please step down and join the group?

The group of NYAIBH members included Stevens's brother, Robert Livingston Stevens, and his brother-in-law, Walter Livingston. Stevens had rounded them all up as soon as the heat ended. It was clearly time for drastic action. As Van Ranst joined them, Stevens said he had the utmost respect for him, but he spoke out of concern for the North's chances. There had to be another jockey on Eclipse; Crafts was not up to the job.

Van Ranst was not about to argue. He had never felt so low. His decision had jeopardized the North's chances. His instincts, honed by decades on the turf, had failed him miserably.

Stevens drove home the point. It was not just that they should consider making a change, he said, it was imperative that they do so. The fate of the North rode on their ability to adjust. Eyes downcast, Van Ranst nodded.

No one spoke for a moment. Finally Stevens himself asked the obvious question. If Crafts was off, who was on? Stevens shouted over to Colden, who was standing nearby eyeing the horses, and asked if Buckley was prepared to take over. Colden's eyes and mouth opened wide. No suggestion could have surprised him more. Buckley was five years removed from the back of a horse, Colden said. It was not possible.

Stevens kept thinking, eyes fixed on the dirt. Then he abruptly looked up. What about Purdy?

Everyone looked at Van Ranst. Stevens asked if Purdy could be persuaded to don the maroon silks and cap. Was there an issue between them that forbade it? Van Ranst shrugged. He had not spoken to Purdy, had no idea where the jockey was. Stevens said it was time to find out. Purdy was the answer; it was just common sense. Thousands of northern dollars had already been lost. The total could triple if Purdy was not found.

Walter Livingston said he had heard that Purdy was on the grounds. A northerner in the stand had said so, none too pleased to see Crafts on the horse for the first heat. The NYAIBH group had no idea if the rumor was true, but they quickly fanned out across the track, calling Purdy's name. Livingston headed from the judges' cupola toward the first turn, walking along the dirt. Stevens walked in the other direction, backward through the stretch, calling for Purdy as if he were a lost dog.

Purdy was packed into the shoulder-to-shoulder crowd along the outer railing not far from the finish, having watched the first heat without saying a word or taking off his coat and hat. His stomach was wrenched with conflicting emotions. He wanted Eclipse to win, being too fond of the horse to wish him anything less than the best. But he also wanted Van Ranst proven wrong for having bypassed him in favor of Crafts. He had thus watched the heat with a strange mixture of sadness and pleasure, feeling sorry for Eclipse but smug about Crafts's miserable performance.

But he had promised himself that he would not put his personal feelings ahead of the best interests of Eclipse and the North. He would answer the call if it came. And it came now, as Stevens shouted his name while slowly walking down the track. Purdy shouted a greeting in return and raised a hand. Stevens found him in the crowd and smiled. The fans around him turned sharply, astonished that a man in such demand had stood among them. Some northerners did not know who he was. Others knew well that he was quite possibly their last chance.

Standing at the railing, Stevens shouted that a change in riders was mandated. Would he take over? A maroon riding costume was waiting for him if he accepted the offer, which was made in humility.

Purdy hesitated, unable to help himself. It would serve the old wizard right if he turned down the offer and let the North crash. A question rushed to the tip of his tongue: "What does the all-knowing Van Ranst say now?" He had every right to ask, he believed. But he did not, keeping his promise to put the North first.

He did not know if he could change the outcome of the race, but he knew he would give Eclipse a better chance. He could not turn his back on the horse. He could not let his pride interfere.

"I accept your offer, sir!" he shouted crisply, cupping his hands to his mouth. "And, might I add, there is no need for a fresh riding costume."

Stevens smiled, anxious to get back and tell the others. But seeing how Purdy was dressed, he could not resist making a comment.

"Mr. Purdy, with all due respect, you are wearing an overcoat that is as suited to the task as a lady's Sunday dress," Stevens shouted. "Shall I get the costume?"

Purdy did not respond. He stepped forward wordlessly and, gripping a lapel with each hand, ripped the coat off his shoulders, revealing the maroon shirt and white breeches. Grabbing his cap and whip from the pocket, he tossed the overcoat to the ground and stepped toward the railing. The fans in front of him moved aside, clearing a path.

Northerners around him shouted his name. "Purdy is to ride!" they exclaimed, their hopes suddenly revived.

The jockey reached the railing and shook hands with Stevens. They eyed each other, their business now also the business of the entire North. Leaping over the railing, Purdy briefly glanced back to where he had watched the first heat. Northern fans caught his gaze and raised their fists. Purdy nodded, turned, and jogged up the track toward the finish. Throughout the sea of fans, northerners turned to their southern rivals and shouted, "Is that six to four for Henry still on the table?"

15

You Can't Do It!

HENRY AND ECLIPSE REMAINED on the track between heats instead of being led away to their barns, which were too far away. The judges gave the sides a half-hour to prepare the horses for the second heat.

Henry's grooms, directed by Taylor, walked him across the track and away from the finish. They held him along the outer railing and methodically sponged him right in front of one of the stands. Barely breathing hard, the horse gazed out at the noisy swarm of fans around him. His eyes danced, his ears flickered. He wanted to move. The grooms held on tight, reining him in. He was excited, not upset. Johnson's concern that he might lose focus had proved unfounded. Minutes after running the fastest four-mile heat in American history, he seemed eager to run again.

Some of the northern fans stared at him incredulously, wondering if he were some freak flying creature. They had briefly panicked about the possibility of the South running such an unbeatable animal after the *Evening Post* reported that Henry had run four miles in six minutes at Newmarket, a physical impossibility. The article had quickly been corrected a few days later, but now some northerners thought it had been right all along. How else to explain Eclipse's defeat? No mortal horse had ever come close to beating him.

Taylor directed Henry's bathing, barking orders at the slaves. Fill the bucket! Careful with the legs! Easy! Badger and Racing Billy watched, their mood euphoric. Billy lamented that Napoleon had not been present to see the record-setting heat, as it was his personal triumph. Badger agreed. Through the noise they heard John Randolph calling their names from the stand. They turned to him. The slender congressman smiled, shook his right fist, and shouted that their victory was nearly achieved. It was rumored that he planned to take his gambling winnings and sail for Europe by the end of the week.

Walden was sitting nearby on an overturned water bucket, a damp towel around his neck. The jockey's shoulders sagged; he was tired from having urged and guided Henry through the long, record-breaking run. But he was smiling inside, exhilarated about a performance he knew was flawless. He did not have to be told.

Billy approached, kneeled beside him, and told him to use the same strategy in the second heat, starting with that fast start, which had knocked Eclipse off balance. Walden did not stand or look him in the eye; staring ahead, he nodded vaguely, thinking he really did not need to be told any of this. Was it not clear that the same strategy should be used?

Still sitting on the bucket, the jockey heard a commotion followed by a burst of shouts and applause somewhere down the track. Squinting into the sun, he could barely make out a small man in a maroon shirt emerging from the crowd and hopping the outer railing. He wondered what was going on there.

Johnson was in agony — not from the lobster but from not knowing what was happening. He was still in bed, staring at the open window, trying to translate the sounds coming from the course. There had been a low rumble of noise until around one o'clock, the race's scheduled start time, and then cheers had suddenly soared and continued for around eight minutes. Johnson checked his pocket watch, which he had put on the nightstand. His frustration mounted. It was like trying to read the wind.

He figured the first heat was over. But how had it ended? The persistent loud cheers suggested Eclipse had won; he was, after all, running in front of his hometown fans. But then the cheers had abruptly

199

stopped, almost as if someone had cued the crowd. Did that mean Henry had won?

As another wave of nausea began to rise in his stomach, Johnson closed his eyes, cursed, raised his right hand, and pounded the bed once, twice, three times.

John Cox Stevens hurried back toward the finish, where the other northern managers quickly gathered.

"Purdy . . . is indeed . . . at the course," Stevens told them breathlessly. "He . . . has agreed to ride."

Purdy arrived moments later, having jogged up the track. He shook hands with each man, ignoring Van Ranst's gaze when their hands clasped.

The old wizard looked in disbelief at the jockey. Where had those maroon silks come from? Had a magician made them appear with a snap of the fingers? Or had Purdy worn them to the course even though he was not going to ride?

"We are . . . thrilled at your addition to our side," said Stevens, unilaterally assuming control. "Have you any ideas about how to approach the second heat?"

Purdy did. He said that while it appeared, alas, that Henry was naturally faster, Eclipse still had superior bottom. The North had to make the most of that.

Van Ranst interrupted, asking how Purdy proposed to do that.

Purdy gave the old wizard a murderous stare.

"The advantage will arise late in the heat," he said. "Henry likely will start fast again, the tactic having worked so well. But I will let him go and trail again without losing contact. Then, in the third or fourth lap" — the seventh or eighth mile of running that afternoon — "I will make the challenge. Henry should be vulnerable then."

Stevens could barely contain his excitement. It sounded like a brilliant plan, he said.

"The North is finally at full strength with your addition," Stevens said. "I hope it is not too late."

Purdy glanced at Van Ranst. Theirs eyes met. The old wizard looked away in shame.

* * *

Van Ranst left the knot of managers and strode over to Crafts, who was standing alone near the horse, whip in hand, unsure what to do. The jockey knew what the old man was going to say. He had watched the managers convene and Purdy arrive. He knew he was being replaced.

He listened numbly as Van Ranst thanked him in a monotone and sent him on his way. The old man sounded awful, Crafts thought. But the jockey felt worse. He was ashamed, utterly and totally humiliated. He had ridden like a lumberjack in front of all these people.

As soon as Van Ranst spun around and left, Crafts grabbed his jacket and whip and walked rapidly toward the entrance, head down, avoiding eye contact. He had no interest in sticking around to see how Purdy fared. He wanted out of here. He wanted to be as far as possible from the Union Course. This had been a nightmare.

A few northerners shouted obscenities at him, furious about having lost their bets. Crafts kept his head down, ignoring the abuse. A thousand thoughts collided in his head. A humming noise buzzed in his ears. He wanted to grab his head, scream, and run. But there were too many people in front of him.

He kept walking until he reached the front gate. Hundreds of late-arriving fans stared at him as he moved against the surge of the incoming crowd. Who was this little man in maroon and why was he leaving?

A few other fans shouted insults. "Our shame rests on your shoulders, sir!" one cried.

Once past the entrance, Crafts found the road to Stevens's estate and started walking. No one shouted at him anymore. Soon he was alone, in silence except for the sound of his boots crunching on the dirt road.

Deep inside, he was relieved.

Eclipse slowly came around during the thirty-minute break.

His grooms worked on him by the inner railing, near the finish. In the beginning, he had been in no shape to run again. His eyes were glassy, his breathing short, his mood somber. Blood trickled down his legs and pooled on the ground. The grooms salved and covered his cuts, holding him tight as he flinched. It was hard to believe this was the great Eclipse. Crafts had whipped him as one might punish a stubborn donkey.

In time, however, he began to recover. His resilience was remarkable. The grooms finished bathing him and walked him in a circle. After five minutes his breathing was back to normal, his eyes no longer glassy. His injuries, in truth, were not that serious — just cuts. The blood on his legs was gone. Showing life, he snorted and stomped when fans on the other side of the railing suddenly shouted about a bet.

He was going to be fine.

Purdy walked over to him, feeling responsible for his sad state. If only he had stood up to Van Ranst and talked him out of changing jockeys! Then he would have been on Eclipse for the first heat. The horse never would have absorbed the odious beating from Crafts. He would have won the heat.

Purdy patted Eclipse and nuzzled his neck. The horse, turning to see who was being kind to him, nickered, seemingly in recognition. Purdy spoke to him in the soft, soothing tone he usually saved for intimate moments in the stall. It was not too late, the jockey said. They could still win. It would not be an easy task against this great southern opponent, but it could be done. In fact, Purdy vowed, it would be done.

The mood inside the course was vastly different now. Northern fans, so cocky before the first heat, had quieted down significantly. Those around the finish watched Eclipse being sponged and walked. They fumed about losing money. They worried about their champion.

Meanwhile, southern fans strutted around the grounds like a pack of hungry roosters, holding wads of bills aloft and daring the northerners to take them on again. A few northerners cursed them rather than take on odds. With the sun now directly overhead, tempers were rising — sheriffs had to step in to stop punches from being thrown.

Hundreds of fans stood on the track by the first turn, having hopped the railing in search of room to stretch their legs. They kept their distance from the horses during the break, but they had to be cleared before the next heat could begin. They were enjoying the view and were not anxious to move. Ridgely did not ask the managers to have their horses rear again, but he sent sheriffs into the throng, threatening to make arrests. Slowly the crowd dispersed. After several minutes, no one was left on the track.

At last it was time for the second heat. Ridgely called out for the horses to approach. Walden and Purdy mounted and jogged over to the judges' cupola. Some northerners cheered when they saw Purdy, whose graying hair fell below the rim of his cap. Fans in the know tried to explain the significance of the change to those who did not understand. Word of the new northern strategy circulated through the crowd.

The jockeys nodded at each other, a show of mutual respect. Walden had never met Purdy, who seldom rode now, but he had heard of him and was not surprised to see him on Eclipse. Gosh, he looks old, Walden thought. But he was surely more adept than Crafts. This heat would be tougher, Walden figured, but he remained supremely confident. How could he not be after Henry's record-setting performance?

Purdy dismounted and stepped onto the track scale. He smiled at Ridgely, whom he had known for decades. Old as he was, the jockey exuded calm. He could have been shopping for apples on a Sunday afternoon. He had ridden in so many races that he was incapable of nervousness. Although he had never seen a crowd like this, he was not worried about it. He was focused on what he had to do once the heat began.

The scale said he weighed 20 pounds more than Crafts, but still less than 126. The judges tethered a pair of lead-pellet pouches to Eclipse's back. It was a break for the horse. Although he would carry the same amount as in the last heat, it was live weight now, able to shift, react, and think, as opposed to dead, pressing poundage.

"Riders up!" Ridgely shouted.

Walden and Purdy remounted the horses and guided them toward the starting posts. The crowd began to cheer. Henry took the inside post this time, his reward for having won the first heat. Walden brought him to a halt along the inner railing, near enough to the fans that they could touch him. Purdy stopped Eclipse twenty feet wide of the railing. Colden later wrote that he "attentively viewed Eclipse and was surprised to find that he had not only recovered but seemed full of mettle, lashing and reaching out with his hind feet, anxious and impatient to renew the contest. Purdy, having mounted his favorite, was perfectly at home, and self-confident."

The shouts of the crowd tailed away as the starter climbed the judges' stairs and stood on the cupola, right hand poised above his drum. After a dramatic pause, he brought down his hand, banged his instrument, and shouted, "Go!" The cheers instantly returned as northerners and southerners tried to drown out each other's voices.

Walden furiously whipped and spurred Henry, asking for another fast start. Again Henry broke sharply and gained the lead. Purdy, making no effort to match the pace, dropped Eclipse toward the inner railing and trailed by three lengths as they reached the first turn. Some northern hearts sank: Was this heat going to be just like the first? Purdy, however, was pleased. This was just what he had planned. He had told the managers this would happen, and he hoped they remembered. The harder Henry ran now, the less he would have later in the heat, when Purdy challenged. And this time there would be a real challenge, unlike the first heat with the hopeless Crafts.

Racing up the back straightaway of the first lap, Henry moved farther ahead than he had been at any point in the first heat. Twenty feet now separated the horses. Henry's muscles strained against his ribs as he bounded across the dirt. He ran effortlessly, wanting to go even harder. He looked invincible. Southerners rejoiced, convinced that victory was imminent. Walden glanced back as he rounded the second turn and briefly thought Henry might distance Eclipse and win in a romp.

But Eclipse was better than that — infinitely better. He was a champion, his bottom deep, his spirit always burning. He just had never been pushed this hard, that was all. He had to dig deeper.

And he did.

He began to rally as the horses came through the finishing stretch and started the second lap. Purdy tightened the reins, signaling it was time to run. There was no miscommunication this time, as there had been when Crafts was aboard. Eclipse, familiar with Purdy's smooth signals, lowered his head. His hooves picked up more dirt as he circled the course a second time. The twenty-foot margin became fifteen, then ten. The northern fans rose, hopes revived, voices raised: "Here he comes!"

Walden did not alter his approach. He knew only one way to ride: steady. He neither whipped nor spurred Henry, and he guided the horse with the same firm tug he had used throughout both heats. He did not look back, but he knew Eclipse was closing on him as he concluded the second lap. He could hear the northern roar growing, and he could feel the vibration of the other horse crowding him. The lead was down to one length,

Could Eclipse vault past Henry and take command? From the stands, Congressman Randolph's shrill voice pierced the crescendo of northern cheers: "You can't do it, Mr. Purdy! You can't do it!"

Purdy brought out the whip as he entered the first turn of the third lap, believing the race had reached a crossroads. Eclipse had rallied, but Henry was still ahead. Eclipse had to dig even deeper, Purdy thought, and it was up to the jockey to bring out that effort. But he had to be careful. Crafts had flogged Eclipse so brutally that the great horse had quit at the end of the first heat. Eclipse was in a precarious state. Purdy could not repeatedly crack the whip on him.

But Purdy understood Eclipse, and, more important, Eclipse understood Purdy. The horse trusted the jockey and was willing to take orders from him. Crafts? No. But Purdy? Sure.

Believing he knew exactly how to get the horse to respond instead of bristle, Purdy flicked the whip once, hoping to jolt Eclipse rather than discourage him. Crack! Then, after five more strides, he flicked the whip again. Crack! That was it. The whip went back under Purdy's arm. And sure enough, Eclipse began to charge harder. He advanced on Henry's outside flank until his nose pulled even with the front-runner's midsection coming up the back straightaway.

The race was on.

Walden brought out his whip for the first time all day, deftly maneuvering it into his right palm. He flicked it twice at the horse, and Henry responded, pulling ahead by a length as he rounded the second turn. But Henry no longer ran with an easy, freewheeling gait. Seven miles of hell-bent racing had taken a toll. When Purdy bore down, digging his spurs into Eclipse's side, the northern horse pulled closer. He crept to within half a length, his nose again parallel with Henry's midsection as they barreled up the finishing straightaway. Purdy had executed his plan perfectly to this point: after laying back early, he was set to charge now, just when Henry seemed on the verge of tiring.

The crowd's roar reached a new pitch, northerners pleading for Eclipse to keep coming while southerners begged for Henry to hang on. As the horses shot past the stands and completed the third lap, Randolph reprised his taunt: "You can't do it, Mr. Purdy! You caaan't do it!"

Eager to see the final lap, Colden and Buckley left their spot at the start of the home straightaway and maneuvered through the crowd to the center of the infield, where the crush of fans was not as intense. "We did so in order to obtain a more distinct view of the struggle for the lead," Colden wrote. "Everything depended on the effort of Purdy [and] well he knew it. His case was a desperate one, and required a desperate attempt."

Actually, Walden was the desperate one. Eclipse's relentless surge had intimidated him, shaken his confidence. Henry was in for a fight on this last lap — a fight with a great horse. It was time for bold action. Circling the first turn, Walden swerved Henry out from the railing and directly into Eclipse's path, cutting off the northern horse. They almost bumped. Some fans gasped. But the tactic worked. Purdy had to tug hard on the reins and move back and behind Henry, his nose almost nestled in Henry's tail.

The southerners cheered. Maybe Randolph was right. Maybe Purdy couldn't pass Henry.

But Purdy's years of experience had taught him to keep looking, keep thinking, and act fast. He saw an opening and quickly hatched a plan. Having failed to pass on the outside, he noted that the inside route suddenly was available, Henry having moved off the rail. Could he pass Henry that way? Running directly behind the southern horse, Purdy measured his chances, eyeing the dirt, the railing, and Henry. He felt Eclipse thundering beneath him, hooves pounding, still full of run. Knowing he could not hesitate for long — Walden might veer back to the railing at any moment, closing the hole — he decided it was worth a try. The risk was minimal; even if he failed, there was still time for another charge before the finish.

Purdy sent his fiercest message yet to Eclipse, flicking his whip twice. He thrust his spurs deep into the horse's flanks and used the reins to veer him toward the railing. There was no time to waste. He had to squeeze Eclipse into that hole on the railing and then get past Henry. It had to happen fast, now, instantly. Surprising Walden was essential if this strategy was to work, Purdy believed.

Walden, as it happened, looked back at the worst possible time, his chin touching his right shoulder as he tried to ascertain Eclipse's position. It was a fateful maneuver. Had he turned the other way, he would have seen Eclipse trying to go inside him. But turning the way he did, he briefly lost track of the northern horse. He turned and, seeing nothing behind him, felt a shock like a blow to the stomach. Where was Eclipse? The question jolted him and he lost concentration. His tug on the reins loosened. Henry took a halting step, then another.

That was all Purdy needed. He crammed Eclipse into the narrow space between Henry and the railing, shouted at the horse, and kicked with all his might. Go, boy!

The audacious move stunned Colden and Buckley, watching from the infield. Buckley stammered, "See Eclipse! Look at Purdy! By heaven, on the inside!" Colden feared for their safety. If Walden tried to move back to the inside, Henry would push Eclipse and Purdy into the railing and possibly over it. "I felt alarmed for the consequences," Colden later wrote.

But the pass was over in a heartbeat. Eclipse, reading Purdy's urgent signals, quickly pulled even with Henry. Coming out of the turn, they ran together for one step, two. And then Eclipse, with more momentum, bulled past Henry and broke into the clear.

Purdy had done it. Eclipse had the lead — his first of the day.

Walden was stunned. He had turned for a glimpse of Eclipse, and when he turned back and faced forward, the horse was ahead of him.

The southern jockey's mind jumped jaggedly as he came up the backstretch, dealing for the first time all day with running behind Eclipse. For the first time, dirt kicked up by Eclipse sprayed his face

— and Henry's. The jockey blinked and quickly rubbed a palm across both eyes. The horse flinched beneath him, a dangerous sign. This was not good. This was not in the plans. Johnson had lectured him about maintaining the lead, being aggressive, controlling Henry. Walden had followed those orders perfectly — until now.

Suddenly he was behind, and very much on his own. He could not recall Napoleon telling him how to proceed in this situation. Behind with a half-mile to go? Walden wondered if he should charge now and try to take back the lead or wait for a final run to the finish? He hesitated, not sure.

Northern cheers echoed across the grounds. Southerners fell silent, shocked by the abrupt reversal. Walden continued to hesitate, allowing Eclipse to gain ground. Purdy went to the whip again. Jolted, Eclipse pulled farther ahead of the now-struggling southern horse. Two lengths separated them as they entered the final turn.

Walden, finally spurred into action, was increasingly anxious. He took out the whip and cracked it. He kicked with his spurs, kicked again. Henry sped up and began to close on Eclipse. The noise of the crowd was almost loud enough to injure a man's ear. One newspaper later reported that the din "seemed to roll along the track as the horses advanced, resembling the loud and reiterated shout of contending armies."

Coming out of the turn, the horses and jockeys eyed the finish, 150 yards ahead. Eclipse was a length ahead, charging hard along the inner railing. Both jockeys flailed nonstop. Henry kept gaining, moving close enough to look Purdy in the eye. Two feet separated the horses. There was no margin for error. One hitch in a single stride meant defeat for either horse. "Although I had not a cent depending, I lost my breath and felt as if a sword had passed through me," Josiah Quincy later wrote.

Suddenly, Eclipse's firmest sense of resolve clicked in, as palpably as a bullet being loaded into the chamber of a gun. Purdy felt it beneath him. Sensing the challenge, the northern horse tensed and dug deeper. Purdy was elated but not surprised. He knew Eclipse would not let another horse pass.

Walden continued to work Henry furiously, needing to gain just a little more ground. Just a little more. Surely, the southern jockey thought, Henry would nose past Eclipse and reach the finish first. Both horses were running all out, and Henry was the faster of the two, wasn't he?

But Henry could gain no more ground.

Eclipse, muscles grinding, eyes almost wild with resolve, met his rival's challenge and threw it back. Racing past the row of stands with fifty yards to go, then thirty, then ten, Henry bounded wildly without gaining an inch. Eclipse held firm, springing across the dirt with Henry at his shoulder.

And to think it had been suggested he was too old for this.

Eclipse reached the finish first, passing the judges with Henry right behind him. Northern fans shrieked. Southerners kicked the ground. The race was even.

Some fans turned to their neighbors with puzzled expressions. How did that happen? It was bizarre, was it not? Henry had led for three laps and the start of the fourth, but Eclipse had somehow passed him and won. When did they change places?

Purdy's inside move would become the stuff of legend, a true-life racing fable. Most fans assumed that Eclipse had passed Henry routinely, on the outside. Few knew he had taken the lead on the inside, through an opening barely broader than his own frame. The vast majority of fans never saw it. The only eyewitnesses were those standing on the first turn, where it happened. Newspaper accounts published immediately after the race made no mention of the move, the reporters themselves apparently having failed to see it.

Not until 1830 did Colden, clear-eyed and authoritative (and citing Purdy), set the record straight, writing in his account that "hundreds" of people saw the inside move and "it is impossible I could be mistaken, notwithstanding the honest beliefs of some gentlemen to the contrary." Purdy's brilliance was confirmed for future generations.

Purdy brought Eclipse to a halt, turned, and rode back to the finish. He jumped off and wrapped his arms around the horse's neck. They shared a brief, intimate moment. "You did it, boy! You did it!" he shouted. Eclipse reacted to the encouraging tone. His ears went back.

Grooms grabbed the horse and took him away. The northern fans continued to cheer. Stevens and the other managers came racing across the dirt with smiles and open arms. They mobbed Purdy, slapping his back and shaking his shoulders. They seemed ready to toast victory now.

Stevens confessed that he had not seen the pass on the first turn, but he had been thrilled to see Eclipse in the lead coming up the backstretch, and he had known Henry would not pass back. Purdy, breathless, gasped that Eclipse had never been pushed so hard. The opponent was formidable, the competition close. But Eclipse had responded as a champion would, Purdy said. There was no end to his bottom.

They turned to listen when Ridgely quieted the crowd and announced the time of the heat: 7 minutes 49 seconds.

A roar went up. No one had ever imagined a second heat being run so fast.

Staggered, the southern managers gathered on the dirt as Walden leapt from Henry near the finish. They eyed each other as grooms led the horse away. No one was smiling now. They did not know what to say or think. What had caused the defeat? Had Walden blown it? Or had Eclipse just come on? The weight of Johnson's absence was suddenly profound. He would have known what happened, where to assess blame, how to respond. But he was not there.

Racing Billy finally broke the silence. He believed Walden had grievously erred in giving up the lead on the final lap. No jockey should allow that to happen. Walden was a decent rider, but it was time to give another the reins. Badger shrugged. He thought Walden was capable enough. He was not sure a change was needed. Taylor, a former jockey, did not comment. Otway Hare, the president of Newmarket, who had left his seat and joined the group, also did not speak.

Billy continued, saying it was inexcusable for a rider to allow his horse to be passed on the inside. Hare asked if indeed that had happened, having not seen the pass himself. Billy nodded. He had seen it clearly. He restated his position. Walden was a capable lad, but Purdy was obviously his superior. The South was at a clear disadvantage in the saddle. They had to narrow that difference or the stakes would soon be gone.

No one responded. Confusion reigned on the southern side. What should be done? Badger was not sure Billy was right. Who could replace Walden? The managers ran through their limited options. Charles Stewart, the slave jockey, was on the grounds and ready, but he was just fifteen, and putting him in now, with so much riding on the final heat, was asking too much. Johnson had brought several other Virginia jockeys, planning to give them mounts in other races during the meeting, but they were not as accomplished as Walden.

The managers needed Napoleon.

Hare tossed out a wild idea. What about putting Arthur Taylor on Henry for the final heat? Johnson's chief assistant was thirty-five years old and long retired from the saddle, but he had been brilliant in his day. He was a better choice than the others in terms of natural ability.

Hare looked at Taylor, who looked at the others, hoping one would step in and say that the idea was ridiculous. But no one stepped in, and Hare continued to implore him to take the reins. He had to do it, Hare said. Thousands of southern dollars were on the line. Walden could not match Purdy, but Taylor could.

Taylor demurred, saying he had not even been on a horse in months, and his last race had been, well, seemingly a lifetime ago.

Just then another horseman, a famous one, joined their circle. John Randolph had pushed his way down from his seat, recognizing that his opinion might be helpful with Johnson absent and the South's chances suddenly dubious. Racing Billy told the congressman they were trying to persuade Taylor to ride. Randolph nodded. He remembered Taylor winning on many of his horses in Virginia. He seconded the notion.

Taylor gave a wan smile.

Randolph unleashed a towering rhetorical volley. Focusing his renowned persuasive powers on Taylor, he stated that the issue was larger than the men standing there or the stakes on the line or the glory of the horses. The issue was the honor of the South itself.

After Randolph put it in those terms, Taylor had no choice. He did not want to ride and thought it was a bad idea, but he said he would do it. Racing Billy shouted. A groom was sent to find a sky blue shirt and cap. The groom soon returned with boots, breeches, cap, and jacket.

Racing Billy broke the news to Walden, who buried his face in a towel. He wanted to keep riding. He knew Henry far better than anyone. But what could he say? Johnson, who surely would have agreed with his assessment, was not there to protect him.

Taylor put on the sky blue shirt. The spectators around the finish watched the drama unfold and passed along the news, which soon circled the entire course: Walden was out and Taylor, of all people, was in.

The switch meant little to the northern fans. Arthur Taylor? Who was he? Whoever he was, he was no Purdy.

The southern fans laughed at the ignorance of the northerners. No Purdy? Please hold that thought and bet accordingly, the southerners said, for your Purdy just met his match.

A mile away, Johnson tried to make sense of the sounds. The cheers had risen, then fallen, then risen again. What the hell was happening?

He pushed himself up from his bed and staggered over to the window, almost doubled over. His damp nightshirt clung to his sweaty body. Chilled and weak, he gripped the window frame with both hands and looked out at the sunny scene. He felt faint, blood rushing to his head. His eyes scanned the countryside, searching for clues. He saw a road, a barn, a grove of trees. He saw the innkeeper's cow munching grass. But was there anyone out there with any news? Were people leaving the course?

He had no idea. No one was out there. The cow was not going to tell him.

Napoleon closed his eyes and pressed his forehead against the window frame. Losing the race was unthinkable. But not knowing was torture.

16

See, the Conquering
Hero Comes

THE HORSES AGAIN REMAINED on the track between heats. Grooms moved them away from the finish and sponged them down, pouring buckets of water on their backs and legs. Eight miles of intense racing, waged in bright sunshine, amid rattling swells of noise, had exacted a toll on both. Their ribs heaved as they drew choppy breaths. Their eyes lacked focus. Their bodies were so overheated that foamy perspiration kept rolling down their flanks during and after their baths.

Unlike the break between the first and second heats, when they seemed eager to run again, now they were plainly exhausted. Grooms tried to walk them in circles, but they initially balked and then began to saunter lazily. They wanted shade and food, not exercise. Forcing them to run another heat in less than thirty minutes seemed a cruel demand.

But run they would. For as much as they had exerted themselves in two heats, they had determined only that they were a dead-even match. They had seldom been more than a few lengths apart and were often close enough to run in each other's shadows. That they would push each other similarly through the final heat seemed certain. Though Eclipse was older and sturdier, and Henry younger and quicker, their overall abilities were amazingly similar. Henry had

213

run the fastest four miles in American history to win the first heat. Eclipse had become the first American horse to surpass 7 minutes 50 seconds in a second heat. The loser of each heat had pressed the winner all the way to the finish.

Now both were on unfamiliar ground. Henry, a racing neophyte, had never run a third heat. But neither had Eclipse, whose undefeated record consisted entirely of two-heat sweeps. The pressure on both was more withering than the sun. The third heat would decide everything — the $20,000 stakes, hundreds of side bets worth tens of thousands of dollars, bragging rights among northerners and southerners. Maybe even the presidency was on the line. The race seemed that important after the soaring drama of the first two heats. Perhaps the third heat would determine whether Crawford of Georgia or Adams of Massachusetts won the 1824 election.

If it boiled down to endurance over speed, Eclipse seemingly had the advantage. But months of bottom-building days had increased Henry's stamina, and as a son of Sir Archie, he was bred to excel at long distances. The heat was a fifty–fifty proposition.

Even the fans were exhausted, both sides having experienced wild emotional swings, joy and despair, success and failure, within the space of an hour. But they continued to shout, argue, bet, and, in a few instances, pray. Some put hundreds of dollars on the final heat. Those who had bet all they owned on the overall stakes waited nervously for the final outcome.

Southerners who had paraded noisily after the first heat now stood quietly. Northerners, having dealt with a stunning defeat in the first heat, giddily held up wads of money, believing the circumstances favored them.

Thousands of latecomers had crowded inside the fence in the past hour, leaving little room for anyone to move. Hundreds of fans jumped the railings and stood on the track after the second heat to stretch their legs. The front straightaway, where the race would be decided, was almost filled with people. Ridgely, believing the situation was nearly out of hand, tried to clear them off. But the fans' passions were inflamed, with money flying back and forth. Ridgely sent sheriffs into the crowd, but their threats failed. The fans refused to disperse. They did not want to push their way back into the sweating, shoulder-to-shoulder hordes.

Ridgely sorted through his options. He knew he could not ask the managers to have Eclipse and Henry rear again; the horses had already run eight miles, with another four to go. Nor did he want to start hauling fans away and throwing them in jail — he would have to arrest hundreds. Going to that trouble would delay the heat and possibly cause a riot.

Ridgely finally decided just to run the heat with the fans on the track. It was absurd, but what choice did he have? No race had ever been run in these conditions, in front of such a crowd. He just had to adjust and hope for the best. Surely the people would move as close as possible to the outside railing and not interfere with the horses.

Ridgely then decided to move up the start of the final heat by a few minutes. Even though the horses were tired and needed the break, it was time to get going. More and more fans were climbing over the railing to stand on the track. Knowing he could soon lose control of the situation, he shouted, "Riders up!"

Both camps were surprised by the early start; they had expected another five minutes. But they moved quickly. The grooms finished walking the horses, gave them final gulps of water, and handed them back to the managers and jockeys. Purdy jumped back on Eclipse and rode over to Ridgely's cupola. Badger and Racing Billy hoisted Taylor up onto Henry. Both horses looked better than they had when the break began. Their eyes were clear, and they had finally stopped sweating. But they did not have the spring in their legs they had had before. They walked more gingerly, the cool-down period having caused mild cramps. Neither would be setting any records in this heat.

Northern fans were confused by the sight of Taylor on Henry. Who was this guy wearing the sky blue shirt and cap? Younger southern fans also wondered, but the older southerners remembered him, his brilliance burnished into their minds. It had been years since he rode, but he had been a bold, intuitive competitor in his prime, the first to see openings and ride through them. His upper body was wiry and strong, and his hands were firm on the reins. Taylor's horses always knew what he wanted. He communicated clearly and forcefully.

"He was a rider equaled by few and surpassed by none," Colden wrote of him.

Now he adjusted himself on Henry, trying to find his bearings. He could barely believe this was happening. When was the last time he had competed in a race? He could not even remember. He fingered the reins, patted the horse, looked at the crowd. The touch and feel of the job were instantly familiar, but he was sure his physical skills had diminished, as Purdy's had. Taylor's hands were still strong, but his belly was soft. When he hopped off Henry and stepped onto the track scale, it registered 110 pounds — two more than Henry had to carry. Taylor looked at Badger and Racing Billy, who stood nearby. They shrugged. They were willing to give up two pounds in exchange for Taylor's expertise. Taylor wondered if Johnson would have made the same decision. Napoleon had obsessed over the weights of the horses in this race, believing the issue would prove decisive. He had discussed it endlessly with Taylor and the others. His entire strategy had been built around maximizing the difference in what the two horses carried. Would he have agreed to give up two pounds after all that? Two extra pounds on a tired horse running a third four-mile heat could set the animal back yards and decide the heat.

But it was a moot point now. Napoleon was not present to offer an opinion, and his surrogates strongly felt that the South needed a better rider to battle Purdy. That was that.

The jockeys greeted each other with wry smiles during the weigh-in. Taylor and Purdy had known each other for years. They had competed in the early 1800s when Purdy was traveling the southern circuit and had occasionally worked together after Taylor retired to become Johnson's assistant. Johnson used only the best riders, and Purdy had worn his colors. But the two were on opposite sides now, a pair of aging jockeys who had started the day on the sidelines and now were thrust into this duel. They were past their prime, their bodies thicker, their reflexes slowed, but they could still tap deep reservoirs of skill, as Purdy had shown in the second heat. Their presence gave the race a fitting final chapter. The best jockeys in each region were pitted against each other.

After Ridgely ascertained that the weights on the horses were correct, he presided over the starting rituals a third time. The horses took their positions, with Eclipse now back on the inside after winning the second heat. The starter's drum reverberated as he shouted, "Go!" Though the voices and emotions of the fans were nearly spent, they roared.

The heat began with a surprise. Purdy kicked Eclipse hard with his spurs while flicking his whip three times at the horse. Crack! Crack! Crack! Eclipse dug deeply into the dirt and accelerated sharply from a standstill, shooting out ahead of Henry. It was a sneak attack!

Purdy had devised the new strategy by himself, without mentioning it to the northern managers, who were busy congratulating themselves after winning the second heat. Sitting in some shade during the break, trying vainly to rest and relax, Purdy decided he should be more aggressive. Eclipse had more bottom, he figured, and while Henry was a dangerous opponent, the older horse was better suited to the extreme circumstances. Eclipse should take control right away, challenge Henry, make the younger horse dig deep just to keep up. Let him worry about catching us this time, Purdy thought. The effort might break the youngster.

Eclipse was three lengths ahead at the first turn. The northern fans howled with delight, for their horse had not led early all day. Taylor silently cursed. He had hoped, and halfway expected, to have the early lead, but now he had to adjust. He moved Henry over to the inner railing and followed Eclipse around the turn and up the backstretch. Purdy kept the pressure on, working the whip and spurs, seeking to move even farther ahead. The northern jockey was "evidently resolved to give Henry no respite, and to cause him to employ all his speed and strength without keeping anything in reserve for the finish," Colden wrote.

Eclipse, energized by the chance to cut loose, bounded through the dirt with renewed sparkle, looking nothing like an old man. His lead swelled to four lengths, then five. Taylor started to panic. Was Eclipse going to run away with it? The jockey had intended to conserve Henry for one major rally on the final lap, doubting the horse was up for much more. But he could not conserve anything at this pace. Worried about losing touch with Eclipse, Taylor whipped Henry once, twice, asking for a sprint. Both horses zoomed through the second turn as if the race were about to end.

Van Ranst smiled as he watched Eclipse dashing through the first lap, daring Henry to keep pace. The old wizard had sat gloomily in his seat for a half-hour after being publicly humiliated between the first and second heats. He had understood that it was necessary to replace Crafts and bring Purdy back, but he was furious that Stevens and the others had ignored him and taken over the management of his horse. For months he had carefully guided Eclipse's training by himself. And he owned the horse! His pride was so injured he had been unable to shake his sadness, even during the second heat when Purdy rallied Eclipse to win. But the cloud was lifting now. His beloved horse was putting on a remarkable show. Who said he was too old? Look at him go! He was going to beat those damn planters and win the purse! Van Ranst could not help but be inspired. Eclipse was his horse, and no other man's horse was faster.

Van Ranst rose from his seat and shouted as Purdy guided the majestic animal past him, heading for the finish. Go, boy! Show the world! Boot those planters out of here by the seat of their pants!

Henry began to gain ground through the run to the finish of the first lap. Taylor's urging helped but, more significantly, Purdy had pulled Eclipse back to a more modest pace. Three miles of running remained, the jockey knew, and no horse could keep up an all-out sprint for that long after having run so far already. Purdy tightened his grip on the reins, signaling to slow down. The fast start had accomplished what he wanted: Eclipse had control of the heat. Though surely disappointed, the horse followed the new orders without complaint, his neck rising as he eased.

Taylor was relieved to see Eclipse slow down in front of him. He did not want to keep pushing Henry so hard, and now he had an excuse. He had been using the whip, trying to stay in touch with Eclipse, but now he tucked it under his arm. He was happy to settle in four or five lengths behind Eclipse as long as the margin did not increase. He would make his run at the end, as planned.

Reaching the end of the lap, Eclipse and Purdy encountered a totally unexpected scene. So many fans stood on the track that it was almost entirely blocked. The only opening was a sliver of dirt along the inner railing, just wide enough for a horse to get through. Purdy almost came out of his saddle. What were these fools thinking? He slowed, fearful of running someone over, but he could not avoid riding into a line of fans pumping their fists and shouting at him. The scene was reminiscent of an earlier era of American racing, when rowdy crowds of colonists had surrounded wild-eyed horses running quarter-mile path races at county fairs. These fans were so close that some could have reached out and slapped Eclipse or Purdy. Fortunately, they did not. But Purdy felt Eclipse tense up, clearly frightened, having never experienced anything like this. The horse's eyes widened. Purdy worried that he might stop running altogether or bolt away at an angle, leaving the race. What a terrible ending that would be. Purdy fiercely gripped the reins.

Henry, five lengths behind, followed Eclipse into the mob. Taylor was more concerned than Purdy about his horse's reaction, for Henry was younger, less savvy, harder to predict. Napoleon had fretted for months that the horse lacked the necessary concentration to compete in front of a noisy crowd. Now the horse was in the midst of the crowd! Taylor, like Purdy, felt his animal tense, seemingly fearful of what might happen next. The jockey yanked the reins and kicked with his spurs, seeking to keep Henry's mind on the business at hand. Keep running! Go!

Amazingly, both horses kept going, squeezed through the crowd, came out the other side, and continued to run, with the same gap separating them. The bizarre interlude had surely affected the horses, but it had not significantly changed the race.

Purdy sought to reestablish a faster pace. Taylor followed. The horses raced around the first turn and through the back straightaway some five lengths apart, matching steps. Horsemen on both sides marveled at their ability to race so hard after covering nine miles and then encountering fans in their way. The pace was astounding given those conditions.

Eclipse sprinted. Henry dug in. They maintained their positions through the rest of the second lap and again plowed through the fans at the finish, more accepting of the experience this time, having survived it once. The fans still shouted and closed in on them, faces purple, voices hoarse, but neither horse tensed, and Purdy and Taylor no longer worried that they would bolt.

During the third lap Eclipse remained some five lengths ahead. Taylor was pleased, believing the pace would allow Henry to charge late. But Purdy too was pleased, figuring that his horse would be able to charge harder. At the end of the lap the horses once again had to push through the mob. They made it through cleanly, came out the other side, and began the final lap. Neither had much left to give. They had raced eleven miles, trading the lead, with the sun and noise hammering down and fans screaming in their faces. They had never experienced such an assault on their senses, or such exhaustion. Fear shone in their eyes. They were crossing a line, racing beyond their limits. They had been pushed too hard for too long. But they were trained for this, and they continued to run as the great swarm of people at the course loosed a roar loud enough to shake a man's faith. Who had ever heard such noise?

Rounding the first turn, Taylor started pumping Henry, bringing the whip down on him once, twice, three times. Go faster, boy! It's now or never! The horse got the message. After the lull of the past two laps, he was pleased by the chance to sprint again. Fighting through his exhaustion, he kicked his legs out as far as they could go, as if trying to fly over as much dirt as possible. His pace quickened. Taylor was thrilled. Henry's powers of acceleration were still functioning. There would be a hard run to the finish.

The distance between the horses began to shrink as the horses charged up the back straightaway a final time. Four lengths separated them. Then it was three lengths. Henry crept closer and closer as Eclipse maintained his modest pace. Purdy remained motionless. The horses curved into the final turn, with a half-mile remaining. Southern fans raised their arms and yelled at Henry. Eclipse is fading! Just a few more yards to go! The southern horse kept coming on the turn. The lead was down to two lengths, then even less. Northern fans shrieked at Purdy, who seemed not to know that the other horse was gaining. Do something, Purdy! Don't just sit there, man!

Rolling out of the turn, the horses pointed for the finish. Each stride brought Henry closer, his head bobbing at Eclipse's midsection, and then his neck. Taylor's heart soared. This was going to happen, he thought. He would pass the tired Eclipse in two or three strides.

But then, abruptly, Purdy whirled into action. He jabbed his spurs into Eclipse's flanks and jabbed again. He had waited all along for this moment, planning to make the charge now, in sight of the finish. The jolts jarred Eclipse, but the horse didn't protest. He responded, taking longer strides, matching Henry's charge. His slim lead held through an agonizing pair of steps.

Then Henry faltered.

Fifty yards from the finish, running almost in tandem with Eclipse, the southern horse reached his breaking point. His fans were bellowing, calling his name, pleading for him to catch Eclipse, finish the rally, and win the stakes. But Henry took a hitched step, awkwardly kicked the dirt, and started to fall back. Eclipse pushed ahead with thirty yards to go, then twenty. It was all over suddenly. Daylight opened between the horses. The urgency drained from Henry. He had nothing left. His final steps were heavy-legged, as if the weight on him had suddenly been doubled.

The fans on the track pulled back this time, apparently grasping that they needed to stay out of the way. The race was on the line.

And then it was over. Eclipse reached the finish first, a full length ahead as he flashed past the cupola. The North had won.

Conflicting emotions rolled though the course. Northern fans raised a racket, slapping each other's backs and shouting the names of Eclipse and Purdy. Southerners went silent, stunned by the finality of the result. The infernal Yankees had beaten them again. It was hard to believe, even harder to accept. How could they lose when they were the superior horsemen, the shrewder breeders, the real experts? How could all that not translate to victory?

The northern fans quickly pulled the southerners' moods even lower, demanding payment on debts owed. All over the grounds, southerners dug into their pockets, pausing, still not believing. For those who had lost their heads and bet too much, the defeat was crushing.

Purdy brought Eclipse to a halt, turned, and jogged back to the finish. The fans on the track were joined by hundreds of others who jumped the railing and raced to put a hand on the winner. Eclipse's grooms grabbed him and led him to the cupola, where the judges declared him the victor. The time of the third heat, they announced, was 8 minutes 24 seconds — 46½ seconds slower than the winning time of the first heat, a testament to the horses' exhaustion.

Van Ranst leapt from his seat and raced across the dirt. He bulled his way through the crowd and came up to Eclipse and Purdy. The horse was weak, almost shaking. Van Ranst hugged him and barked at a groom to bring water. The old wizard was the only one of the northern managers who was thinking of the horse. Purdy looked down at him. Their eyes met. They smiled.

In the end, the great horse they shared had brought them back together.

A brass band struck up "See, the Conquering Hero Comes," from a famous Handel oratorio. Northern fans crooned the well-known chorus, their voices wafting across the Jamaica plain: "See, the conquering hero comes, sound the trumpets, beat the drums!"

The southern fans watched sullenly. Badger and Racing Billy wordlessly shook Arthur Taylor's hand when he jumped off Henry. The old jockey had almost — but not quite — pulled off a victory.

John Randolph stood alone in the grandstand, speechless for once.

A mile away, sweaty with fever and back in bed, William Ransom Johnson heard the brass band through his window. He knew what it meant, and his heart sank.

17

Ours Was the Best Horse

EVEN BEFORE THE BRASS BAND had played the last note of its tribute to Eclipse, Flying Childers was sprinting toward Brooklyn, his rider urging him down dirt roads with a steady whipping. It took him less than a half-hour to race from the Union Course to the foot of the Liberty Pole, where the rider announced that Eclipse had won. Up the pole went a white flag signifying victory for the North.

Hundreds of New Yorkers had gathered around the pole, awaiting the flag raising. They cheered the sight of the white flag and began to celebrate. Applause also sounded across the East River at the Fulton Market, which had advertised its view of the pole. Another flag signaling the northern victory soon flew over the Bank Coffee House.

The news quickly spread through the city, happily ending what had been a long, tense afternoon. Earlier, John Pintard had sent a young relative named Andrew to the East River to scrounge for information from ferry operators. "I almost palpitate. What an old foo!" Pintard wrote in his diary while waiting. At four o'clock he added, "Andrew has returned. Huzza for New York! Thus settles the account of the ancient dominion."

The *Evening Post* published a truncated description of the race in a second edition of that day's paper. A reporter who had been at the course returned to the city in William Niblo's carriage, scribbling an account that he handed to editors when he reached the newspaper office. "We have at this very moment received the following letter from a gentleman at the course, which can be relied on as perfectly accurate," the editors wrote at 4:30 P.M.

The nameless reporter wrote:

I dispatch this by Mr. Niblo's Express to inform you that, at one o'clock on this day, the great match race took place between Eclipse and Henry. About ten minutes past one, both horses set off in fine style. Henry, taking the lead and keeping ahead, came in ahead. Time of the first heat: seven minutes and 40 seconds. Eclipse then took the second and third heats. Time of second heat: seven minutes, 49 seconds. Victorious Eclipse was then marched off the field, followed by an immense cavalcade of gentlemen on horseback, to the popular 'See the conquering hero comes.' Thus has ended the greatest race ever run in this country, and the result has shown that the challenge may be again fearlessly repeated: Long Island Eclipse against the world!

All evening impromptu celebrations sprouted in bars, taverns, and homes across the city. Fans just returning from Jamaica recounted the drama to those who had missed it, eyes wide as they described the great crowd, the ear-splitting noise, and the heroism of Eclipse and Purdy — and Henry, too.

Reaction among the thousands of southern visitors in New York spanned the emotional spectrum. Some just gathered their belongings and left town, choosing to start the long trip home rather than witness the northerners celebrating. Others swallowed their pride and waded into the enemy camp with a smile and, in some cases, an offer to buy drinks. A few took out their frustrations, taunting the winners and picking street fights.

It was a loud night across New York.

An hour after the race, Badger and Racing Billy knocked on the door of Johnson's room and poked their heads inside. Napoleon was just where they had left him, in bed, looking pale. But he stared back at them with sharp eyes, not the glazed-over slits of that morning. He was recovering.

Badger and Billy did not have to say a word. Their dour expressions told Johnson which side had won. Johnson already knew, anyway. A brass band would not have played for so long and with such obvious joy after a southern victory.

Badger finally asked if Johnson wanted to hear the sad details. Napoleon nodded. He was, in fact, quite anxious to hear. Badger sat at the foot of the bed and slowly recounted the afternoon's astounding ebb and flow — Henry's spectacular first heat, the substitution of Purdy for Crafts, Eclipse's decisive inside pass late in the second heat, the substitution of Taylor for Walden, the surge of spectators onto the course, and the drama of Henry's failed final charge.

When Badger finished, a silence enveloped the room. Napoleon did not know where to begin. America's most knowing, accomplished horseman was shocked by the afternoon's developments. Henry had run the fastest four-mile heat in American history and still lost the stakes? Taylor, not Walden, had ridden the deciding heat for the South? And the horses had been forced to run through spectators in the final heat? What on earth?

Now Napoleon spoke as the others listened wordlessly. He was enormously proud of Henry. The time of the first heat was astonishing. Walden had obviously heeded his instruction to go fast. It would be years before another horse ran four miles so quickly. That was some consolation. But the overall defeat was crushing. Bitter medicine. It should not be blamed on Badger and Billy and their decision to replace Walden. Napoleon liked Walden, but Taylor was magnificent and surely the South had put forth its best effort. On the other hand, it was unsporting and unfair that the final heat had been run with fans on the course. Their presence was doubtlessly more upsetting to a young horse such as Henry than to a veteran such as Eclipse. It was typical of the pitiful caliber of northern racing that such outrageous conditions had been tolerated. One would never see fans on the track at Newmarket!

Having vented his fury, Napoleon suddenly closed his eyes and sank back into his pillow. He was still weak, still battling waves of nausea. He mumbled thanks to his visitors for bringing him the news, as sad as it was, and then motioned for them to leave. Badger and Billy crept out of the room as the sounds of the thousands of fans leaving the Union Course wafted through the open window. Johnson, his mind in a haze, began plotting his response.

That evening Niblo put on another sumptuous dinner in the tent adjacent to the Union Course. The northern and southern managers sat down with judges, jockeys, officials, and friends as the sun set. A sociable tone prevailed. It was as if that afternoon's intense competitiveness was a tide that had temporarily ebbed.

After dinner the tables were cleared and the toasting began. Judge William Van Ness, president of the NYAIBH, rose and raised his glass: "To Eclipse — still the best courser of his day." Everyone raised a glass and drank.

A southern planter named Emmet spoke next: "To Henry, the best four-year-old in the country." Horsemen from both sides nodded.

Then a northerner named Barnum spoke with his glass raised: "To our opponents of the South — gentlemen in prosperity and in adversity."

John Cox Stevens rose next. "To the better health of William Ransom Johnson," he said, "the trainer of the first four-year-old to run a four-mile heat in seven minutes and forty seconds."

A southerner named Field toasted "the spirit and emulation and liberality and magnanimity of our rivals of the North."

Back and forth it went. After a northerner toasted "the New York Association," a southerner raised his glass to "southern pluck and northern bottom."

Nathaniel Coles, the Long Islander who had bred Eclipse, said, "Since we good friends have met here, let us drink to the success of the turf, the only means of promoting the breed of fine horses."

Isadore Hone, a prominent New York auctioneer whose brother, Philip, would become mayor of the city, recited a poem: "Let others praise the rising sun, we worship that whose race is run."

Van Ranst stood, drink in hand, and said, "To the turf, may it continue to have its zealous votaries."

A Virginian named Wyche followed: "To the state of New York — unrivaled in her population and in her enterprise for internal improvements, and, so far, victorious on the course."

Standing next was Purdy: "To Eclipse! Too fast for the speedy and too strong for the stout."

After Purdy, Charles Ridgely took a turn. "To the conqueror and the conquered — neither needs praise," he said.

After a final toast saluting Van Ness and the NYAIBH, the men shook hands and departed in their carriages. Packs of fans remained at the course, and the road to Brooklyn was still hopelessly clogged eight hours after the race. It would take all night for the crowd to disperse.

Johnson awoke in a hateful mood the next day. His stomach was fine, but losing to the North sickened him more than any spoiled lobster could. Handing over $20,000 to Stevens, Van Ranst, and the others was unpleasant enough, but listening to them brag about Eclipse was worse — more than he could stand.

Burning with thoughts of revenge, he grabbed a quill pen, sat down at the wooden desk in his room, and furiously scrawled a letter to Stevens, proposing yet another race that, he believed, would restore the South's honor. Deep lines creased his forehead as he wrote with bold strokes.

Long Island, May 28, 1823

To John C. Stevens, Esq.

Sir: I will run the horse Henry against the horse Eclipse at Washington city, next fall, the day before the Jockey Club purse is run for, for any sum from $20,000 to $50,000; forfeit $10,000. The forfeit and stake to be deposited in the Branch Bank of the United States at Washington, at any nameable time, to be appointed by you.

Although this is addressed to you individually, it is intended for all the bettors on Eclipse, and if agreeable to you and them, you may have the liberty of substituting at the starting post, in place of Eclipse, any horse, mare, or gelding, foaled and owned on the northern and eastern side of the North River; provided I have the liberty of substituting in the place of Henry, at the starting post, any horse, mare, or gelding, foaled and owned on the south side of the Potomac. As we propose running at Washington city, the rules of that Jockey Club must govern, of course.

I am respectfully yours,
William R. Johnson

It was not Napoleon's finest hour. He was widely respected for his sportsmanship, but, perhaps owing to his recent illness, this proposal was anything but sporting. Not only did the South have far more territory from which to choose horses — all of the South and West, as opposed to a strip of Long Island for the North — but Washington was much closer to Virginia than to New York, and the course's scale of weights was better suited to a young horse such as Henry. The conditions plainly favored the South.

Stevens received Johnson's letter that afternoon at the Union Course, where the racing meeting had resumed. He conferred with Van Ranst and quickly wrote a reply.

Dear Sir:

The bet just decided was made under circumstances of excitement, which might in some measure apologize for its rashness, but would scarcely justify it as an example; and I trust the part I took in it will not be considered as a proof of my intention to become a patron of sporting on so extensive a scale. For myself, then, I must decline the offer. For the gentlemen who with me backed Eclipse, their confidence in his superiority, I may safely say, is not in the least impaired. But even they do not hesitate to believe that old age and hard service may one day accomplish what strength and fleetness, directed by consummate skill, has hitherto failed to accomplish.

For Mr. Van Ranst I answer, that he owes it to the association who have so confidently supported him, to the State at large, who have felt and expressed so much interest in his success, and to himself as a man, not totally divested of feeling, never, on any consideration, to risk the life or reputation of the noble animal whose generous and almost incredible exertions have gained for the North so signal a victory, and for himself, such well-earned and never failing renown.

I remain, sir, your most obedient servant,

John C. Stevens

It was a magnificent response, gently putting down a challenge that had obviously been made in desperation. There would be no rematch. Stevens and Van Ranst knew they had pushed Eclipse to his limit, if not beyond it, in the match race, just as the old wizard had feared. He was not about to push his luck again. Eclipse had ventured onto the turf for the last time.

Johnson's proposal and Stevens's reply eventually were reprinted in newspapers across the country. The *New York American* commented:

The proposition is denied not from any want of confidence in the superiority of Eclipse, but from a sense that his well-earned reputation should not be exposed to even the possibility of diminution. Eclipse is nine, Henry but four; the difference in weights is six pounds greater in Washington than here; and Henry is improving while Eclipse is at least stationary. We do not undervalue the southern horse, but although we do not doubt Eclipse can beat him even with the advantages spoke of, the distance to travel, the possibility of accident and the uncommon properties of Henry as a young horse warrant a hesitation in accepting.

The North's refusal to submit to a rematch infuriated southerners. Their magnanimous toasts and generally civil behavior in New York after the race belied their true opinion: that bad luck, not Eclipse, had beaten them. Back on home soil, they quickly erected a bonfire of excuses and rationalizations. If only Johnson had not fallen ill and missed the race. If only John Richards had not bruised a heel. If only the fans had not been on the track during the final heat. If only Purdy had ridden for the South, which a high fee might have tempted him to do. If only the Yankees would let Henry and Eclipse race again.

Admit defeat? Never.

Johnson himself, in a letter to the *Virginia Times,* wrote: "Had we an open course to run upon, and not upon the crowd, as was the case, we should have beat the race, as ours was the best horse." This attitude angered New Yorkers. The *Evening Post* wrote:

We are surprised, we must confess, to find such a letter making the rounds. We are sorry any thing should have been thrown out to disturb the good feelings which were apparently manifested by the friends of both horses, or to create any suspicion that the race was not fairly run. The course, we are free to admit, was not as clear as we could have wished, but it is denied in the most direct manner that this prevented Henry from winning. If he was the best horse, how did it happen that in the third heat, he never once in four miles came close enough to touch Eclipse even though he made repeated dashes?

Back came a southern reply in the *Baltimore Federal Gazette:* "Had Henry not carried 12 pounds beyond what his age and general sporting regulations justify, he would have distanced Eclipse in the first heat." The *Baltimore Patriot* commented, "We are heretic enough to believe that if Purdy had ridden him, Henry would have won."

In response, the *New York Spectator* wrote, "We have no doubt that our southern friends believe Henry ought not to have been beaten. It is very natural that they should think so. But the truth is they did not know the power of Eclipse. Henry was fairly beaten, and here we think the matter ought to be put to rest."

The rest of the Union Course meeting belonged to the South, although the victories only added to the southerners' frustration, emphasizing the superiority they believed they held over the North. On Wednesday, the day after the great race, Betsey Richards easily defeated Eclipse's full younger brother in a four-mile event, winning the first heat by four lengths and the second heat by two hundred yards. Then, after rain postponed Thursday's race, the South won two events on Friday. Flying Childers won a three-mile event in successive heats over a northern colt named Slow and Easy. In a two-mile event that followed, Johnson, obviously to make a point, entered Henry against a pair of northern horses. Racing superbly just three days after the great race, Henry fended off a challenge late in the first heat to win by several lengths, then distanced both horses in the second heat. The southern fans on the grounds shouted that they would like to see old Eclipse try to match that success.

Henry's victory ended the meeting. The North had won just one race — but it was the one that counted.

"Our southern competitors have shown no lack of knowledge or judgment," the *Evening Post* conceded. "They have indeed lost the match race, but they have won all three purse races, amounting to $1,900. This was to be expected. They have had six months to search the whole southern country for first-rate horses, and try their speed and bottom against each other in order to find one to contend with Eclipse." The left-handed compliment did not make the southerners feel any better.

* * *

John Randolph was a more gracious loser than most southerners. On Tuesday morning, before the race, he had told friends it was a good day to hold a presidential election because so many people from so many states would be present. When asked about his idea that evening, he said, "I'm relieved my proposition was not acceded to, for if an election had taken place today at the Union Course, Purdy would have been elected president."

The Virginia congressman lost more than most on the event — a $1,000 personal bet, a portion of the $20,000 stakes, and a trip to Europe. But he did not complain as bitterly as Johnson and the other southerners. He did say in a speech that "lobsters did in the South," but he also paid Purdy perhaps the greatest compliment ever accorded an American jockey, praising him in a speech on the floor of Congress:

> I call the attention of the House to a man who knows, in his vocation, no superior. He was the last and only hope of the North in a struggle between it and the South, where pride and skill were at stake. I was opposed to him; I joined the general wish of every true son of the South that his great knowledge of his vocation should fail him. But we were all doomed to disappointment. I believe we lost by the absence on the occasion of one of Virginia's best sons [Johnson], who had a "rascally ague" at the time. I speak of Samuel Purdy, the rider of Eclipse!
>
> Had you witnessed the exultation of the South when Henry came out ahead in the first heat of that memorable contest, you might form some idea of the consternation which prevailed in our ranks when it was announced Purdy was to ride the next heat. The breathless anxiety and silence with which we eyed him, as he threw his leg over the noble animal, were only broken by the murmuring applause with which the adverse party greeted his appearance. The skill of the Virginia rider was undoubted, but it required something more than human to compete successfully with Purdy. The horses went off, and as all the world knows, Eclipse won. The renown of the performance that day will go down with the history of civilized society, and transmit the name of Samuel Purdy as the most skillful of jockeys.

The day after the race, a New York man committed suicide. "He had lost all his money in betting on the southern horse," the *New York*

Spectator reported. There were also reports of southerners who had lost all they possessed.

That a horse race could lead to deaths and bankruptcies led many commentators to reflect negatively on the epic event that had gripped the country. The consensus opinion was that the race, though exciting, had become too large, too important, and too divisive. Even turf fans wondered if the nation's greater good had been served. "Never did a case happen before, perhaps, in which state pride was so much at stake. It might be excited, we think, by more laudable objects. The money expended or lost, and time wasted on the occasion, is not far short in its value of half the cost of cutting the Erie Canal," commented *Niles' Weekly Register.*

Even the *New York Commercial Advertiser,* which had enthusiastically promoted the race, wrote, "We should regret to see another heat run in this country on which such sums of money depend. The experiment is a dangerous one, and if pursued, may introduce a uniform spirit of gambling."

America's introduction to sports fever had frightened the public. A Maryland man wrote to the *Baltimore Patriot:*

> It seems strange that so much feeling can be excited about two horses, both Americans. I sincerely hope this is the last sectional event of any kind that we shall ever have, and this wish, I am much pleased to find, is generally expressed. Horses may run, and candidates for office may appear on the political turf, but let not the contest be between the men and horses of the North, South, East, and West, but between merits and talents. We Marylanders, placed in the center, wish to cherish union.

Such desires were naive. The North and South had already started down the long road to a tragic civil war. Slowly, ominously, their union continued to dissolve as their profound differences became more entrenched. The Missouri Compromise, which had headed off a rising conflict in 1820, was repealed and declared unconstitutional in the 1850s. Bloodshed became inevitable. South Carolinians fired on a Union ship in January 1861, beginning a war that would result in more than 600,000 American deaths, a northern victory, and the abolition of slavery.

When Eclipse died in 1847, one New York newspaper recalled the event that in its view had first crystallized the nation's differences:

There is no one who witnessed the great Eclipse race in 1823 . . . who will ever forget the clear and distinct manifestation of . . . North and South . . . that was embodied by that contest. The agitation over the Missouri question, and of the discussion relative to slavery, had indeed provoked the expression of earnest and conflicting views; but the horse race, and the huzza which rang through the air as Purdy mounted Eclipse for the second heat, attested the depth and intensity of the feeling with which the race was watched, and the confidence that the North, properly guided at least, could not be beat.

Years after the Civil War, the race was still recalled. In 1881 Josiah Quincy, the Bostonian who had watched the race as a young man, wrote:

Never was there a contest more exciting. It was the first great contest between the North and South, and one that seems to have foreshadowed the sterner conflict that occurred 40 years afterwards. The victory, in both cases, resulted from the same cause — the power of endurance. It was, in the language of the turf, bottom against speed. The North had no braver men than were found in the Confederate ranks. It had no abler generals than Lee and Jackson. It had only greater resources.

Epilogue

The aftermath of the great race was just as remarkable as the event itself in one way: Henry was eventually bought by John Cox Stevens's brother and became a stud based primarily in the North, while Eclipse was bought by William Ransom Johnson and stood in the South. After having so famously represented their regions in Jamaica, the horses changed sides in retirement.

Henry continued to race after his defeat at the Union Course, winning races in 1823 and 1824, but he went lame and was retired at age six. Robert Livingston Stevens bought him and stood him on Long Island, near the Union Course. Henry sired his share of winners, but his stud career was not nearly as successful as that of Sir Charles, as evidenced by the demand for their services. Henry sired 109 colts, Sir Charles 417.

Eclipse never raced again after beating Henry. Van Ranst commented that he hoped Eclipse would become the "founder of a stock which shall never disgrace their sire." He sold the horse at auction for $8,000 to a New Yorker who then leased him to James Junkin Harrison, the Virginia planter whom Eclipse had shamed at the National Course in 1822. Harrison took Eclipse to Virginia, where Johnson later bought him.

Eclipse stood for many years in Virginia, Maryland, and Kentucky, and died in Shelby County, Kentucky, in 1847, at thirty-three. Although he did not stand in New York, northern breeders remained intensely loyal to him. His sons and daughters represented the North in many intersectional races. He fulfilled Van Ranst's hope of siring high-quality animals, producing many winners, including a filly named Ariel and a colt named Medoc that became a top sire.

In 1825 Eclipse was bred to Lady Lightfoot, the southern mare he had beaten at the Union Course in 1821. (John Cox Stevens had bought her and taken her to Long Island.) After giving birth to a black filly, Lady Lightfoot died. The filly, Black Maria, became a fine runner known as the "Twenty-Mile Mare" after winning a brutal race consisting of five four-mile heats.

Although Stevens turned down Johnson's immediate proposal for a new challenge, match races between northern and southern horses became popular after 1823. The majority were held at the Union Course, with some at the National Course and at Baltimore's Central Course. Stevens and Johnson often managed the opposing sides, controlling the matchmaking, stakes, and training.

The South initially gained revenge for Henry's loss by winning nine of fourteen intersectional races at the Union Course in the five years after the 1823 event. But only one of these races was a major event — an 1825 match between the northern mare Ariel, Eclipse's daughter, and the southern mare Flirtilla, a half-sister to Henry. The stakes were $30,000 a side, and emotions ran high. Northerners, buoyed by Eclipse's success, fully expected the fleet Ariel to win. Thousands of southerners again traveled to New York. Ariel won the first heat, but Flirtilla came back to take the next two heats and the stakes, winning the final heat by sixty yards, as Ariel was discouraged by incessant pounding from an inexperienced jockey. Southerners rejoiced, while northerners blamed Ariel's owner for grossly mismanaging their side.

With each side now having won one major race, Stevens and Johnson arranged a third and supposedly deciding event in 1829. Black Maria, the Twenty-Mile Mare sired by Eclipse, represented the North. The South put up a colt named Brilliant, sired by Sir Archie. When Black Maria won, northern newspapers proudly claimed the "superiority of the blood of Eclipse." Johnson and the other Sir Archie devotees fumed.

The North's success mirrored the social and political drift across America, as the South absorbed numerous blows to the vision of supremacy that had prevailed during the Virginia presidential dynasty. The opening of the Erie Canal, connecting the Hudson River to Lake Erie, left no doubt that New York was now the nation's leading port and financial center. John Quincy Adams of Massachusetts won the 1824 presidential election, and Andrew Jackson of Tennessee won in 1828 and served two terms. A New Yorker, Martin Van Buren, succeeded Jackson.

Van Ranst retreated from the turf after Eclipse's victory. More than a decade later, however, still basking in the nation's memory of the moment, he surfaced again, offering to lend the winners of another major race Purdy's maroon shirt and whip, which he viewed as the quintessential symbols of racing excellence. The items later became valued artifacts.

John Cox Stevens emerged as the North's leading horseman. He won many major stakes in the 1820s and 1830s with a stable of runners based at his compound near the Union Course. Stevens was keenly involved in the daily operation of his stable, demanding to know the weights of his horses before and after their workouts and races.

One of his greatest victories came in an event called the Produce Stakes at the Union Course in 1838. A race of one-mile heats for three-year-olds, it drew forty-four nominations. Just five eventually ran, but almost $15,000 in entry and forfeit fees were collected, making it the richest "futurity" sweepstakes (for young horses) in American history. Stevens's chestnut colt Fordham won on a muddy track.

Ever the forward-thinking sportsman, Stevens also promoted other events. In 1835 he put on a ten-mile foot race at the Union Course that drew a crowd. He built a cricket patch and "base ball ground" at Elysian Fields in Hoboken, New Jersey, where his family ran an amusement park intended to increase ferry traffic. In 1846 the first organized baseball game was played at Elysian Fields.

Stevens abruptly lost interest in racing in the early 1840s and turned his focus to yachting. As commander of the New York Yacht

Club, he crossed the Atlantic and won the first America's Cup in 1851, beating eighteen English yachts.

Within months of Eclipse's victory over Henry, Van Ranst gave a written account of the horse's career to a New York publisher named Ephraim Conrad, who wrote and published *An Authentic History of the Celebrated Horse American Eclipse.* At the front of the twenty-seven-page book Van Ranst wrote, "The utmost pains have been taken to give these as correct as possible; I therefore vouch for their authenticity."

The book included details about Eclipse's upbringing and accounts of his races. Conrad printed a quote from Act III of Shakespeare's *Henry V* on the title page: "He trots the air; the earth sings when he touches it; the basest horn of his hoof is more musical than the pipe of Hermes."

American horse racing boomed in the 1830s, especially in the South, where many planters backed major stables and crowds of many thousands filled tracks. The sport's popularity spawned a market for racing journals such as the *American Turf Register* and *Spirit of the Times,* both of which reported on races and helped establish bloodlines, quantify record-setting performances, and organize the sport.

Although the North–South rivalry continued in the early 1830s, many of the races were minor events with small financial stakes. Southerners stopped going north to the Union Course when it declined under the shoddy management of Cadwallader Colden, the horseman who had written so observantly about the race between Eclipse and Henry. (New managers took charge in 1833 and cleaned it up.) Increasingly divided on social issues such as the possible emancipation of slaves, southerners became more interested in beating each other rather than the North. Grudge matches between horses representing various states drew large crowds.

Not until 1842 did another intersectional race involve the public with the ferocity of the great match race. A four-mile event between Boston, a nine-year-old southern hero, and Fashion, a five-year-old northern mare, evolved into the biggest national race since 1823. It was held at the Union Course for $20,000 a side, and fifty thousand fans attended. Johnson, now sixty, was brought in by Boston's owner to manage the southern side. A winner of thirty-five of thirty-eight previous starts, Boston was heavily favored, but he lost in successive heats to Fashion.

As usual, the defeat stirred outrage across the South, where horsemen refused to admit that the North could produce comparable horses. When a rematch of sorts was arranged in 1845, pitting the now-aging Fashion against a southern mare named Peytona at the Union Course, southerners rose up with a passion unseen since 1823. They lined the streets to applaud Peytona as she traveled from her home in Alabama to New York; one newspaper reported that "the feeling of the South against the North was aggravated to almost fury." Again a huge crowd gathered at the Union Course. Southerners cheered when Peytona won in successive heats.

That was the last of the great intersectional races. While northern and southern horsemen remained friendly enough, the regions they represented had become too antagonistic to meet at the racecourse.

Samuel Purdy never rode again after guiding Eclipse to victory at the Union Course. He spent the rest of his life in business and politics and was twice elected alderman of New York City's tenth ward. When he died suddenly at age sixty-two in December 1836, his ward members said of him, "We have sustained a loss in the removal of an able and efficient magistrate, a sound democrat and a worthy and upright citizen."

He was such a prominent New Yorker that he was buried in the historic yard of St. Paul's Church in Manhattan. His son, John, followed him into racing, becoming a winning coach driver and then a steward and handicapper for the American Jockey Club, a national organization that helped revive the turf after the Civil War.

The attention Purdy received for winning at the Union Course in 1823 signaled a dramatic change of fortune for all American jockeys. Never again would they be relegated to the background, deemed insignificant. Although they did not really become prominent until after the Civil War, they always received a share of the spotlight whenever a major race interested the public.

In a bitter irony, northern racing emerged as superior after the Civil War; southern racing almost had to start from scratch because of the wartime devastation to the region. Befitting the war's great moral lesson, many of the best jockeys at the northern tracks were black.

A slave's son named Isaac Murphy, born as the Civil War began, won more than a third of his races, including the Kentucky Derby three times. Willie Simms, born in Georgia shortly after the Civil War, was the first American rider to win the Kentucky Derby, Preakness Stakes, and Belmont Stakes, the races that later composed the modern Triple Crown. Jimmy Winkfield, the youngest of seventeen children born to Kentucky sharecroppers, rose to stardom in America and later rode in Russia, Poland, and France. He was the last black jockey to win the Kentucky Derby, in 1902. As the politics and practice of segregation spread, black jockeys were driven out of the sport.

On the one hundredth anniversary of the great race — May 27, 1923 — a group of horsemen went to St. Paul's and placed on Purdy's headstone a maroon cap and riding shirt, replicas of the colors he wore to victory on Eclipse. Even though much of his riding career had taken place before accurate records were kept, he was elected to the National Museum of Racing's Hall of Fame in 1970.

Shortly before the Civil War, the new sport of baseball became popular enough to rival horse racing in its ability to draw crowds. Although no leagues existed, the ball-and-stick game was wildly popular in northern cities. Hundreds of people routinely gathered to watch others play, and newspapers covered the games.

Crowd sizes increased after the Civil War. The Cincinnati Reds of 1869, the first truly all-professional baseball team, drew thousands on a nationwide tour, which helped heal the fractured nation. The National Association of Professional Base Ball Players, a league of teams representing cities, was organized in 1871. Ballparks that could hold thousands of spectators became commonplace.

Other spectator sports also gained legitimacy and popularity. The first football game, between students from Rutgers and Princeton, was played in 1869. The first U.S. men's tennis champion was crowned in 1881 in Newport, Rhode Island. The next year boxing crowned its first heavyweight champion, John L. Sullivan. The public was transfixed by games, matches, and bouts; stars, schedules, and champions. America's sporting age was under way in earnest, never to wane.

Horse racing was still the most popular, having regained prominence after a steep decline before the war, when trotting events, of all things, had stolen the spotlight. The American Jockey Club set up shop at New York's Jerome Park in 1866, declaring it would "promote the improvement of horses . . . and become an authority on racing matters." As many as forty thousand people paid admission to watch top horses run at northern tracks increasingly ruled by gamblers.

Through it all the Union Course race of 1823 remained a vivid memory, faithfully recalled as an epochal starting point, the first time a sports event gripped the American public.

William Ransom Johnson operated a top racing stable for most of his life, although its power slowly drained away in the 1830s as he became more involved in Virginia politics and a huge Texas land deal.

He continued to manage the southern side in most of the challenges against the North, but his entourage slowly shrank. John Randolph died in 1833, leaving $25,000 to Johnson. Bela Badger died in Bristol, Pennsylvania, in 1839. Racing Billy Wynne remained an enthusiastic breeder and owner (and served a term as sheriff of Dinwiddie County, Virginia). But in 1839 one of his daughters was found dead at his Raceland estate, which reportedly caused him to flee Virginia "for a distant state." He was never again seen at the races.

Johnson retired from politics in 1838 and cut his racing operation to little more than a few horses, and then none at all for a time in the early 1840s. His intersectional-race career ended with Boston's disappointing loss to Fashion in 1842. (The owner of Peytona managed the southern side in the 1845 rematch victory.) Johnson remained "a fascinating companion and friend, the perennial bon vivant and devotee of sport," according to the historian John Hervey. In 1847 he returned to racing in charge of just one horse, a formidable colt named Revenue. Johnson, now known as "Old Nap," won seven races with Revenue in Louisiana in 1847 and 1848.

On a trip to Mobile, Alabama, in February 1849, Johnson died suddenly at age sixty-seven. It was believed for almost a century that he was buried beside his wife at Oakland, but according to Hervey, the city of Mobile examined its records and found that Johnson, one of the greatest figures in American racing history, actually had been buried ingloriously, far from home, in a public cemetery in that city.

When Johnson was inducted into the National Museum of Racing's Hall of Fame in 1986, the museum's historians wrote that his reputation as the finest horseman of his era withstood his failures in the North–South races of 1823 and 1845. Johnson himself surely came to terms with both defeats, but given the circumstances of the 1823 race — his absence due to illness, the confusion that reigned on the southern side without him, and the presence of hundreds of fans on the track — one can only wonder if he ever truly accepted the result of the most famous race of his career.

On many nights, one imagines, Johnson dreamed that he did not eat the fateful lobster the night before, that he watched the race on horseback from his usual vantage point near the finish, and that, to his great joy, Henry triumphed in successive heats. Northerners would have had to admit that southerners were the superior horsemen and Sir Archie was the finest of all stallions.

But alas, it was just a dream.

Author's Note

Writing this book turned me into a serial library lurker. For my previous four books and for a quarter-century of columns and articles for the *Baltimore Sun* and the *Dallas Times Herald,* I learned to rely on as many eyewitnesses as possible when reconstructing events, but I obviously could not depend on a single one for this book. Seeking to maintain the level of reportorial certitude I am accustomed to, I studied the newspapers of the era, the personal papers and correspondence of my characters, and the work of writers who had previously studied the Union Course race. I lurked in the stacks and the microfilm archives of the Library of Virginia and the Virginia Historical Society in Richmond; the New York Public Library and the New-York Historical Society in Manhattan; the Library of Congress in Washington, D.C.; the Enoch Pratt Free Library in Baltimore; the Duke University Library in Durham, North Carolina; and the Wilson Library at the University of North Carolina, in Chapel Hill. I also asked for help from the Bucks County Historical Society in Bristol, Pennsylvania; the Richard Bland College Library in Petersburg, Virginia; the Keeneland Library in Lexington, Kentucky; and the library at the National Museum of Racing and Hall of Fame in Saratoga Springs, New York.

The books, magazines, newspapers, personal papers, and Web sites that I used as sources are listed in the Bibliographical Notes. I am grateful to all of the historians and journalists who have written accounts of the race. Like many of those who have walked the same ground, I found the work of the late John Hervey, America's preeminent horse-racing historian, to be singularly helpful. His series Racing in America stands as a definitive source, as does his book about the sire Messenger, a copy of which Joe Goldstein graciously loaned me.

I am also indebted to the many unnamed newspaper and magazine reporters from the 1820s who in effect became my eyewitnesses. Few of their publications were entrenched institutions, and none of the hundreds of articles I found about the race and its horses and personalities came with a byline — journalism was a decidedly different creature in the 1820s — but they provided a solid factual foundation. Where differences of opinion surfaced, I went with the consensus view.

In a way, researching a book is like playing a role in a detective story: you follow leads down an endless succession of dark alleys, never knowing what you might find. I had no idea what to expect when my trail led me to the Wilson Library at the University of North Carolina and the papers of Elizabeth Amis Cameron Blanchard, coauthor of *The Story of America's Greatest Thoroughbred: The Life and Times of Sir Archie*, published by the University of North Carolina Press in 1958. What I found was a story almost worthy of a book itself.

Blanchard was a wealthy New Yorker descended from the family that owned the great sire. She became fascinated with the Sir Archie story and spent years traveling and doggedly researching every tendril. She befriended Hervey, among others, and she intended to turn her findings into a book, but the task of trimming her voluminous material apparently became too great — several publishers turned her down — and then she died, leaving to a coauthor the responsibility of getting the manuscript published. But she left behind what proved to be a treasure trove for me: thick books of meticulous stud records she had compiled, hundreds of letters to and from sources, reams of newspaper articles and historical data about horse racing in the early 1800s, and stacks of primary source material. Blanchard died in 1956, but her life's work greatly informed this book.

While my reflexive goal as a journalist is to use multiple sources to support and corroborate whatever I write, I was unable to fully satisfy my standard at some places in this narrative. In those cases I applied a dramatist's license, strictly for the sake of advancing the story, while always seeking to remain faithful to the characters and the facts. The responsibility for every word is mine alone.

I am especially indebted to several people. Susan Canavan at Houghton Mifflin saw the potential in the story from the beginning and then shepherded me through the writing process with incisive line-by-line direction. She pushed all the right buttons. Peg Anderson of Houghton Mifflin carefully edited the manuscript and saved me in countless ways. My agent, Scott Waxman, not only made the book happen, as always, but also stepped in at a key juncture and provided keen advice about the manuscript. At every library I visited, the staff was kind and accommodating. Finally, my wife, Mary Wynne, and my children, Anna and Wick, allowed me to turn the computer room we ostensibly share into my lair and were kind enough to smile at me instead of pointing out that I seemed to be taking an awfully long time. I cannot thank them enough for their love and patience.

Bibliographical Notes

The following sources helped me learn and write about the Union Course race and its time, place, and people.

BOOKS AND ARTICLES

Adelman, Melvin L. *A Sporting Time: New York City and the Rise of Modern Athletics 1820–1870.* University of Illinois, 1990.

Alexander, David. *The History and Romance of the Horse.* Cooper Square, 1963.

Anderson, James Douglas. *Making the American Thoroughbred.* Plimpton Press, 1916.

Blanchard, Elizabeth, and Manly Wellman. *The Story of America's Greatest Thoroughbred: The Life and Times of Sir Archie.* University of North Carolina Press, 1958.

Bracey, Susan L. *Life by the Roaring Roanoke: A History of Mecklenburg County.* Mecklenburg County, Va., 1877.

Brasch, Rudolph. *How Did Sports Begin?* David McKay, 1970.

Bruce, William Cabell. *John Randolph of Roanoke: 1773–1833: A Biography Based Largely on New Material.* Two vols., 1922; reprint, Octagon Books, 1970.

Bush, Doreen. "First Battle Between the North and South." *American History Illustrated,* April 1976.

Carruth, Gorton. *Encyclopedia of American Facts and Data.* Harper Collins, 1993.

Commager, Henry Steele, and Samuel Eliot Morrison. *The Growth of the American Republic.* Oxford University Press, 1962.

Crego, Robert. *Sports and Games of the 18th and 19th Centuries.* Greenwood Press, 2003.

Culver, Francis Barnum. *Blooded Horses of Colonial Days.* Privately published, Baltimore, 1922.

Dabney, Virginius S. *Richmond: The Story of a City.* University of Virginia Press, 1990.

Dictionary of American Biography, vols. 1–20. Charles Scribner's Sons, 1928–1936.

Dictionary of Virginia Biography. Library of Virginia, 1999.

Dizikes, John. *Sportsmen and Gamesmen.* Houghton Mifflin, 1981.

——. *Yankee Doodle Dandy: The Life and Times of Tod Sloan.* Yale University Press, 2000.

Fehrenbacher, Don E. *The South and Three Sectional Crises.* Louisiana State University Press, 1980.

Gorn, Elliott, and Warren Goldstein. *A Brief History of American Sports.* Hill and Wang, 1993.

Green, Doron, and C. S. Magrath. *A History of Bristol Borough.* C. S. Magrath, 1911.

Guttmann, Allen. *Sports Spectators.* Columbia University, 1986.

Harrison, Fairfax. *Roanoke Stud 1795–1833.* Old Dominion Press, 1930.

——. *The Equine FFVs.* Old Dominion Press, 1928.

Herbert, Henry William. *Frank Forester's Horse and Horsemanship of the United States and British Provinces of North America,* vol. 1. Stringer and Townsend, 1857.

Hervey, John. *Messenger: The Great Progenitor.* Derrydale Press, 1935.

——. *Racing in America: 1665–1865,* vols. 1 and 2. Jockey Club, 1944.

Hickok, Ralph. *Encyclopedia of North American Sports History.* Facts on File, 2002.

Holliman, Jennie. *American Sports (1785–1835).* Porcupine Press, 1975.

Hotaling, Edward. *Great Black Jockeys: The Lives and Times of the Men Who Dominated America's First National Sport.* Forum, 1999.

Irving, John Beaufain. *South Carolina Jockey Club.* Russell and Jones, 1857.

Jones, Richard L. *Dinwiddie County.* Dinwiddie County, Va., 1976.

Kweskin, Steve. "The Great Race of 1823." *Turf and Sport Digest,* December 1976.

Longrigg, Roger. *History of Horse Racing.* Stein and Day, 1972.

Lutz, Francis Earle. *Chesterfield: An Old Virginia County.* William Byrd Press, 1954.

Lyttle, Richard B. *The Games They Played: Sports in History.* Atheneum, 1982.

MacLeod, Duncan. "Racing to War." *Southern Exposure,* Fall 1979.

Montgomery, E. S. *The Thoroughbred.* A. S. Barnes, 1971.

Neale, Gay. *Brunswick County.* Brunswick County, Va., 1976.

O'Dell, Jeffrey. *Chesterfield County History Sites and Structures.* Chesterfield County, Va., 1983.

Parmer, Charles B. *For Gold and Glory: The Story of Thoroughbred Racing in America.* Carrick and Evans, 1939.

Pintard, John. *Letters from John Pintard to His Daughter: Eliza Noel Pintard Davidson, 1816–1833.* New-York Historical Society, 1940–1941.

Porter, David L., ed. *Biographical Dictionary of American Sports.* Greenwood Press, 1988.

Powell, William S., ed. *Dictionary of North Carolina Biography.* University of North Carolina Press, 1979–1988.

Quincy, Josiah. *Figures of the Past.* Roberts Brothers, 1883.

Rader, Benjamin. *American Sports: From the Age of Folk Games to the Age of Spectators.* Prentice-Hall, 1999.

Robertson, William H. P. *The History of Thoroughbred Racing in America.* Prentice-Hall, 1964.

Ryland, Elizabeth Lowell, ed. *Richmond County, Virginia.* Richmond County, Va., 1976.

Scott, James G., and Edward A. Wyatt IV. *Petersburg's Story: A History.* Petersburg, Va., 1960.

Shaw, David W. *America's Victory.* Free Press, 2002.

Stang, Phil. *Horses in America.* Frederick Stokes, 1939.

Stevens, A. D. *John Stevens: An American Record.* Century, 1928.

Struna, Nancy L. "The North–South Races: American Thoroughbred Racing in Transition 1823–1850." *Journal of Sport History,* Summer 1981.

Sydnor, Charles S. *The Development of Southern Sectionalism.* Louisiana State University Press, 1948.

Untitled article on the Eclipse–Henry race. *Harper's New Monthly Magazine,* June–November 1870.

Virginia Writer's Project. *Dinwiddie County.* Virginia Writer's Project, 1942.

Weeks, Lyman Horace. *The American Turf.* The Historical Company, 1898.

Who Was Who in America, 1607–1896, rev. ed. Marquis Who's Who, 1967.

NEWSPAPERS OF THE 1820S

Albany Daily Advertiser
American Farmer
American Turf Register and Sporting Magazine
Baltimore American
Baltimore Morning Chronicle
Charleston Courier
Franklin Gazette (Philadelphia)

Georgetown Metropolitan
Long Island Star
Nashville Whig
National Intelligencer (Washington)
New York American
New York Commercial Advertiser
New York Evening Post
New York Gazette
New York Spectator
New York Statesman
Niles Weekly Register (Baltimore)
Pennsylvania Correspondent
Petersburg Intelligencer
Petersburg Republican
Richmond Enquirer
Southern Patriot and Commercial Advertiser (Charleston, S.C.)
Spirit of the Times (New York)
Washington Gazette
Virginia Times

PERSONAL PAPERS

Elizabeth Hooper Blanchard Papers, Southern Historical Collection, Manuscripts Dept., Wilson Library, University of North Carolina at Chapel Hill

William Ransom Johnson papers, Rare Book, Manuscript and Special Collections Library, Duke University

WEB SITES

bloodlines.net
census.gov
derbypost.com
earlyrepublic.net
tbheritage.com

Index

CPSIA information can be obtained
at www.ICGtesting.com
Printed in the USA
LVOW12s1215200416

484500LV00001B/167/P